Hollywood Diplomacy

Hollywood Diplomacy

Film Regulation, Foreign Relations, and East Asian Representations

HYE SEUNG CHUNG

Rutgers University Press
New Brunswick, Camden, and Newark, New Jersey, and London

Library of Congress Cataloging-in-Publication Data

Names: Chung, Hye Seung, 1971– author.
Title: Hollywood diplomacy : film regulation, foreign relations, and East Asian representations / Hye Seung Chung.
Description: New Brunswick, New Jersey : Rutgers University Press, [2020] | Includes bibliographical references and index.
Identifiers: LCCN 2019014922 | ISBN 9781978801561 (hardcover) | ISBN 9781978801554 (paperback) | ISBN 9781978801592 (pdf) | ISBN 9781978801578 (epub)
Subjects: LCSH: East Asians in motion pictures. | Motion pictures—Political aspects—United States. | Motion pictures—Censorship. | East Asia—In motion pictures. | United States—Foreign relations—East Asia. | East Asia—Foreign relations—United States.
Classification: LCC PN1995.9.E23 C48 2020 | DDC 791.43/65295—dc23
LC record available at https://lccn.loc.gov/2019014922

A British Cataloging-in-Publication record for this book is available from the British Library.

∞ The paper used in this publication meets the requirements of the American National Standard for Information Sciences—Permanence of Paper for Printed Library Materials, ANSI Z39.48-1992.

www.rutgersuniversitypress.org

Manufactured in the United States of America

Contents

Hollywood Diplomacy

Introduction

On October 16, 1950, the day before the Battle of Pyongyang, which was one of the most significant United Nations offensives during the Korean War to capture North Korea's capital after successfully taking back Seoul from communist enemies the previous month, Hollywood's Production Code Administration (PCA) sent a letter to Robert L. Lippert. Having established himself in the industry as an independent producer and theater owner of note, Lippert was now in the midst of producing a low-budget combat picture set in Korea, one directed by the up-and-coming firebrand filmmaker Samuel Fuller and titled *The Steel Helmet*. The PCA raised several objections to the submitted script, based on the standards of what contemporary commentators might call "political correctness." It opposed the racially derogatory expression "gook," a term that General Douglas MacArthur—then the commander of U.S./U.N. forces in Korea—had recently cautioned against using due to its offensiveness to locals. The PCA also disliked the Japanese American character Tanaka's nickname "Buddhahead," owing to its insensitivity to the "religious sensibility of certain people." The agency was furthermore concerned about the film's claim that "Auld Lang Syne" was the tune of the Korean national anthem and urged the producer to seek "proper technical advice for [this] story point."[1]

Among the many constructive pieces of advice given by the industry's self-regulating body, the most surprising and progressive recommendation pertains to the depiction of North Korean enemies, rather than to minority soldiers or South Korean allies. Exhibiting a prudence that might surprise some, the PCA's Morris Murphy advised Lippert on the phone the following day, saying, "In view of the critical war situation in the Far East and the unusual circumstance that this story is about a war which is presently being fought, it was the feeling of this office that [you] should protect [yourself] and the industry and should handle [your] portrayals of the North Koreans with extreme care and delicacy lest the picture be a stumbling block to our State Department in reaching a peaceful settlement with the North Koreans."[2] On October 19, representatives of the PCA had a story conference meeting with Fuller's assistant and went out of their way to restate their concern about the "serious damage to the international relations of the United States as well as serious embarrassment to the motion picture industry" that might be caused by the inappropriate treatment of North Koreans in the script. As the PCA weighed in, "Some of the material in *The Steel Helmet* might cause serious embarrassment to our State Department at a later date."[3]

This anecdote from midcentury motion picture production culture, buried deep in the history of Golden Age Hollywood (an industry best remembered for its glamorous stars, ruthless moguls, and rebellious artists), has remained inaccessible to the general public for years. There are exceptions, of course: a small number of historians and academics who might travel to Los Angeles on a research account and toil through long hours in the Academy of Motion Picture Arts and Sciences' Margaret Herrick Library Special Collections Reading Room, going through the PCA's voluminous archival documents. For most Americans, especially those who have not pored over such documents, the word "censorship" is synonymous with political oppression and unconstitutionality, regardless of who imposes it (whether the government, state and foreign censorship boards, or the industry itself). Contrary to that preconception, the PCA's intervention during the production of *The Steel Helmet*, as documented in the above-cited files preserved by its parental trade organization, the Motion Picture Producers and Distributors of America (MPPDA, which changed its name to the Motion Picture Association of America [MPAA] in 1945), demonstrates that self-regulation was a productive process that contributed valuable feedback to producers and allowed them to make preemptive revisions at an early stage of production without incurring additional costs of reshooting. From a poststructuralist standpoint, this material evidence also corroborates or lends credence to Michel Foucault's theory of power, repression, and resistance.

As with other types of power-based relationships, censorship is not simply a "mode of subjugation" or "a general system of dominance," as one might presume. Rather, in a way that is indicative of Foucault's notion of discursively constructed and deployed power, film censorship can be best understood as "the multiplicity of force relations immanent in the sphere in which they operate"; or, in other words, "the process which, through ceaseless struggles and confrontations, transforms, strengthens, or reverses them." As Foucault explains, "Where there is power, there is resistance . . . . [The existence of power relationships] depends on a multiplicity of points of resistance."[4] When applied to censorship studies, this idea can assist in theorizing filmmakers' creative circumvention of prohibitions and rules through textual ambiguity, visual symbols, distant framings, the use of offscreen space, and narrative strategies steeped in allegory and displacement. Talented filmmakers such as Alfred Hitchcock reportedly "*enjoyed* his negotiations with [the PCA]" and found the "spirited give-and-take" in the formalized process of Hollywood's self-regulation as thrilling as "competitive horse trading."[5] Film historian Thomas Doherty argues that formal restrictions imposed by PCA censorship were "preconditions for the creative act," just as the fourteen-line (stanza, quatrain, and couplet) rule was an inspirational, rather than limiting, structural form for Shakespearean sonnet poets (or, to update Doherty's metaphor, the 140- and then 280-character limit for Twitter users).[6] In a sense, the give-and-take negotiation process between studios/filmmakers and censors can be likened to Foucault's description of the mutually reinforcing pleasure of exercising and evading power: "The pleasure that comes of exercising a power that questions, monitors, watches, spies, searches out, palpates, brings to light; and on the other hand, the pleasure it kindles at having to evade this power, flee from it, fool it, or travesty it."[7]

In the years since the MPAA opened its PCA files to the public at the Margaret Herrick Library (beginning in 1983), American film censorship studies have focused on the issue of self-regulation. Subsequent research and scholarship drawn from the archive, as Daniel Biltereyst and Roel Vande Winkel argue, enabled "a much more sophisticated view on film censorship [as a] key mediating factor in discourses that govern American film industry and film culture."[8] Lea Jacobs's *The Wages of Sin: Censorship and the Fallen Woman Film, 1928–1942* (1991), Ruth Vasey's *The World According to Hollywood, 1918–1939* (1997), Thomas Doherty's *Pre-Code Hollywood: Sex, Immorality, and Insurrection in American Cinema, 1930–1934* (1999) and *Hollywood's Censor: Joseph I. Breen and the Production Code Administration* (2007), Stephen Prince's *Classical Film Violence: Designing and Regulating Brutality in Hollywood Cinema, 1930–1968* (2003), and Ellen C. Scott's *Cinema Civil Rights: Regulation, Repression, and Race in the Classical Hollywood Era* (2015) are among the major studies that have extensively consulted and cited PCA files. These and other previous studies prove that the U.S. film industry's self-regulation was not simply prohibitive but also productive in generating more nuanced representations of sex, violence, race, ethnicity, and nationality.

In his introduction to *Controlling Hollywood: Censorship and Regulation in the Studio Era*, Matthew Bernstein divides movie censorship into two categories: (1) the type that is "external to the film industry," or, in trade terms, a form of "political censorship" such as that associated with state, municipal, and foreign censorship boards; and (2) the type that "is frequently categorized as 'self-regulation,'" such as that overseen by the PCA and eventually baked into the MPAA rating system.[9] According to Doherty, "Under the law school definition of censorship (a restriction on freedom of expression enforced by a state power), [the latter] was not a censor."[10] One could argue the same about so-called government censorship, in the form of advisory script consultation and preview print review by the Office of War Information (OWI) from 1942 to 1945 and the Department of Defense (DoD) from 1949 to the present. Because neither of those two organizations commanded jurisdiction over commercial film distribution and exhibition, there was no way that these external advisors could enforce their views and suggestions unless production companies voluntarily adopted them to advance their own economic and political agendas. Therefore, their "friendly advisory services" (provided pro bono, unlike the fee-based review of censorship boards and self-regulatory agencies) should be distinguished from the binary of censorship that Bernstein lays out. Another missing category is censorship that is induced by audience boycotts and protests over offensive images detrimental to the self-esteem of their group identities. In the context of this study, I will focus on the resistance of Chinese and Korean audiences to Hollywood's Orientalist representations, which not only distort languages, costumes, cultures, and geographies but also erect an ideological dichotomy between the good/West/self and the evil/East/other. All of these types of often-conflated censorship will be comprehensively addressed in this book, with attention to their subtle differences.

To clarify, the aim of this book is neither to celebrate the productive capacity of censorship nor to prove whether it is "good" or "bad," sweepingly progressive or regressive. What needs to be stressed is that, depending on the administrating institutions (federal authorities, foreign governments, trade organizations, organized consumer groups, etc.), censorship has varying degrees of enforcing or bargaining power and diverse aims, purposes, and ideological imperatives. For example, as stated previously, federal government agencies such as the OWI (the Roosevelt administration's World War II propaganda agency) and the DoD had limited means of changing Hollywood's scripts on the grounds of "good policy," be it equitable images of racial minorities and foreign nationals or authentic, realistic depictions of war and military personnel. Their institutional leverage was almost exclusively confined to the financial gains that they could bring to studios, as in the OWI's influence on the Office of Censorship's selection of film export titles and the DoD's in-kind service of equipment rentals and technical advising.

While the OWI explicitly discouraged jingoism and white supremacy on wartime U.S. screens for political purposes (mobilization of minority soldiers, protection of national reputation against Axis propaganda, and improved diplomacy with allies), their initiatives led to mixed results at best. As observed by Clayton R. Koppes and Gregory D. Black, the OWI all but discontinued its earlier efforts to improve Hollywood's images of African Americans by 1943 in the face of conservative Southern and congressional backlash.[11] On the other hand, the authors argue that the same agency could achieve relatively greater success in inducing sensitivity toward Filipino and Chinese allies.[12] This does not necessarily mean that there was an intra-minority racial hierarchy in Hollywood that put African Americans on the bottom and Asians or Asian Americans on the top. This disparity is indicative of the strong economic incentives studios had to portray Asian nationals in a more positive light to preempt diplomatic crises with allied governments and gain unrestricted access to foreign markets. In other words, the American film industry's financial and diplomatic, not racial, priorities determined the effectiveness of regulatory interventions.

When we turn our attention to foreign governmental censorship—the power to ban films and demand cuts of certain scenes based on arbitrary standards of national insult—it is tempting to take the stance of defending Hollywood filmmakers' civil liberalities and their freedom of expression. However, as demonstrated in chapter 1 (as well as the Conclusion of this book), the Chinese government's censorship of Hollywood's degrading images of China and its nationals can also be construed as an equalizing deliberative process through which foreign audiences and authorities were able to talk back and air their grievances to more powerful political and cultural entities (the U.S. government and Hollywood executives) for perceived detriments to their country's prestige in the world arena. This international perspective on censorship as cultural resistance can further enrich the idea of "good censorship" put forth by Francis Couvares and Ellen C. Scott in the context of domestic civil rights. As stated by Scott, "censorship can come from society's weakest members as an expression of their oppression" and as a political tool to counter Hollywood's dominant cultural narrative of misogyny, homophobia, and racism.[13]

As documented in this book, the long history of productive censorship of American motion pictures on behalf of and by East Asian countries (China, Japan, North Korea, and South Korea) from the 1930s to the present is a fertile intellectual ground wherein debates about screen Orientalism and Asian/Asian American stereotypes can be reshaped and modified. As a specialist in Asian and Asian American representations in American popular culture, I am indebted to pioneering scholarship in the field by Eugene Franklin Wong, Gina Marchetti, Darrell Y. Hamamoto, Robert G. Lee, and Peter X. Feng, whose work continues to guide my own research and teaching. These scholars' studies of Asian American representations (*On Media Visual Racism: Asians in the American Motion Pictures* [1978], *Romance and the "Yellow Peril": Race, Sex, and Discursive Strategies in Hollywood Fiction* [1993], *Monitored Peril: Asian Americans and the Politics of TV Representation* [1994], *Orientals: Asian Americans in Popular Culture* [1999], and *Screening Asian Americans* [2002]) share a common critical methodology of historicizing and examining

Oriental stereotypes through textual analysis. This dominant approach to representation studies can be complicated and expanded when the heretofore neglected factor of film censorship and regulation is taken into consideration. There is currently no book-length study concerning the ways in which film censorship and industry regulations influenced Hollywood's representations of East Asian countries and their people. *Hollywood Diplomacy: Film Regulation, Foreign Relations, and East Asian Representations* fills this gap in film regulation studies and makes the case that, rather than simply reflect the West's cultural fantasies of an imagined "Orient," images of East Asian ethnicities (Chinese, Japanese, and Korean) have long been contested ideological sites where the commercial interests of Hollywood studios and the political mandates of U.S. foreign policy collide, compete against one another, and often become compromised in the process.

This book owes its existence to pioneering scholarship in the area that explores the understudied connection between film regulation and race, ethnicity, or nationality. The most influential was Vasey's *The World According to Hollywood*, which I first encountered as a doctoral student in film and television studies at UCLA. In many respects, I have emulated Vasey's method of examining, through primary documents, the ways in which Hollywood producers modified their scripts to accommodate the demands of foreign markets. However, her study covers an earlier period (1918–1939) and is not focused on East Asian representations (although one of its chapters compares Chinese influence with British, Mexican, French, and Italian interventions). While it draws heavily upon PCA and studio files, Vasey's book does not consult unpublished government documents housed at the National Archives to cross-reference and complement Hollywood's archive. Ellen C. Scott's excellent *Cinema Civil Rights* has also been a source of influence, insofar as it explores the role of ethnic audiences (African American activists and lobbyists) in responding to Hollywood's portrayals of race. Like the current study, Scott's book uses both PCA and OWI files. Her exclusive focus on African American representations, Classical Hollywood, and domestic contexts of race (civil rights rather than foreign relations) ultimately distinguishes her work from mine. One of my earlier books, *Hollywood Asian: Philip Ahn and the Politics of Cross-Ethnic Performance*, devotes a chapter to the subject of state interventions (on the part of both the Chinese government and the State Department) in the construction of Chinese images in two Pearl S. Buck adaptations, *The Good Earth* (1937) and *China Sky* (1945). As a more comprehensive industry review than that offered in my previously published work (which was tied to the filmography and career of Korean American actor Philip Ahn), *Hollywood Diplomacy* addresses itself to a larger readership. It also endeavors to contribute a much-needed historical perspective to current national debates about foreign censorship on American media, not simply through traditional means (as will be discussed in my first chapter) but also through networked protests, cyber vandalism, and the acquisition of U.S. media corporations (which I will address in this book's second half).

This project differentiates itself from earlier scholarship on the subject in both film studies and Asian American studies on two fronts. First, it draws upon archival research in Los Angeles (the Margaret Herrick Library) and Washington, DC (the National Archives and Records Administration and the Georgetown University Special Collections Research Center) in order to uncover often-overlooked connections between public policy and cinematic representations. I have consulted a variety of primary documents, including the PCA files, studio production files, State Department files, Bureau of Foreign and Domestic Commerce files, OWI files, the DoD Film Collection, and duplicates of MPAA rating documents (which are included in the Richard Heffner papers at the Columbia University Oral History Archive). The first three chapters of the book, which focus on Classical Hollywood cinema from the 1930s to the 1950s, cite from these sources in order to present authoritative historical narratives. These chapters make a unique scholarly intervention by redefining external censorship or advisory entities (the Chinese government, the OWI, and the Pentagon) as productive contributors pushing for increased cultural authenticity and/or more egalitarian racial/ethnic/national images in Hollywood's Orientalist productions.

Second, this book is the only publication of its kind to compare and contrast the representational crises specific to Classical Hollywood productions and contemporary Hollywood productions. The final two chapters focus on North Korean representations in recent films and East Asian resistance to the spread of global Hollywood. In doing so, they present a case for reconsidering the concept of power in relation to a "third" kind of censorship (neither official state censorship nor the industry's self-regulation) imposed by consumer boycotts and activism against hegemonic, imperialistic, or outright racist representations of foreign nationals and cultures in contemporary American films. Given Hollywood's century-long dominance of global markets and the United States government's trade policy targeting protection quotas for indigenous film productions, it would be shortsighted to interpret international audiences' protests as merely a form of repressive censorship against the freedom of expression exercised by American artists. In this context, local censorship efforts around the world, but particularly in East Asia, can be read as resistance to Hollywood hegemony and unequal racial ideology in Western/American culture.

The book is divided into two parts: "Part I: Diplomatic Representations in Classical Hollywood" (chapters 1, 2, and 3) and "Part II: The War on Terror, Contemporary Hollywood, and Its Global Discontents" (chapters 4 and 5). The first chapter, "Censorship as Cultural Resistance: The Chinese Government's

'Uplift' of National Images in 1930s Hollywood," offers comparative historiographies of film censorship in the United States and China from 1927 to 1934. It then attends to specific case studies of the Republic-era Chinese government's reactions to degrading national images in 1930s Hollywood comedies such as the Harold Lloyd vehicle *Welcome Danger* (1929) and cinematic exotica such as the Josef von Sternberg–directed *Shanghai Express* (1932). Unlike its status as a form of commercial entertainment in the United States, the Nationalist (Kuomintang) government in China saw cinema as a medium of national "uplift" and were determined to suppress representations contrary to its public interests in both domestic and foreign productions. Article Two of the Motion Picture Censorship Law of 1930 empowered the state-controlled film censorship board to ban any films deemed "injurious to the dignity of Chinese people." Using this provision as a weapon, the governmental body put a halt to censorship review for the entire output of offending Hollywood studios or filmmakers, demanding that they withdraw insulting films from worldwide markets while the Chinese foreign service lobbied to other governments to bar "anti-Chinese" films from their territories. These hardline measures invited diplomatic dialogue among the Chinese government, State Department representatives in China (consuls in Nanjing and Shanghai and legation counselors in Beijing), and studio spokespeople, as all involved players worked together on negotiations and compromises (which often resulted in premature withdrawal of controversial films and conciliatory letters of apology or pledges not to offend China in the future).

Hollywood's internal records suggest that the MPPDA's Foreign Department and the PCA were frustrated by the recurring "China problem" throughout the 1930s, despite the State Department's hands-on involvement in film diplomacy. The fact that Paramount Pictures encountered a repeated crisis in China over *The General Died at Dawn* (1936), merely four years after a similar warlord film produced at that studio, *Shanghai Express*, enraged the Chinese government and public, attests to the force of racial ideology and cultural entitlement that sometimes overruled the industry's commercial and diplomatic interests. The final section of the chapter discusses the shifting power dynamics of the early 1940s, when China, after the wartime dissolution of its centralized censorship board, had lost its bargaining chip to penalize Hollywood producers for inflammatory images and the State Department was pushing for pro-American propaganda in the region through nonprofit, "cultural relations" films.

Titled "Justified Patricide and (Im)Properly Directed Hatred: Regulating the Representations of Chinese and Japanese in Doolittle Raid Films," the second chapter charts out the development of foreign relations protocols in Hollywood's self-regulation process from the MPPDA's silent-era Open Door policy to the Production Code's "National Feelings" clause. The chapter puts forth the argument that there was an unexpected confluence of interests between the PCA and the OWI when it came to images of foreign nationals and racial minorities, despite radical differences in their purposes, goals, and ideological orientations. At the center of this chapter is a study of 20th Century-Fox's Doolittle Raid film *The Purple Heart* (1944), which was opposed by both the PCA and the OWI, for different reasons. Directed by a seasoned veteran in Hollywood, Lewis Milestone, this unusual war film spotlights a Chinese collaborator and his patriotic son, who kills his own father (whose betrayal led to the Japanese capture and trial of eight Doolittle flyers). Whereas representatives for the Production Code disapproved of the film's treatment of patricide for revenge on moral grounds, the OWI frowned upon the depiction of allies as collaborators from a wartime policy perspective. Despite their contradictory suggestions to Milestone and other studio figures attached to this production, the two organizations were united in their vision of eliminating racial stereotypes of Chinese allies and joined forces in gently pushing filmmakers in a progressive direction. While Chinese representations improved to a certain extent, thanks in part to regulatory interventions, the OWI's "properly directed hatred" policy failed to be upheld in Japanese portrayals, despite the film's evasive evocation of enemy torture in a displaced manner (through offscreen sound and metonymic montage). Based on reception data gathered by both the studio and the OWI, the chapter demonstrates that the film incited intense hatred for the Japanese people as a whole rather than the fascist military system of the enemy nation, as government propagandists had hoped for. Archival documents consulted in this chapter shed light on the government's priority of countering negative images of allies harmful to America's wartime alliances rather than toning down excessive propaganda against enemies, which would have had adverse effects on postwar foreign relations.

Chapter 3, "Beyond the Propaganda Model: The Pentagon as a Technical Advisor for Brainwashing Films of the Cold War Era," challenges both popular and academic understandings of the Pentagon's "technical advising" role (script consultation and print review in exchange for military assistance to commercial film productions) as a form of government censorship. Drawing upon archival documents in the DoD Film Collection housed at Georgetown University and focusing on the case studies of POW brainwashing films set during the Korean War (e.g., MGM's *Prisoner of War* [1954] and Columbia's *Bamboo Prison* [1954]), this chapter reevaluates the role of the Pentagon as a technical advisor. Challenging Edward S. Herman and Noam Chomsky's theory of the "propaganda model" (relating to the filtering of media messages to advance the interests of government officials or economic elites in democratic societies), this chapter emphasizes that the primary impulse of military advising was to enhance the realism and authenticity of war-related representations in Hollywood's otherwise fanciful scripts (notorious for their authors' geopolitical fabrications) through constructive feedback to studios seeking military cooperation.

After reviewing the script of *Prisoner of War*, for example, the Army and the DoD opposed the film's depiction of a diabolical Russian colonel (played by Oscar Homolka) as a senior advisor to North Korean prison officials' brainwashing program for American POWs. The military insisted that the role should be changed to Chinese in order to be technically correct and factual. Although MGM accommodated some other suggestions made by military reviewers, the studio kept the colorful Russian villain despite the DoD's demand that they adhere to known facts of Soviet involvement in Korea (e.g., no Russians were in POW camps). As in the power relationships described by Foucault, the Pentagon had limited leverage in terms of asserting control over Hollywood's private enterprise industrial structure, and filmmakers were free to adopt military advice selectively. After offering MGM full military cooperation, the government had no choice but to decline an acknowledgment in the credits and distance itself from the completed film, which retained objectionable elements. The chapter also introduces a novel perspective on Pentagon film regulations by emphasizing the agency of Donald Baruch, a former Broadway producer and studio employee who served as a liaison between the military and the film industry between 1949 and 1989. Toward the end of the chapter, the Pentagon's technical advising on contemporary Hollywood blockbusters is briefly discussed as a counterpoint to Cold War–era B-movies analyzed earlier.

Part II begins with chapter 4, "*From Die Another Day to 'Another Day'*: The Anti-007 Movement, Pan-Asian Nationalism, and Protests as Censorship." It examines South Korea's "Do Not See 007" movement spearheaded by civil groups and internet users from December 2001 to January 2002. As the twentieth installment in the James Bond franchise, MGM-UA's *Die Another Day* (2002) offended much of the Korean public due to its depiction of North Korea as an "axis of evil" terrorist state and of South Korea as a provincial backdrop under U.S. military control. The boycott movement gained momentum quickly due to an emergent protest culture of candlelight vigils, which coincidently started in November 2001, one month prior to *Die Another Day*'s Korean release, igniting a nationwide anti-American fever more generally. Tens of thousands of citizens flocked to a public square in downtown Seoul carrying candles to protest the U.S. military court's acquittal of two American soldiers who were responsible for running over two Korean schoolgirls with an armored vehicle and killing them. Street protests soon morphed into consumer boycotts against American products such as McDonald's fast food, Coca-Cola, and Hollywood films. It would be disingenuous to categorize *Die Another Day* simply as an "American" film since it is officially a U.K./U.S. coproduction based on Ian Fleming's series of novels romanticizing the exploits of Her Majesty's Secret

Intelligence Service (SIS or MI6) as a bulwark of the NATO alliance during the Cold War. However, networked Korean protests against the film (consolidating online activism and theater picketing) can be better understood within the broader geopolitical context of U.S.-Korean relations at that time. Any censorship that resulted from this boycott movement, such as the change of the Korean title to *Another Day* and cancellations or reduction of theatrical screenings, is thus connected to that local resistance to U.S. military, political, and cultural hegemony. This chapter argues that, beyond expressing an inter-Korea cultural "bond" (pun intended), the anti-007 movement represents pan-Asian nationalism precisely because of the interchangeability of different Asian ethnicities, locations, and icons in the 007 series in particular and Euro-American cultural productions in general.

The final chapter is titled "*The Interview* as a Twenty-First-Century *Great Dictator*? Rethinking Film Regulation and Foreign Relations through the Sony Crisis." This most recent case study is an indicator of how far we have stepped back from the PCA era (1934–1968) in terms of Hollywood's foreign relations and how the discourse surrounding a foreign government's protest and punitive action has shifted from a diplomatic crisis to a threat to American constitutional rights to free expression. The chapter provides historical context of the industry's transition to the MPAA rating system with the narrowed purpose of serving American parents with children under the age of seventeen. As a result, matters concerning foreign representations fell out of the purview of the industry's self-regulation. With the discontinuation of the PCA's established protocol of advising studios to clear scripts and preview prints through official channels of foreign government representatives (embassy and consulate staff) in the United States to preempt diplomatic fallouts, studios have been left to their own devices and have been forced to do their own risk assessments. When North Korea, with characteristic fury, denounced Seth Rogen and Evan Goldberg's *The Interview*, owing to its ludicrous assassination plot targeting their incumbent leader Kim Jong-un (based on a teaser trailer released in June 2014), Sony Pictures contacted State Department officials through a less dependable back channel (RAND Corporation) and sent review copies to its Asian branches, which uniformly submitted negative reports on the film.

Confidential studio memoranda made public on WikiLeaks reveal that the studio was pressured by its parent company's CEO, Kazuo Hirai, to eliminate the gory assassination scene (in which Kim Jong-un's face melts away in fire) in fear of diplomatic repercussions. Leaked internal documents and trade interviews collectively suggest that Sony executives became hostages of star power and were afraid to go against the will of Rogen, who insisted that Kim's real name be used in the film despite the studio's misgivings and that the "comic" shot of Kim's head popping be retained despite the Sony CEO's opposition. Ultimately, though, it is President Barack Obama who pressured Sony to release the film in small independent theaters and on digital platforms on Christmas Day of 2014, one week after the studio announced its plan to shelve it indefinitely due to canceled multiplex bookings in the wake of cyberattacks and bomb threats to theaters by a group called the "Guardians of Peace" (allegedly a front for the North Korean government). Although it is not clear what, if any, ulterior motive lies behind the presidential interference—the executive branch's decision to weigh in on a private enterprise's self-protective decision—Obama publicly admonished Sony for setting a bad precedent of allowing a foreign dictator's censorship on American culture. Even after partially recuperating production costs from the film's limited distribution, Sony lost an estimated $30–$40 million on *The Interview* (not counting the indirect cost of repairing its vandalized network system).[14] A hard lesson was learned from this costly crisis. Indeed, as I hope to reveal in this book, the past should be looked back at with fresh eyes, not out of nostalgic yearning but as an inspiration for establishing future regulatory protocols concerning Hollywood's biggest customers: foreign audiences, who contribute 70 percent of the industry's total revenues today.

The book's Conclusion discusses China's current rules of film regulation and Hollywood's efforts to increase access to the world's second largest movie market (on the path to overtake the U.S. box office in the not-too-distant future). Several members of Congress as well as policy analysts have expressed concerns about the recent Chinese acquisition of American media companies and theater chains, and also about Hollywood's tendency to change film content to please Chinese censors. In particular, Marvel Studios' *Doctor Strange* (2016) came under fire due to its "whitewashing" of a sorcerer character called the Ancient One. The Disney subsidiary, under the leadership of producer Kevin Feige, allowed the filmmakers (including director Scott Derrickson) to change the comic book character's ethnicity from Tibetan to Celtic and cast British actress Tilda Swinton in the role, in hopes of circumventing an uncomfortable political confrontation with Chinese censors over any Tibet reference. After examining the alarmist rhetoric of the "freedom defense" against Chinese authoritarian censorship on American culture, the conclusion weighs in with an alternative view on the issue. It is there, in the book's Conclusion, that I point out an opportunity for Hollywood to renovate its long-engrained racial stereotypes through a negotiation process involving Chinese regulators, who are sympathetic to nuanced ethnic representations.

In bringing this Introduction to a close, I would like to share a personal story, one that, I hope, will illuminate how this book project came about and why I structured it in a way that combines classical and contemporary case studies. Some skeptical readers might, at first glance, blanch at my decision to mix two different periods in this way. I decided to undertake the book project and visit the National Archives several times to study more historical case studies because of the controversy surrounding *The Interview* and because I believe that a new framework for understanding Hollywood diplomacy is needed in the wake of the Sony hacking scandal.

On December 1, 2014, one week after the Sony hack and three weeks prior to *The Interview*'s planned release, I received an email from a producer of an NPR-affiliated Los Angeles radio station who was in charge of a daytime call-in talk show. She invited me to join her program the following day to discuss the controversy surrounding the film. In that email, the producer shared her personal opinion about the film's premise, which she found distasteful and problematic. She did not think that it was appropriate to ridicule a foreign head of the state with racialized jokes, on the grounds that he is a despotic figure who perhaps deserves more serious and thoughtful criticism for his regime's suppression of individual freedoms and violation of North Koreans' human rights. However, it was not the "satire" part of *The Interview* that bothered her most (as she had previously laughed at Margaret Cho's impersonation of Kim Jong-un's father, Kim Jong-il, in an episode of *30 Rock* [NBC, 2006–2013]), but rather the film's assassination plotline. The producer stated that she could not imagine a comedy film about an assassination attempt on President Obama or German chancellor Angela Merkel being made without inciting public outrage. She posed a rhetorical question, asking why there was no such public reaction to *The Interview*, and wanted to tackle that question with her listeners. Despite the short notice, I heartily agreed to join her show because I appreciated her thoughtful email and wanted to chime in from my academic position to help shed light on an issue that had entered the public sphere. She said that she was still looking for another expert with whom to pair me in the twenty-minute segment devoted to the topic. The next morning the producer called me to go over the logistics of that afternoon's interview. She informed me that she was able to locate another guest, who was an editor/critic for a trade news website, someone who strongly believed in Sony's right to satirize Kim using his real name and would be quite vocal about it.

On air, what I believed to be an opportunity to question and critique the film from an Asian American perspective transformed into a test on my patience while listening to my fellow guest's one-note defense of artistic creativity and free speech and support of the film's heavy-handed approach to totalitarian dictatorship in North Korea. What particularly bothered me as a film historian was his logic that the kind of satire being mobilized in *The Interview* is above reproach because something similar had been done years earlier by comedian-filmmaker-icon Charlie Chaplin in *The Great Dictator* (1940), a PCA-regulated motion picture that, it should be noted, did not even mention Adolf Hitler's name. This struck me as a false equivalency, the kind that has since been offered by numerous other commenters and which will be examined in chapter 5. My effort to interject a Korean/Asian American perspective on the controversy (explaining why, for example, Hollywood's previous anti–North Korean films such as *Die Another Day* and *Team America: World Police* [2004] were not welcomed in South Korea, and how the premise of assassinating a current leader does not sit well with Asian sensibilities) was challenged by my fellow guest, who, despite his professed love for Korean culture, would not budge from the position that advocates filmmakers' unrestricted freedom, particularly in their use of satire as a weapon against tyrants.

Two listeners called in and asked solid questions. The first caller critiqued the American double standard about offending other nations without putting ourselves in their shoes (i.e., Americans would likely detest a foreign satire about an assassination of their president, regardless of their own potentially ill feelings about that leader). My fellow guest, of course, disagreed and said that assassinating (or attempting to assassinate) a fictional American president is a perennial theme in popular culture (without clarifying that, in *The Interview*, the CIA is the good guy and covert assassination is accepted as a viable foreign policy option, while in American political thrillers the president, rather than malicious criminals, is often the object of audience empathy). The second caller opined that ridiculing Kim Jong-un in American popular culture blinds viewers from the harsh realities experienced by North Korean people. How could we take the suffering of North Koreans seriously without taking Kim seriously? The other guest responded that satire/comedy is the best way to reveal brutal dictatorships and shame them (the point being that *American* freedom, not North Korean, should be protected). I was struck by this online journalist's deeply held conviction, which blinded him from seeing the validity of any opposing views expressed by other participants on the program.

This experience motivated me to develop the project and seek out archival materials both in Washington, DC, and in Los Angeles to spotlight the current situation from a historical perspective. *Hollywood Diplomacy* is an invitation to scholars to look back at the historical context of Hollywood's foreign relations, which reflect the current crisis. It is also a call to cultural producers who might seek inspiration in shaping new representational modes conducive to international dialogue in the future. I believe that this study can be beneficial not only to film and media scholars but also to industry practitioners and policy makers facing the challenges of increasingly competitive global markets. Rejecting a clear-cut binary between "us" and "them" and resisting the temptation to celebrate the rhetoric of American liberties being threatened by foreign governments or rogue terrorist groups, my project invites scholars and industry professionals to rethink the current North Korean crisis in the larger historical context of Hollywood's diplomatic negotiations and self-regulation. Drawing upon archival evidence, I use the past as a reflection of the present and as a lesson for the future. In addition to offering an analysis of the current crisis through historical contextualization, I call for a long-term policy of foreign representations in terms of mitigating racial and ethnic stereotypes and respecting international audiences.

On March 15, 1927, in his address to students of the Harvard University School of Business, the MPPDA president Will H. Hays affirmed the American film industry's will to fulfill its responsibility in representing all nations and people fairly as the provider of 85 percent of motion pictures on the world's screens. With a mixture of empathy and barely disguised pride, the industry leader declared Hollywood's international commitment, stating, "We cooperate with the governments of all nations, that our pictures may correctly portray the habits and customs of every country to the citizens of every other country . . . . Our own government is cooperating closely, and we are ourselves determined that at every opportunity a true portrayal of American life and ideals shall be given to the world and that to the nationals of all countries shall go a true message of the lives of the nationals of all others."[15] Ninety years later, Hays's grand vision—articulated at the dawn of the American studio system—might sound overly idealistic and ambitious. However, if Hollywood is determined to hold on to its global leadership into the new century, it may be time to renew its youthful vow to respect the people of all nations and represent them fairly to the best of its ability.

Part I

Diplomatic Representations in Classical Hollywood

1

Censorship as Cultural Resistance

The Chinese Government's "Uplift" of National Images in 1930s Hollywood

While previous studies on the Production Code Administration (PCA) highlight the productive function of in-house self-regulation as a cost-effective, preemptive defense against external censorship (both domestic and foreign), such obliging discourse has rarely been extended to censorship boards operating outside of the American motion picture industry's jurisdiction. *Banned in Kansas: Motion Picture Censorship, 1915–1966* (2007), authored by Gerald Butters Jr., is the only book-length attempt to historically frame one of the seven state film censorship boards that existed in the United States.[1] In-depth academic studies on foreign censorship boards' impact on Hollywood film content are equally rare and limited to a few book chapters (e.g., "Diplomatic Representations: Accommodating the Foreign Market" in Ruth Vasey's *The World According to Hollywood, 1918–1936* [1997] and "Regulating National Markets: Chinese Censorship and *The Bitter Tea of General Yen*" in Eric Smoodin's *Regarding Frank Capra: Audience, Celebrity, and American Film Studies, 1930–1960* [2004]).

Drawing upon files housed at the U.S. National Archives, where I consulted documents of the State Department and the Bureau of Foreign and Domestic

Commerce, this chapter examines the pivotal role that Chinese censors played in pressuring Hollywood to improve the images of China and its people throughout the 1930s. That pressure, it should be noted, was applied soon after the industry-wide implementation of synchronized sound and in the wake of the 1929 stock market crash, a period of recalibration and transformation for the major motion picture studios and for U.S. society as a whole. In March 1931, the Chinese government set up a centralized, national film censorship board, the National Board of Film Censors (NBFC, later reorganized and renamed the Central Motion Picture Censorship Committee).[2] All motion pictures, whether domestic or foreign, were required to pass through the NBFC's censorship body before screenings could take place in China. Consisting of members appointed by the Ministry of Education and the Ministry of the Interior, the board could suppress any films deemed "injurious to the dignity of Chinese people" (Article Two of the Motion Picture Censorship Law of 1930). Although Hollywood's own Production Code had a self-regulatory provision mandating respect for foreign governments and nationalities (Article Ten, "National Feelings"), a number of China-themed films (such as *Welcome Danger* [1929], *East Is West* [1930], *Shanghai Express* [1932], *The Bitter Tea of General Yen* [1933], and *The General Died at Dawn* [1936]) were banned in China due to their negative images of the Chinese. Instead of simply suppressing offensive films case by case, the Chinese government actively sought to "uplift" images of China in Hollywood cinema through diplomatic pressure on the State Department (also known as the Department of State) and economic pressure on the studios. The NBFC put a moratorium on censorship review for the entire output of individual studios until they withdrew the insulting films from worldwide circulation and pledged to improve Chinese images in their future productions. Although studio personnel and American diplomats often saw these demands as capricious and severe, Orientalist representations in Depression-era Hollywood could have been far more damaging without such interventions.

State Department documents of the 1940s demonstrate that the Chinese government lost its voice in this capacity due to the United States' "protective" role in China during and after World War II, as well as to the wartime dissolution of its centralized censorship board in 1938. Unfettered by such political inequality, the Chinese government of the 1930s was able to demand that Hollywood contribute to New China's nation building and international publicity rather than harming it with racial stereotypes. At this historical juncture, film censorship was a crucial mechanism through which to enable diplomatic dialogue between the two nations, with the mediation of the American legation in Beijing (then Peiping) and the consulates general in Nanjing (then Nanking) and Shanghai, representing Hollywood studios.

The Pre-Code Rise of Hollywood's Self-Censorship and Foreign Relations Protocols

A comparative look at the consolidation of centralized film censorship in China and the United States between 1927 and 1934 highlights fundamental philosophical differences in the national consensus as to why—and by whom—motion pictures needed to be regulated. The United States remains one of the few countries in which the federal government has not censored motion pictures in the medium's history (although, through the Federal Communications Commission, it has taken the responsibility of regulating radio and television broadcasts on public airwaves).[3] Even after the nation's Supreme Court denied First Amendment protection for motion pictures in the 1915 *Mutual v. Ohio* ruling, in effect legally sanctioning the arbitrary banning of films by local, municipal, and state film censorship boards across the country,[4] the U.S. government steered clear of outright film censorship. Instead of regulating individual film content, the government was more interested in breaking up the oligopolistic business structure that hindered fair competition. The Justice Department filed antitrust suits against Hollywood twice: first, against the Motion Picture Patents Company, a trust created by Thomas Edison and nine other motion picture patent holders and technology manufacturers, in 1915; and second, against the vertically integrated "Big Five" companies (Paramount, MGM, 20th Century-Fox, Warner Bros., RKO), which were forced to divest themselves of studio-owned theaters by the Supreme Court's 1948 Paramount Decree. Ever vigilant against Washington's potential intrusion into film production, industry leaders formed a new trade organization, the Motion Picture Producers and Distributors of America (MPPDA), in 1922 and hired Will H. Hays, postmaster general of Warren G. Harding's administration, as its president. As Hollywood's respectable front man and capable lobbyist, Hays was responsible for developing an internal regulatory regime to preempt trouble with various external censorship boards, both domestic and foreign.[5]

Drawing up a set of guidelines for industrial self-regulation, the MPPDA published a list of "Don'ts and Be Carefuls" on May 17, 1927. The list was agreed upon in a meeting between Hays and the Sub-Committee of Eliminations (consisting of MGM head of production Irving Thalberg, Fox Film Corporation producer Sol Wurtzel, and film editor E. H. Allen). Prefacing the document is a statement of purpose: "In suggesting scenes and titles which should be entirely eliminated, the Committee has in mind not only the fact that these are habitually condemned by censoring boards in this country and abroad but more importantly that audiences observing them in non-censorship states and countries are aroused to demands for censorship. By eliminating these scenes and titles we not only save footage and the possibility of a mutilated picture when they are eliminated but also effectively forestall the demand for further censorship and further develop the ground work for the repeal of such censorship as now exists."[6] This statement underscores the industry's belief in preemptive self-regulation not only as a means of protecting their financial interests but also as a shield from hostile external censorship. The eleven prohibited subjects included profanity, nudity, drug trafficking, sex perversion, white slavery, miscegenation, venereal diseases, scenes of childbirth, children's sex organs, ridicule of clergy, and offense to any race, nation, or creed. The twenty-five subjects or activities that required "special care" included the use of the flag, international relations, arson, the use of firearms, theft, robbery, safe-cracking or dynamiting (trains, mines, buildings), brutality and gruesomeness, technique of committing murder, methods of smuggling, third-degree methods, hangings or electrocutions as legal punishment, sympathy for criminals, attitude toward public characters or institutions, sedition, cruelty to children and animals, branding of people or animals, the sale of women, rape or attempted rape, first night scenes, man and woman in bed together, seduction of girls, the institution of marriage, surgical operations, the use of drugs, scenes with law enforcement, and excessive or lustful kissing.

Three years later, the MPPDA expanded this list into an elaborate treatise with general principles, particular applications, and supporting reasons in the form of the Production Code, coauthored by Father Daniel Lord, a Jesuit priest, and Martin Quigley, a Catholic publisher of the *Motion Picture Herald*. Evaluated in retrospect from a contemporary perspective, the Code has been seen as being "responsible for the trivialization of American movies" and has been "blamed for Hollywood's timidity and lack of realism."[7] David A. Cook, for example, grumbles that "the Code as a whole was obviously restrictive and repressive . . . and in a very real sense, kept [American films] from becoming as serious as they might have been, and perhaps should have been."[8] However, it is important to acknowledge that, as pointed out by cultural historian Thomas Doherty, in "the context of its day, the Code expressed a progressive and reformist impulse" which "evinced concern for the proper nurturing of the young and the protection of women, demanded due respect for indigenous ethnics and foreign peoples, and sought to uplift the lower orders and convert the criminal mentality."[9]

Despite the lofty moral aims of the Code, its adoption could be best described as "a public relations gesture, designed to placate the bluenoses and to curtail agitation for state censorship."[10] To borrow an analogy put forth by film historian Richard Maltby, the MPPDA's promise of Code-conforming "pure" entertainment—motion pictures that would be harmless to all consumers regardless of their age—was comparable to the Food and Drug Administration's guarantee of pure, untainted meat.[11] Hollywood's crafting of an internal cleansing system between 1930 and 1934 was a response to external pressures, including a series of Payne Fund studies exploring the potentially negative effects of motion pictures on children (1929–1932), the looming threat of federal censorship by Roosevelt's New Deal government, and the Catholic Legion of Decency's nationwide boycott campaign against indecent movies. In 1927, the MPPDA organized the Studio Relations Committee (SRC) in Los Angeles in order to tighten the industry's self-regulation through script and print supervision. Although the SRC was in charge of implementing the Code after its 1930 publication (the submission of scripts became mandatory from 1931 onward), the organization was apparently ineffective and was replaced by a more powerful successor, the PCA, on July 15, 1934. This transitional period (1930–1934) is known as the "pre-Code era" and is reputed to have given rise to more permissive expressions of sex, violence, and immorality. In many historical accounts, both professional and amateur, pre-Code Hollywood is imagined as a vice-filled hinterland populated with gangsters, floozies, and gold diggers whose criminal and libidinal impulses went unchecked by the Production Code's strict moral order. In his book-length study of pre-Code cinema, Doherty goes so far as to say that early 1930s films were more "unbridled, salacious, subversive, and just plain bizarre than what came afterwards," and that "they look like Hollywood cinema but the moral terrain is so off-kilter they seem imported from a parallel universe." "In a sense," he concludes, "pre-Code Hollywood *is* from another universe."[12]

A close investigation of archival documents related to film regulation during the SRC era (available as part of the PCA files housed at the Academy of Motion Picture Arts and Sciences' Margaret Herrick Library) demonstrates that there is greater continuity between SRC and PCA guidelines than commonly believed. As Maltby argues, the Academy's records "reveal that this period actually saw by far the most interesting negotiations between the studios and the Code administrators over the nature of movie content, as the Code was implemented with increasing efficiency and strictness after 1930."[13] The myth of a "pre-Code cinema," for him, was created for "the need to situate Hollywood within a critical melodrama of daring creative heroes and reactionary villains, because the only version of Hollywood its critics can truly love is an 'un-American' anti-Hollywood, populated by rebel creators challenging and subverting the industrial system."[14]

Along with the issues of sex, crime, and morality, the topic of foreign relations was a regulatory priority for the SRC. Ruth Vasey elaborates on the agency's special interest in representations of foreign nationalities:

> By 1928, the SRC was fully operational in Hollywood, allowing Colonel Joy to accommodate the sensitivities of the foreign market in the course of his general supervision of production, not just in response to specific expressions of concern. Offenses to national groups were technically guarded against by the Don'ts and Be Carefuls . . . . This clause [about foreign relations] was something

> of an anomaly in the document, as it was the only stricture which did not refer to sex or crime. . . . The interests of foreign nations, especially those that were important or sensitive customers, received regular consideration, the objective being less to respond to criticism than to obviate it.[15]

Such perceived sensitivity of Italian customers is well documented in PCA files. For example, SRC director Jason S. Joy repeatedly cautioned Paramount against the caricatured portrayal of overexcited Venetian police detectives in Ernst Lubitsch's romantic comedy *Trouble in Paradise* (1932), reminding the studio that "the Italian point of view is . . . far from being a silent one" and that "the Italians are getting more than a little sensitive about all this hand-waving and jabbering that is almost constantly portrayed as the main characteristic of their race."[16] Following a series of high-profile Italian protests against pre-Code gangster films such as *Scarface* (which I will discuss in chapter 2), Hollywood started to suppress the representation of Italian bad guys altogether unless they appeared in a kind of "closeted" manner. In 1939, Warner Bros. named one of its gangster characters in *The Roaring Twenties* Nick Brown (Paul Kelly), although this seemingly Anglo-Saxon criminal is introduced by a shot of spaghetti, and his love for the dish is explicitly observed by another character in dialogue.[17]

Censorship as National Uplift: China's Motion Picture Censorship Law of 1930

Along with Italy, at the top of the SRC watch list (and later that of the PCA) of demanding foreign censors was the Republic of China, which centralized film censorship around the same time when the MPPDA developed the Production Code and its enforcement system. It is important to understand that, unlike in the United States (where film censorship was institutionalized as self-regulation *within* the industry in order to protect the financial investments of studios), in China it was developed as a part of a nation-building project of the Nationalist (Kuomintang, KMT) government during the Nanjing decade (1927–1937). Under the leadership of Generalissimo Chiang Kai-shek, the Nationalists unified China following the Northern Expedition (1926–1928) and consolidated state power with Nanjing as a new capital. That nation-building endeavor went beyond modernizing state infrastructures and reforming laws to prohibit feudal customs. It also involved propagandizing new national ideals represented by the founding father Sun Yat-sen's Three Principles of the People (democracy, nationalism, people's welfare/livelihood) through cultural, educational, and ideological indoctrination.[18] For this reason, the Nationalist government took the role of cinema seriously and sought to suppress undesirable subjects harmful to public morals, national unity, and international prestige, such as explicit sexuality, superstition, local dialects, and Japanese and Western imperialism. As historian Zhiwei Xiao asserts, "Confrontations with Western and Japanese imperialism on issues related to film censorship during [the Nanjing decade] were an important part of the Chinese struggle for equality, freedom, and sovereignty in the international community."[19] This nationalist view of film censorship was a logical extension of the uniquely Chinese concept of national cinema which, as Jubin Hu points out, was viewed as "a kind of 'good medicine' that could and should be used to save China."[20]

Before the 1927 inauguration of the new Nanjing government, film censorship in China from the late 1910s to the mid-1920s fell within the jurisdiction of police departments of regional governments.[21] During this period, as in the United States, Chinese films remained uncensored by a central government. In November 1927, the Education Department of the Shanghai Municipal Government established a film censorship committee. Unlike previous local film censors with geographically limited power, the Shanghai board not only had "much broader ramifications for the entire country" (due to its connection to the central government as well as its location in the center of the Chinese film industry) but also expanded its authority to foreign concessions areas.[22] The Shanghai Board of Film and Theater Censors appealed to the Nationalist Party to set uniform standards for film censorship across the country. In an attempt to nationalize film censorship, the Ministry of the Interior published the "Thirteen Regulations on Film" in September 1928 and declared the central government's right to censor motion pictures. However, the legislation granted sole authority of prescreening and approval to the police. This plan was both impractical (due to police departments' lack of necessary manpower and resources to enforce systematic censorship) and controversial in the eyes of other ministries, such as Propaganda and Education, which saw themselves as being better suited for the task. As a result, in April 1929, new legislation—"Sixteen Regulations"—coauthored by the Ministry of Education and the Ministry of the Interior, replaced the earlier document and "stipulated that film censorship should be conducted jointly by officials from the departments of police, social affairs, and education at all levels of government."[23] Under the Sixteen Regulations, the central government was to provide guidelines and to rule on controversial cases, while film reviews and censorship decisions were to be left to local censorship boards. This contradiction resulted in "arbitrary, inconsistent, and whimsical" variations of local rulings despite the principal of centralized censorship.[24]

In November 1930, the Nanjing government proclaimed the Motion Picture Censorship Law and finally legalized film censorship rules, strengthening state control. Article One states, "All motion picture films, either domestic or foreign production, are not allowed to be shown unless they have passed censorship in accordance with this Law." Article Two mandates, "Motion picture films will not be approved if they are: [1] injurious to the dignity of Chinese people; [2] contrary to the Three Principles of the People; [3] detrimental to good morality and public order; and [4] promoting superstition or heterodoxy." Article Three specifies, "The censorship of films shall be done by a Motion Picture Censorship Committee consisting of four members appointed by the Ministry of Education and three members appointed by the Ministry of the Interior."[25] The remaining articles (Four to Fourteen) explain the process of applying for a permit to show a motion picture and note censorship fees and fines for violating the law. To implement the new law, the Chinese government formed the NBFC in March 1931 and mandated that the national censorship board's seal be a requirement for exhibition of any film in China. The local censors were still allowed to exist, but "their job was not to censor films, for that was to be done in Nanjing . . . but to ensure that all films shown in their jurisdictions carried a seal of approval" from the NBFC.[26]

Although the China-themed films discussed in this chapter were censored on the basis of the most controversial first clause of Article Two, Hollywood's biblical epics, horror films, and fantasies featuring no Chinese connections—from *The Ten Commandments* (1923) and *Ben Hur: A Tale of the Christ* (1925) to *Frankenstein* (1931) and *Alice in Wonderland* (1931)—were likewise banned as "superstitious films" (*shenguai dianying*).[27] China's Motion Picture Censorship Law aroused the anxiety of many American producers and distributors, who feared that their films might be blocked in the Chinese market on arbitrary grounds, such as being "injurious to the dignity of Chinese people" or "promoting superstition or heterodoxy." In his September 16, 1931, meeting with Vice Minister of Education Chen Pu-lei, Consul General Willys R. Peck (at the United States consulate general in Nanjing) addressed this issue. According to a report from the United States legation in Beijing to the State Department, Consul Peck pointed out to the vice minister that "the four reasons given in the Motion Picture Censorship Law for possible refusal to issue permits were . . . matters of personal opinion" and inquired if more detailed guidelines or explanations could be provided to American film distributors, "so that they could avoid incurring the expense of bringing to China pictures which would be certain to be disapproved by the Committee." While the vice minister acknowledged "a certain amount of personal opinion involved in the censorship of films," he argued that substituting local censorship boards with "one national committee" would remove "the uncertainty attaching to possible differences of opinion among the local committees." He further advised that "it would be impossible for the Censorship Committee itself to issue any official definition of the meaning of the four reasons for the rejection of films as found in the censorship law" as only the government could issue such a definition.[28] As Xiao explains, the Chinese Motion Picture Censorship Law was purposefully "vague and elusive" so that "it would allow the government censors nearly arbitrary authority to interpret the law, placing filmmakers in a more vulnerable position."[29] The Production Code and its implementation were detailed and precise, so that studios could benefit from opportunities to rewrite and reedit as preemptive measures. By contrast, the Chinese Motion Picture Law was intentionally broad in its prohibitive provisions so that government officials could have interpretative leeway in serving public or national, rather than commercial, interests. Therefore, it is unsurprising that the American industrial demand for specificities conflicted with the Chinese bureaucratic preference for generalities as the two sides had fundamentally different understandings of the purposes and utilities of film censorship.

This difference was perceptively observed by Consul Peck, who mediated many disputes between the Chinese censors and Hollywood studios throughout the 1930s. In his June 21, 1933, report to Nelson Trusler Johnson, American minister (ambassador after 1935) in Beijing, Peck opined,

> It is evident . . . that motion picture censorship by the [Chinese] National Government is performed in the belief that motion pictures are a powerful influence on the public and an efficient agency either for assisting or retarding the political program of the Nationalist Party and the National Government. The attitude taken officially by the American Government seems to be that the motion picture industry is merely a money making enterprise, like the sale of a commodity, and . . . it appears that the American Government takes no steps to control the production or exhibition of motion pictures, either in a negative way by eliminating objectionable features, or in a positive way to further its own policies. Nevertheless, it seems awkward for a foreigner to question the right of the Chinese Government to exercise legitimate control over an agency which, potentially at least, will influence the Chinese population as profoundly as will public education.[30]

Enclosed in this report is a resolution entitled "The Standard of Foreign Motion Pictures Needed in Our Country," which was passed by the Central Executive Committee of the Nationalist Party on December 1, 1932. The resolution indicates the Chinese government's preference for subjects that have pedagogical value to its people (e.g., science, communication technologies, Western industries, modern machinery and armaments, social education), as well as those deemed morally and politically appropriate (e.g., conforming to Party principles, encouraging oppressed people's struggle for freedom, demonstrating respect for morality and public order).[31]

In his September 1, 1933, meeting with Kuo You-shou, a delegate of the NBFC chairman, and Peng Beh-chuan of the Ministry of Education, Consul Peck was presented with a leaflet ("An Open Letter to European and American Film Producers") that had been drafted by the National Educational

Cinematographic Society of China and distributed by the Ministry of Education in July 1933. Fifty copies of this document had been sent to the Chinese vice consulate in Los Angeles, where Vice Consul Kiang Yi-seng acted as the Chinese government's representative in charge of supervising China's images in Hollywood cinema. And, most importantly, it was to be distributed to Hollywood producers. This manifesto/petition is suffused with the resentment that comes from the perceived affront of foreign films exhibited in China that exploit the subjects of "adultery and robbery" and whose chief attribute is "the prevalence of so much social immorality." Identifying desirable motion picture subjects as "development of national spirit, promotion of productive and constructive enterprises, inculcation of scientific knowledge, cultivation of the revolutionary spirit, and establishment on the moral standards of people," the open letter cites a few American titles that are deemed acceptable—namely, that are in accordance with regulatory standards: Fox's *7th Heaven* (1927; a tunnel sweeper's triumph over obstacles), United Artists' *Resurrection* (1927; positive moral influence), United Artists' *Abraham Lincoln* (1930; expression of the national spirit), and Universal's *Captain of the Guard* (1930; encouragement of the revolutionary spirit). Toward the end, the letter explains that China, under national reconstruction, is "in great need of sympathy and cooperation from the advanced nations," not "international scorn and open insult." It indicts the recent trend in foreign films to depict China as a "disorderly and disorganized state" in order to "amuse the audience with imaginary and false impressions." Denouncing this trend as "international propaganda" at the service of "Japanese intrigues," the National Educational Cinematographic Society reminds Western producers of financial consequences for such national affronts, as the Chinese government "has decided that no films of these companies which do not respect our national honor are to be screened in our country."[32]

In a November 4, 1933, letter to the MPPDA's foreign manager Colonel Frederick L. Herron (who had earlier written to the consulate general in Nanjing, inquiring about reliable information on China-related film subjects that would likely meet with objections from the Chinese government), Consul Peck offered a perceptive interpretation of this document:

> This "open letter" explains a great deal of the difficulty which has arisen over American films relating to Chinese subjects. You will note that the "National Educational Cinematographic Society of China," which guides Government section in these matters, not only insists that films shall contain nothing derogatory to China or the Chinese people, but also nothing which is calculated to corrupt the public morals. The letter announces that filmmaking in China has certain definite "uplift" objects and it is clearly intimated that foreign films which pursue the same subjects will be favored, and those which do

> not will be censored. I have explained to the Chinese that American films are designed to amuse their audiences and have no avowed educational purpose. Nevertheless, the Chinese authorities seem determined to regard motion pictures as a means for improving the Chinese public and advancing the interests of the nation.[33]

As correctly pinpointed by the consul, the Chinese government saw cinema as a medium of national "uplift" that served public educational purposes, a view fundamentally at odds with how commercial motion pictures were perceived by the industry and the government in the United States. In 1915, the nation's Supreme Court denied First Amendment protection to motion pictures as, to quote Justice Joseph McKenna, they were deemed "business, pure and simple, originated and conducted for profit like other spectacles and, not to be regarded as part of the press of the country or as organs of public opinion."[34]

I have not found any evidence that the Chinese view of cinema as a tool of "national uplift" was influenced by the African American philosophy of "racial uplift," the black elite's leadership for the community's collective progress that was advocated by such influential thinkers as Booker T. Washington and W. E. B. Du Bois. It appears that the Chinese concept was propelled instead by popular resentment against foreign films' gross distortions of their national character and custom and wanton vilification of the Chinese as a people. As Jubin Hu notes, early Chinese film producers "saw the establishment of a positive image of the Chinese nation as their national duty."[35] Similarly, government bureaucrats conceived of themselves as enablers of national uplift by censoring negative images of China in both domestic and foreign motion pictures. The Chinese "uplift" theory is supported by the constitution of the NBFC itself. Although the committee was supposedly a joint venture between two ministries, the imbalance of board members (four from Education and three from the Interior, as specified in Article Three of the Motion Picture Censorship Law) demonstrated the Nanjing government's emphasis on positive enabling functions (education) of film censorship over negative prohibitive matters (policing). Some of the NBFC censors hailing from the Ministry of Education had impressive academic backgrounds. For example, Guo Youshou, who served as the board's coordinator from 1932 to 1934, received a PhD in economics from the University of Paris and was well connected to the leftist intellectual community in Shanghai.[36] Although Hollywood industry leaders and American diplomats suspected the NBFC's propaganda agenda (in the above-quoted letter to the MPPDA, Consul Peck referenced Soviet propaganda films as more extreme examples of an "uplift" cinema promulgated by the Chinese government), the board sought to maintain its autonomy and was lenient toward leftist Shanghai films despite the Nationalist Party's official anti-communist policy. Xiao argues that the NBFC's "defiance of Party control must be understood in the context of 'democratic endeavors' that marked the early years of the Nanjing government" founded on Sun Yat-sen's ideals of constitutional democracy.[37] It is precisely because of the NBFC's disobedience to the Party and its liberal attitude toward socially conscious leftist films that, in March 1934, the board was dissolved and reorganized as the Central Motion Picture Censorship Committee (CMPCC) under the direct control of the Nationalist Party.[38] The CMPCC discontinued its operations and was dissolved in 1938, one year after the Sino-Japanese War broke out.

The transition from the NBFC to the CMPCC signaled a move toward more stringent, restrictive censorship that paralleled a similar shift from the SRC to the PCA occurring around the same time in the United States. In response to the American legation's lobbying to the Chinese Ministry of Foreign Affairs, in December 1931 the NBFC agreed to describe objectionable portions, if it were only one or two scenes, and allow American importers and distributors to eliminate them rather than rejecting entire films.[39] By 1936, two years after the CMPCC replaced the NBFC, "fewer and fewer foreign films were given the option of editing."[40] According to unofficial statistics, as many as thirty American films were banned in China between 1936 and 1937.[41] Similar to that of the SRC, the NBFC's legacy tends to be brushed off as a short-lived, ineffective institution that is more or less forgotten in Chinese film historiography. However, the copious State Department files on the subject of the Chinese government's motion picture censorship in the early 1930s is a testament to the board's prowess in generating diplomatic crises that required interventions of American consular staff acting on behalf of Hollywood studios. Its vocal criticism of national and ethnic stereotypes in American cinema was shared by other countries such as Germany and Italy, both of which enlisted China's assistance in their own fights to safeguard national images (as will be demonstrated in the next section).

From *Welcome Danger* to *Shanghai Express*: Mitigating National Insults through Diplomatic Negotiations

It is noteworthy that the push for national film censorship in China, in particular the suppression of foreign films deemed "injurious to the dignity of Chinese people," came from both the film industry and the movie-going public. Throughout the 1920s, newspapers and studio-backed film magazines published numerous articles denouncing offensive images of the Chinese in Western films and calling for the government's intervention.[42] Perhaps no American film contributed more to the strengthening of Chinese film censorship than Harold Lloyd's first talkie, *Welcome Danger* (1929), a Clyde Bruckman–directed throwback to the comedian's better-known silent classics *Safety Last* (1923) and *The Freshman* (1925). The slapstick-infused romantic comedy tells the story of

Harold Bledsoe (Harold Lloyd), a nerdy botany enthusiast who travels to San Francisco to take his recently departed father's post as a police captain. He is assigned to the case of a Chinese opium smuggling ring that uses a flower shop in Chinatown as their front. The gang abducts the Chinese American doctor Gow (James Wang), who has been privately investigating their criminal organization. The gentle physician happens to be an attending doctor for the crippled brother of Harold's love interest, Billy Lee (Barbara Kent). Disguised as a Chinese man, Harold infiltrates the smugglers' joint, ambushes bumbling henchmen Keystone Cops–like fashion, and knocks their heads with a police baton one by one. Harold saves the doctor and exposes the incognito ring leader, an outwardly respectable local reformer named John Thorne (Charles Middleton).

This much-anticipated sound film premiered to Chinese audiences in two Shanghai theaters (the Grand and the Capitol) in the International Settlement on February 21, 1930. The following day, the Nationalist Party claimed that "the picture ridiculed and disgraced the Chinese nation" and pressured the theater management to stop its exhibition.[43] It also took preemptive measures to stall future screenings throughout China by instructing major newspapers not to print advertisements of *Welcome Danger* and requesting various government agencies to prohibit the film's exhibition within their jurisdiction. Governmental actions went hand in hand with consumer boycotts. On February 22, Hong Shen, a Harvard-educated playwright and professor at Fudan University, addressed a full house shortly before the film's 5:30 P.M. screening at the Grand Theater (Da Guangming). He stated that he had already seen the 3:00 P.M. screening and found the film to be "unfit for his countrymen to see," owing to its "anti-Chinese" sentiments.[44] The professor urged fellow theatergoers to walk out and demand refunds of their admission costs. According to reports, many audiences did just that, and Hong was soon arrested by police (who had been called by the management to quell the disturbance). After this incident, the film was withdrawn from both theaters. Upon being released on bail, Hong wrote a letter to the Shanghai branch of the Nationalist Party, demanding that the Grand Theater be penalized for showing *Welcome Danger* and citing stateside African American protests against D. W. Griffith's *The Birth of a Nation* (1915) as his inspiration. Hong is quoted as saying, "We [Chinese people] and the black people are both oppressed.... How can we Chinese fall behind American black people in reacting to this kind of humiliation and racism?"[45] Apparently, Party officials were responsive to Hong's call for action and stipulated that all future screenings of Lloyd's films be prohibited until the actor/producer officially tendered his apology to the people of China.

According to State Department documents, Edwin S. Cunningham, the American consul general in Shanghai, expressed his sympathy for the Chinese indignation over Lloyd's comedy in his official report on the incident:

"*Welcome Danger* does ridicule the Chinese and it should not have been exhibited in China. That the producer knew this to be true and anticipated trouble is believed to have been substantiated by the fact that the most wonderful character in the entire play was a Chinese doctor, which the producer probably thought would be sufficient to counteract the criticism of the Chinese in general. It is unfortunate that an effort was made to display such a picture in China at the present time; it is exceedingly humorous but not suitable for the entertainment of Chinese."[46] The staff in the Bureau of Foreign and Domestic Commerce (later the Department of Commerce) disagreed with Consul Cunningham. For example, Nathan D. Golden, assistant chief of the Bureau's Motion Picture Division, wrote to Addie Viola Smith, American trade commissioner in Shanghai, on April 1, 1930, stating, "There is no question but this agitation was probably created by one of the local producing concerns. Having seen the picture, I hardly could see anything that would be derogatory to the Chinese. I believe it is just another instance of a starving domestic producing company agitating for the showing of more of their own pictures at the expense of good American product."[47]

The sharp contrast between Consul Cunningham's respect for the Chinese perspective and Golden's cynically commercial view on local protests against Lloyd's film is a good barometer as to why the State Department, not the Bureau of Foreign and Domestic Commerce, was the right agency to step in to mediate censorship crises abroad. Although many studio executives and publicity managers at that time might have privately sided with Golden's opinion, such a parochial view is insensitive to the depth of injury that silver-screen racism could inflict on the collective psyche of a nation under "semi-colonization by European and Japanese powers."[48] It is also oblivious to the bottom-up nature of audience boycotts, a popular demand that no doubt influenced government leaders' punitive action against American producers. On April 17, 1930, Jay C. Huston, consul in Shanghai, visited Yu Hung-chun, chief secretary to the mayor of the Special Municipality of Shanghai, to object to the temporary ban on all Lloyd comedies in China as a penalty for derogatory Chinese images in *Welcome Danger*. The American consul was informed that "the opposition to the Harold Lloyd film . . . was a matter of public sentiment [of] such widespread indignation" and "the ridiculing of the Chinese in the scene where they were all knocked out, and in the opium smuggling act were especially offensive." Consul Huston defended the film as "purely a comedy" with no intention of offending the Chinese people. He further insisted that the Chinese community in San Francisco and his Chinese friends in the Rotary Club expressed no objection to it.[49] The State Department even dispatched the consul to Hollywood in order to facilitate the Harold Lloyd Corporation's reconciliation with the Chinese government. Based on Huston's advice, Lloyd wrote a letter of apology to China, dated May 29, 1930, addressed specifically to Henry K. Chang, consul general of China in San Francisco. After claiming that no offense was intended and "a staff of Chinese experts" was consulted throughout the production, Lloyd ultimately capitulated: "What I am anxious to do is to offer my sincere apologies to China and her people, through you, if I have in any way reflected upon her national pride and dignity."[50]

The effect of the *Welcome Danger* scandal went deeper than what might have been expected. In January 1936, the Chinese government banned another Lloyd film, the Sam Taylor–directed comedy *The Cat's Paw* (1934), on the grounds that it was "derogatory to China and the Chinese."[51] Chinese sources of government censorship documents explicitly indicate that "Lloyd's previous offense [*Welcome Danger*] was a factor in the ban on [*The*] *Cat's Paw*."[52] Furthermore, the widespread public outrage and sense of national disgrace must have spurred the government's effort to consolidate film censorship and eliminate local variants as well as the exemption status of foreign concession areas in Shanghai, where the trouble started. The Chinese government learned a valuable lesson from the incident, realizing that even the whiff of an economic threat (i.e., the chance that *all* products of an offending producer or production company might be banned) could elicit the desired response, be it an apology or a pledge not to offend local sensibilities again.

U.S. State Department files concerning motion pictures in 1930s China demonstrate that the latter country collaborated with other governments in barring the exhibition of certain American motion pictures for offenses to non-Chinese nationalities/ethnicities. For example, Universal's antiwar drama *All Quiet on the Western Front* (1930) and United Artists' aviation epic *Hell's Angels* (1930) were prohibited in China for being "anti-German," at the request of the German legation. According to a May 1932 MPPDA report to the State Department, the German government attempted to ban the latter film in different parts of the world (including France, England, New Zealand, Turkey, Canada, Argentina, Australia, Mexico, Singapore, and Cuba), but only China and Spain were responsive to such a diplomatic call.[53] In June 1936, the management of Paramount Films of China, the American studio's local branch in Shanghai, was dismayed when the advertised exhibition of *Give Us This Night* (1936), a romantic melodrama-musical set in the world of opera, was suspended at the request of the Italian consul general in Shanghai even though the film had already passed the CMPCC's review. In his report to the State Department dated July 2, 1936, George H. Merrell Jr., first secretary of the United States embassy in Beijing, stated that "the film had been returned to the [Nanjing] for re-screening before the National Motion Picture Censorship Committee with a representative of the Italian Embassy present. . . . the [Italian] objections were based on some comic representations of Italian policemen."[54] The crisis was resolved in August, when Paramount Pictures and the Italian government agreed upon cuts of derogatory parts prior to the film's showing in China.

From an American perspective, a foreign government's attempt to influence other countries' censorship decisions on Hollywood films would be seen as unjust obstructionism, an obstacle to international commerce. In August 1933, William Phillips, acting secretary of state, issued official policy instructions to Minister Johnson in Beijing when the NBFC threatened to exclude all Columbia films from the Chinese market until the studio withdrew the warlord film *The Bitter Tea of General Yen* from worldwide circulation. The United States State Department recognized "the right of any government to prevent within that government's jurisdiction the exhibition of any motion picture which it may regard as contrary to its interests" but declared that it "could not admit the right of any government to demand the suppression of an American picture outside the jurisdiction of the government making the demand."[55] In the aforementioned November 1933 letter to the MPPDA's foreign manager, Consul Peck described the difficulty of upholding Washington's policy in the local market:

> You will note . . . that if an American film contains matter which the Chinese regard as exposing China to ridicule or insult, it does not improve matters merely to refrain from exhibiting such a film in China. If it is exhibited anywhere, the producing company will be visited with penalties in China. I have attempted to prove to the Chinese authorities that this constitutes an unwarranted assumption of authority by the Chinese Government over the film industry in other countries, but my arguments seem to have had little effect. One reason that the Chinese seem to be convinced of the correctness of their attitude is, I imagine, that authorities in other countries generally lend a ready ear to complaints by Chinese consuls abroad. Each nation seems to be entirely willing to cultivate the good will of China, if this can be done merely by suppressing a portion of an American film.[56]

From Chinese, Italian, or German perspectives, allied market pressures were seen as effective consumer weapons in battling Hollywood's already entrenched racial, ethnic, and national stereotypes. As Vasey points out, "Although China's contribution to the American companies' foreign revenue was miniscule, its cultivation of diplomatic channels of protest had a significant impact on the industry."[57] For example, as studied by Eric Smoodin, "Chinese lobbying efforts designed to keep people away" from regional theaters screening *The Bitter Tea of General Yen* (in Batavia [now Jakarta], Singapore, Manila, Calcutta [now Kolkata], and others) did more fiscal damage to Columbia's overseas revenue than the banning of the film in China itself and thus gave the studio a strong incentive to withdraw it prematurely.[58]

Although in May 1931 Universal Studios got into hot water with the Shanghai film censorship board thanks to *East Is West* (1930), a sordid potboiler about the human trafficking of women from China to San Francisco, and had to publish an apology in Chinese newspapers with a promise to produce no more films that might be insulting to China, no film since *Welcome Danger* enraged the Chinese government and public more than Paramount's *Shanghai Express* (1932).[59] Directed by Josef von Sternberg, a master of expressive melodrama whose penchant for ornate visual flourishes and atmospheric lighting (not to mention his gravitation toward his frequent muse Marlene Dietrich) had already earned him a reputation for excellence, this pre-Code film was a prestige production that took thirty-six days to shoot with a budget in excess of $700,000. It revolves around a captivity narrative, one that spotlights a group of Western first-class passengers aboard the titular train who become hostages of the Eurasian rebel warlord Henry Chang (Warner Oland) and his troops. Among the ill-fated hostages are Shanghai Lily (Marlene Dietrich), a woman of easy virtue, and her former lover and English army surgeon Donald "Doc" Harvey (Clive Brook). The two are apparently still in love despite their icy demeanors toward one another. Lily is accompanied by a fellow prostitute of Chinese ancestry, Hui Fei (Anna May Wong), who is later sexually assaulted by Chang and kills him in revenge. Before his demise, Chang displays barbaric tendencies, such as branding a German opium dealer as payback for insolence, attempting to torture and maim Harvey, and coercing sexual favors from Lily in exchange for leniency toward the man she loves.

Paramount touted Harry Hervey's original story ("Sky over China," also known as "China Pass") as an authoritative account of the Orient in its press sheet written for *Shanghai Express*'s marketing and publicity. Searching for an inspiration for exotic stories with an "oriental flavor," Hervey traveled extensively throughout the region—from China and Japan to Vietnam and Malaysia. *Shanghai Express* is loosely based on his own "thrilling experience of . . . being held by revolutionaries" on the train which, according to the writer, was "a common occurrence" during the warlord era. However, Hervey's literary Orient is a Western cultural construct that, as the studio admits, is "shrouded by age-old mysteries and fretted with a kaleidoscopic change of color and pattern of millions upon millions of strange, fascinating peoples."[60] Likewise, Sternberg's cinematic Orient, as described by Carole Zucker, is "at once China—we know this because the series of images have a connotative value which accretively means China; and, it is Not-China, a fictive world marked 'exotic,' a landscape capable of spawning and supporting an elaborate dream, delivered to the audience through symbol and surface."[61] Gina Marchetti further contextualizes the Orientalist construction of China in Sternberg's film, stating, "A product of the uncertainties and social crises of the depression, *Shanghai Express* . . . titillates the viewer with the allure of forbidden sexuality, exotic adventure, 'Oriental' opulence, and decadent self-indulgence at a time when the promised security of the bourgeois home seemed like an empty illusion for the majority in the audience taunted by the very real possibilities of bankruptcy, unemployment, domestic strife, and complete moral and physical ruin."[62]

As a relatively cosmopolitan studio known for its polished, continental house style (largely attributed to its employment of European émigrés like German-born Ernst Lubitsch and the Armenian American filmmaker Rouben Mamoulian), Paramount gave the Austria-born Sternberg tremendous creative leeway, allowing his production team to build a faux Chinese village in Chatsworth, California, and to transform the Santa Fe railway station and adjoining streets in San Bernardino into the Beijing terminal. In his 1965 autobiography, Sternberg reminisced, "A China was built of papier-mâché and into it we placed slant-eyed men, women, and children [extras], who seemed to relish being part of it."[63] The director "thought the canvas of China, as evoked by [his] imagination, quite effective" and did not anticipate that he would be blacklisted by the Chinese government. Despite the alleged threat of arrest and punishment, Sternberg traveled to China "some years later" and rode the actual Shanghai Express, which he found "thoroughly unlike the train [he] had invented."[64] The Svengali-like auteur, whose reputation for putting style ahead of story preceded him, retrospectively commented, "I was more than pleased that I had delineated a China before confronted with its vast and variegated reality [because there was] quite a difference between fact and fancy."[65] This striking admission confirms Edward Said's classic definition of Orientalism as a structural set of Western ideas about the Orient, "despite or beyond any correspondence, or lack thereof, with a 'real' Orient." As such, Orientalism "has less to do with the Orient than 'our' world"—that is, Depression-era America, in the case of *Shanghai Express*.[66]

In addition to its tendency to foreground flamboyant art direction and set design, another side of silver-screen Orientalism—the *performative* side—is worth noting. The studio's press sheet celebrated the cross-racial casting of Warner Oland, a versatile character actor who specialized in playing "swarthy villains and Chinese mystery men of sinister portent," as a Chinese warlord. The publicity copy even claimed that an aged Chinese extra on the location set mistook the Swedish American performer as his countryman. Through Sternberg's interpreter and technical advisor, Tom Gubbins, the Chinese man reportedly asked the Caucasian actor if he came from Canton. Paramount endeavored to present Oland as an authentic interpreter of the Orient, someone who acquired "a manner that suggests an Asian ancestry . . . from constant study of the manners and customs of the East."[67] Larded atop the visual Orientalism of Oland's yellowface performance is yet another side of this reductive representational schema. Taking a translation sequence (in which Hui Fei translates Cantonese spoken by rebels to English for other passengers) as an example, film scholar Yiman Wang observes that "a major incongruence is that the train is staffed by people who speak Cantonese, a Southern Chinese dialect, despite the fact that it departs from a Northern Chinese city, where Mandarin and its variants are spoken." Wang further distinguishes Anna May Wong's hereditary language—Taishan dialect—which gets lumped together with Cantonese on the soundtrack, a mishmash of sonic signifiers.[68] As an Orientalist text created by and for "outsiders" that hinges upon the binary opposition between West and East, *Shanghai Express* not only lacks geopolitical fidelity and cultural authenticity, as evidenced by linguistic mishaps, but also signifies "a relationship of power, dominance, of varying degrees of complex hegemony" between the United States and China through its deeply problematic politics of representation.[69]

In his memorandum to Colonel Jason Joy dated September 18, 1931, the SRC reviewer (and future screenwriter) Lamar Trotti listed three objectionable plot points in Paramount's script: [1] the depiction of Chinese rebels appearing to be victorious over the government; [2] the unsympathetic treatment of a clergyman/missionary character named Reverend Carmichael; and [3] explicit references to Lily's profession.[70] While the latter two subjects (religion and sex) are more typically targeted as "usual suspects" of American film censorship, PCA files on *Shanghai Express* indicate that the SRC's top priority was the issue of Chinese characterizations. In his letter to the Paramount head of production B. P. Schulberg dated September 28, 1931, Joy stated, "We have read your script *Shanghai Express* [and] our first thought about it, from the point of view of the Code and of censorship, is that it would be advisable by all means to have some authoritative Chinese opinion regarding the conflict between the government and the rebels."[71] In a follow-up letter dated October 8, 1931, Joy reemphasized, "It is our understanding that you will . . . screen the finished film [to the Chinese minister in Washington, DC] to make certain that there are no objections." He reminded the Paramount executive of the SRC's regulatory protocol by adding, "It is a policy matter, the question of censorship abroad being the major consideration" despite the fact that his office did not think that the "Chinese people are placed in an unfavorable light."[72]

Despite the SRC's cautionary approach regarding international relations, it is clear that the self-regulation agency failed to predict the ferocity with which Chinese officials would oppose Sternberg's film. One month prior to the film's stateside release, on January 14, 1932, Paramount's vice president of production, Jesse Lasky Jr., wrote to Joy and shared a translation of an article recently printed in a Chinese newspaper. Titled "Paramount Utilizes Anna May Wong to Produce Picture to Disgrace China," the translated article read:

> Recently Paramount has made a picture showing the darkest side of Chinese politics. It is called *Shanghai Express*, in which Anna May Wong plays the part of a contemptible Chinese prostitute. This picture has the Chinese revolution

> as its background, depicting a conspiracy between rebels and foreigners.... The picture, when completed, will further expose all the evils of Chinese society, and as the Occident knows very little of Chinese and always entertains a contempt for things Chinese, the pictures always exaggerate the truth. If any Chinese character is included, he has to wear a queue and Chinese boots, long discarded.... We hope the Chinese Minister in America will immediately file a protest with the Paramount Company.[73]

Although Lasky brushed off the report as being unjustifiable and misinformed, the Paramount executive demanded that he meet with Joy to discuss the possibility of contacting the Chinese minister on this matter. Even after reading this preemptive Chinese press objection to the unreleased Paramount film, a blindsided Joy reported to Hays the following week, "I am pretty sure... that Paramount has handled *Shanghai Express*... in a way that will please the Chinese although we are planning to show it to the Chinese Consul General in order to make sure."[74] After conducting a preview of the completed film, Joy wrote to the studio on January 21, 1932, informing its representatives that they found *Shanghai Express* to be "satisfactory under the Code" and anticipated that "the Chinese will have a favorable view of the picture... since you have respected their point of view throughout."[75]

Despite the existence of the Production Code's Article Ten ("National Feelings"), which mandated that "the history, institutions, prominent people and citizenry of other nations shall be represented fairly" and the SRC's prioritization of this provision, the case of *Shanghai Express* highlights the difficulty of internal regulators defining, identifying, and preempting offensive national images across cultural barriers. It did not help that the NBFC's own criteria were vague and overly generalized, as discussed earlier. According to Xiao,

> There were no clearly stated rules delineating what was considered offensive, but judging from the list of banned foreign films and segments of foreign films that Chinese censors penciled for deletion, one can infer what qualified as taboo representations. These seem to include scenes that showed China as a backward country and her people as an uncivilized race; scenes in which the Chinese appeared as villains, as morally corrupt (smoking opium and gambling) or even as servants; and dialogue that ridiculed the Chinese and the Chinese way of life or referred to the Chinese in a less than respectable way.[76]

In his report to the State Department dated December 7, 1936, Ambassador Johnson similarly stated, "With Oriental susceptibility, the Chinese regard motion pictures portraying Chinese 'warlords,' banditry, civil war, natural disasters, epidemics and widespread poverty as among the worst of the agencies by which China is lowered in prestige before the nations of the world and they seem determined to combat such portrayals at any cost."[77]

What is noteworthy is that the Chinese censors did not object to the performative aspects of Classical Hollywood representations, such as the convention of racist cosmetology (i.e., yellowface) or the kind of linguistic inauthenticity that results from the mangling of different dialects. The controversial Charlie Chan film series (which was adapted from the novels of Earl Derr Biggers and produced at Fox [20th Century-Fox after 1935] during the 1930s and early 1940s, and which cast three successive Caucasian actors—Warner Oland, Sidney Toler, and Roland Winters—as the titular Honolulu detective speaking in fortune cookie–style vernacular) was "accorded a near hero's welcome in China" and surprisingly did not encounter any censorship problems.[78] Chinese producers even remade five Charlie Chan films from 1937 and 1941, starring Xu Xinyuan. Instead of the kind of racial issues (including Detective Chan's phony accent and genuflectory attitude) that agitate many Asian American critics and activists today,[79] the Chinese censors' attention was focused on broader themes, narrative elements, and characterizations outside of the Charlie Chan series that, in their eyes, were contrary to national interests and damaging to China's standing on the world stage. Warlord films and bandit pictures were among the most detested materials as far as Chinese film censors were concerned. This important distinction between Asian American and Chinese reactions to Hollywood pictures highlights the fact that the Republic-era censorship board saw stateside representations as a matter of foreign rather than race-based relations, although many intellectuals regarded the Chinese as oppressed people comparable to African Americans (as evidenced by the playwright Hong Shen's protest letter against *Welcome Danger*, cited earlier).

Shanghai Express's first fifteen minutes provide ample evidence of the sort of derogatory images and dialogue frowned upon by the Chinese censors. Shortly after the train departs from the Peiping (Beijing) central train station, its passage is blocked by a nursing cow and her baby calf, which refuse to budge from the track on a busy urban street. Watching the scene of a frustrated conductor arguing with the cow's owner from the window of the first-class compartment, Chang, a half-Chinese rebel leader traveling incognito, answers Reverend Carmichael (Lawrence Grant)'s question—"Can you tell me what's wrong now?"—with self-contempt: "We are in China now, sir, where time and life have no value." This dismissive sentiment is echoed by his fellow passenger, an American bookmaker named Sam Salt (Eugene Pallette), who says in a later scene, "What future is there in being a Chinaman? You're born, eat your way through a handful of rice, and you die. What a country!" As the train finally resumes its course, Lily and Hui Fei are seen settling down in their compartment, luxuriating in the jazz music coming from a portable gramophone and taking out a deck of cards. The relaxing duo is visited by Mrs. Haggerty

(Louise Closser Hale), an elderly prig from the next compartment who introduces herself as the owner of a Shanghai boarding house. Claiming that she only accepts respectable guests, the uptight woman glances suspiciously at a sultry, cigarette-smoking Hui Fei and asks, "I am sure you are very respectable, madam?" The young Chinese woman replies with words drenched in cynicism. "I must confess I don't quite know the standard of respectability that you demand in your boarding house," she says, to the shock of Mrs. Haggerty, who hastens her exit in a show of contempt. During an earlier scene, an outraged Reverend Carmichael similarly refuses to share train space with Hui Fei, barking at the porter, "I haven't lived for ten years in this country not to know a woman like that when I see one. Get me another compartment." Although Lily and Hui Fei sustain themselves through the same vocation, it is obvious that the former outclasses the latter with her racial privilege. In the opening scene set in the station, Harvey's fellow soldier informs him with excitement that Shanghai Lily is on the train. When the army doctor does not recognize the name (he knows her by another name, Madeleine), his friend enlightens him, "Everyone in China knows her. She is a notorious coaster . . . a woman who lives by her wits along the China coast." While Shanghai Lily is a local

FIG. 1.1 The opening scene of Josef von Sternberg's *Shanghai Express* (Paramount Pictures, 1932) abounds in the kind of derogatory images that the Republic of China's National Board of Film Censors saw contrary to their national interests, such as a nursing cow and her calf blocking the titular train's passage on a busy urban street.

FIG. 1.2 Hollywood's self-regulatory agency, the Studio Relations Committee, cautioned Paramount against an unsympathetic portrayal of Reverend Carmichael (right: Lawrence Grant), who protests his seat assignment in the compartment occupied by Hui Fei (left: Anna May Wong), a woman of ill repute.

celebrity flanked by a legion of admirers, Hui Fei is a fallen woman who eventually becomes a rape victim after being ostracized in her own country by Western moralists such as Mrs. Haggerty and Reverend Carmichael.

Despite the SRC's cautionary advice, Paramount made few adjustments to the original script in order to improve the characterizations of Hui Fei and Henry Chang. By contrast, it made significant changes to Reverend Carmichael, following the SRC's recommendation to make him "a sympathetic figure who, through his very bearing, suggests a streak of decency" in order to preempt Protestant church protests. In the early script, the "picayune, irascible and narrow-minded" man is an imposter who uses the holy garb as a cover for his crime, whereas in the final print he is a respectable clergyman who defends Lily's honor to Harvey and tries to help the estranged lovers reunite.[80] In Hervey's original story, Carmichael, a bigoted doctor (not a minister), sexually attacks Hui Fei and is stabbed by his victim. As such, this character came a long way and was "purified" in the adaptation process. The studio did make some changes to Chinese representations. Based on Joy's feedback that "the scene of the human heads hanging from poles in the Chinese street [is] gruesome . . . and will invite the opposition from the Chinese," Paramount eliminated the scene.[81] Also gone is a heavy-handed passage of dialogue that would have perpetuated Chang's Fu Manchu–like anti-Western ideology if it had been retained: "My fellow brothers are eating their rice—in comparative happiness—an existence they have enjoyed for many centuries—you see, our civilization was highly developed long before Christ was born—before the whites made history—before the grandeur that was Greece and the glory that was Rome—and we Chinese have not changed while the white man formed Europe—while your churches were being built—while you had a thousand years of ignorance and chaos—while you borrowed our knowledge of the stars, gunpowder and printing—and conquered every continent except this."[82] Earlier scripts feature another line spoken by Chang—"I belong to a gambling people"—that might have been offensive to the Chinese people and which was stricken from the final print.[83] In the original script, Chang takes Harvey as a hostage in hopes of exchanging the English surgeon (whose skills are needed to save the life of the British governor-general in Shanghai) for his own son, a prisoner of government troops. In the completed film, the object of exchange is Chang's spy. This subtle transformation further dehumanizes Chang by turning him from a concerned father into a calculating militia leader.

Scholars drawn to gender theory and cultural studies–based approaches to cinema might find the middle-aged character's celibacy suggestive of a queer(ed) positionality. In her discussion of Chang's ambiguous biracial identity (which prompts his fellow passenger to question, "Are you Chinese or are you white or what are you?"), Marchetti argues that "Chang stands as the emblem of the ideological question of difference. Neither Asian nor white, homosexual nor heterosexual, his potential threat comes as much from his existence outside the distinct, hierarchical boundaries on which Euro-American society is based as it does from the fact that he is a vicious warlord." Marchetti continues her cultural analysis, stating, "It is the uncertainty and the potential duplicity of Chang's existence, the possibility that rigid social distinctions based on race or gender are essentially meaningless, that creates Chang's disturbing allure."[84] Chang is one of the many cinematic offshoots of Sax Rohmer's serialized icon Dr. Fu Manchu, the somewhat demonic embodiment of the Yellow Peril stereotype. As Robert G. Lee observes, "Fu Manchu . . . is invariably described physically in feline and androgynous terms: [his nemesis] Nayland Smith . . . is the imaginary archetype of the Anglo-Saxon hero . . . . Fu Manchu's power to incite the fevered imagination lies in his ambiguous sexuality, which combines a masochistic vulnerability marked as feminine and a sadistic aggressiveness marked as masculine."[85] While *Shanghai Express* similarly contrasts Chang's fluid identity with Harvey's rugged Anglo-Saxon masculinity, inviting a queer reading, it seems that there was a more practical reason to cast Chang as a Eurasian (born to a Chinese mother and a white father) rather than a full Chinese character.

There were two Production Code clauses that would have stood in the way of depicting him as a Chinese: the anti-miscegenation clause (under Article Two: "Sex") as well as the foreign relations clause (under Article Ten: "National Feelings"). Although the Code specifically defined miscegenation as "sex relationships between the white and black races," in practice the exclusion extended to other racial minorities such as Asians, Latinos, and Native Americans.[86] Chang's interracial lust for Lily, however, would have been a less egregious violation as it remains unconsummated and he is punished for his devious sexuality (Frank Capra's *The Bitter Tea of General Yen* follows an almost identical narrative trajectory but retains the title character's full Chinese identity). The latter clause would be the primary reason for Chang's biracial identity, so that his non-Chinese, European half could be blamed for his criminality in the event of Chinese objections (this plot point was indeed cited in the film's defense to the Chinese minister in Washington, DC, an anecdote that will be discussed in the following pages). As was the case of *Welcome Danger*, which features a morally admirable Chinese doctor as a significant supporting character to counterbalance negative images of opium smugglers, the producers of *Shanghai Express* (including studio boss Adolph Zukor) must have predicted trouble with the Chinese censors when they intentionally drew attention to Chang's mixed race identity in the script without clear narrative rationale being given otherwise.

In a manner that recalls the frosty reception given to *Welcome Danger*, the Chinese government's punitive action against *Shanghai Express* originated from people's protests. After Paramount released the film in February 1932, the Chinese legation in Washington, D.C., received letters of disapproval from Chinese residents in the United States who saw the film. Although the studio did not submit a censorship print to the NBFC (the Paramount Shanghai office determined that the film's "certain amusing anachronisms made it unsuitable for use in China"), the censorship committee was alerted when Chinese students in Germany who were offended by the Sternberg-Dietrich collaboration sent angry missives to the board.[87] In his meeting with Consul Peck on June 21, 1932, NBFC member Beh Chuan Peng argued that *Shanghai Express* "would give foreigners an incorrect impression of the Chinese people and would hurt the feelings of the Chinese people" because of its objectionable subject matter and unsubtle portrayals of bandits and prostitutes. In response to the American consul general's defense of the plot, the Chinese censor went on to insist that, "in the case of a 'strong' country like the United States, everybody would know that bad characters in a film, even if true to life, represented an occasional phenomenon, but in the case of a 'weak' country like China, people might suppose that Chinese bad characters were typical of the bulk of the population."[88] Peng requested Peck's aid in suppressing *Shanghai Express*'s exhibition around the world, assuring him that the board would

FIG. 1.3 The producers of *Shanghai Express* deliberately call attention to the biracial identity of Henry Chang (left: Warner Oland), a Fu Manchu–like Oriental villain with a transgressive sexual desire for Shanghai Lily (right: Marlene Dietrich), in order to blame his European half for his criminality.

return the favor if another country's motion picture mispresented the United States in a similar way.

One week later, Peck was visited by a local representative of Paramount Films of China, who reported that the committee "had passed a resolution barring all Paramount films from exhibition in China unless all copies of *Shanghai Express* throughout the world were destroyed."[89] This "unusual demand," as Consul Peck puts it in the title of his report to the State Department dated August 9, 1932, alarmed the studio, which claimed that such an arrangement would be impractical and costly due to contractual obligations with distributors around the world. However, Paramount discontinued making new prints and committed to retrieving existing prints as soon as its contracts were fulfilled. Consul Peck mediated the friction between the Nanjing censors and Paramount Studios as both parties gravitated toward a resolution on July 27, 1932, when the former agreed to recommence censorship of Paramount films in exchange for the latter's withdrawing of *Shanghai Express* from circulation within two months. The studio also provided an assurance of future compliance, as suggested by the consul: "It is the desire and intention of Paramount to refrain from producing any film which may be regarded as injurious to the dignity of the Chinese people."[90]

Examining the *Shanghai Express* scandal through archival documents contained in PCA, State Department, and Bureau of Domestic and Foreign Commerce files illuminates the inherently U.S.-centric bias that prevented the industry from fulfilling its professed commitment to respect national feelings of overseas audiences. Paramount representatives, SRC regulators, and consular staff collectively claimed that there was nothing offensive about Chinese images in *Shanghai Express* and that the Chinese censors as well as general audiences were being inordinately sensitive about commercial American entertainment, known for its stock characters and formulaic narratives. For example, in the aforementioned meeting with the NBFC representative, Consul Peck tried to persuade him that the "Chinese should [not] feel over sensitive if the bad characters in a film were occasionally Chinese, just as they often were Americans and persons of other nationalities."[91] In his report to the State Department about the *Shanghai Express* incident, the otherwise sympathetic Peck could not mask his patronizing attitude toward NBFC members, whom the consul general identified as "comparative young 'returned students'" with overseas degrees who were "keenly alive to reflections on the dignity of the Chinese people." Consul Peck candidly opined that "there is something not unattractive in the naive realism with which [they spring] to the defense of the Chinese people, as well as something pathetic in [their] hypersensitiveness to real or imagined insult and oppression."[92]

On December 12, 1932, the Bureau of Foreign and Domestic Commerce's Motion Picture Division hosted a special screening of *Shanghai Express* in Washington, DC, for guests from the Division of Far Eastern Affairs of the State Department and the Chinese legation. The Chinese minister (ambassador after 1935) Dr. Alfred Sao-ke Sze and the first secretary of the Chinese legation Dr. Anching Kung were in attendance. According to the Bureau's Motion Picture Division chief Clarence J. North's report to the MPPDA's foreign manager, the event purported to show to the highest Chinese officials in the United States that "the picture not only was remarkably faithful in its attention to detail but was exceedingly careful not to offend Chinese susceptibilities." North boasted that they were able to make an argument to the Chinese minister and his attaché that "the bandit leader is not even a Chinese but a half-caste and also that it is mentioned on numerous occasions that the Chinese Government has put a price on his head and is trying in every way possible to catch him."[93] It is ironic that mid-level government bureaucrats, so sure about the cultural correctness of Chinese images concocted by Caucasian writers (screenwriter Jules Furthman and original story author Harry Hervey) and filmmakers (executive producer Zukor and director Sternberg), attempted to lecture prominent Chinese diplomats on why their compatriots' protests against Chinese misrepresentations were misguided. There is no way to know how Minister Sze privately felt about Washington's effort to persuade him to approve of Hervey/Sternberg/Paramount's Orientalist version of his own country. At least the Bureau's Motion Picture Division chief felt certain that the minister left with a more positive impression of a film blacklisted in China. North even suggested that the motion picture industry should adopt a policy to screen to foreign legation or embassy officials any films that they might protest "entirely on hearsay evidence."[94]

The fact that the Chinese minister did not agree with North and State Department staff can be conjectured from reports about the following event. On June 26, 1933, the Chinese legation in Washington, DC, took an extraordinary step by appointing Vice Consul Kiang Yi-seng in Los Angeles as the "Chinese representative in Hollywood to whom the film producers may seek" advice on the production of China-related pictures with the singular "duty" of seeing that they do not make any works that might "offend the sensibilities of the Chinese audiences."[95] In his letter to Consul Peck dated May 31, 1933, the MPPDA's foreign manager Herron had already complained about the new vice consul's "pugilistically inclined" and "obstreperous approaches to studios" as well as his open demand "to be appointed official supervisor of all studios in regard to matters pertaining to China and the Chinese." The foreign manager believed that this was "something that cannot be done" as the industry had been fighting against similar demands from other countries for many years.[96] In his report to the State Department dated September 21, 1933, Consul Peck contradicted Herron and observed, "The appointment of Mr. Kiang seems to have been made at the request of Mr. Hays . . . and if this was the case, seems . . . to have been the only way of enabling the American film producers to obtain any advanced Chinese criticism of films which might possibly arouse Chinese antagonism." The diplomat continued, "It is natural that American film producers should desire to obtain as early as possible in the making of any film authoritative information whether such a film will meet with official criticism in China."[97] If Vice Consul Kiang's appointment was indeed made at the request of the MPPDA president himself (despite the widespread dissatisfaction with his "dictatorial" disposition in the industry, as reported by Herron), it attests to the seriousness of the Chinese problem in Hollywood after the high profile crises of *Welcome Danger* and *Shanghai Express* as well as the urgent need for authoritative opinion on Chinese images in advance of the NBFC's censorship review.

Peck's predictive description of the Chinese representative in Hollywood as an *enabler*, rather than an obstructer, for American producers turned out to be prophetic. Within seven months of Kiang's appointment, on January 26,

1934, Herron sent a positive report to Peck, stating, "Vice Consul Kiang . . . is really helping in a very constructive way . . . . I know that a number of our companies are consulting with him right along on pictures containing Chinese situations." Although the MPPDA foreign manager was reluctant to establish a precedent to make all scripts and preview prints available to foreign representatives in the United States (as the vice consul initially expected upon his arrival in Los Angeles), he conceded that "the Chinese Government representatives in this country should have authority enough to say whether or not a picture should be sent to China." Acknowledging the sensitive disposition of the Nanjing censors, Herron blamed press members for printing only negative news of China (focusing on war and banditry). He reasoned, "As long as the newspapers carry this type of news in every day's issue, naturally the public is interested in that side of Chinese life, and it makes it very difficult for our people to treat that side of life so that it will meet with the approval of the Chinese."[98] On the other hand, American diplomatic representatives in China saw the question as the industry's own responsibility. In his letter to Herron, dated January 5, 1934, Peck opined, "There is no advantage to be gained . . . in irritating Chinese public opinion. It is, of course, essential that scenario writers should retain their literary independence and not be compelled invariably to depict China as the one perfect country and all Chinese as free from fault, but a little attention to Chinese susceptibilities will probably bring worthwhile returns in avoiding annoyance."[99] One of the most insightful commentaries on Hollywood's Chinese problem can be found in Ambassador Johnson's December 7, 1936, report to the State Department: "It seems to me that this problem is one which can be solved only by American motion picture producers themselves . . . . The fact is that the American producers are producing a product which, if it is to find a market, must please as many people as possible and displease as few people as possible, and no official action can take the place of conformity to this fundamental rule of merchandising."[100]

"We Cannot Go on Forever with Murder of This Sort": Overridden Rule of Merchandising and the Persistent Chinese Problem

Paramount got into trouble with the Chinese government again when its producers disregarded Vice Consul Kiang's endeavors to change the offensive sections of another warlord film set on a Shanghai-bound train, *The General Died at Dawn* (1936). Directed by Lewis Milestone, the film stars Gary Cooper as an American newspaperman-turned-mercenary on a dangerous mission to deliver smuggled arms to underground patriots resisting General Yang, a megalomaniacal warlord played by Akim Tamiroff in grotesque yellowface. This monstrous Chinese villain destroys his own province when poor farmers fail to pay taxes and orders the mass suicide of his loyal guards when his own death is eminent. An agitated censorship board sent an official notification to Paramount Pictures on November 23, 1936:

> Paramount . . . has lately produced two consecutive films insulting China, *Klondike Annie* and *The General Died at Dawn*. The Committee, as its archives show, has repeatedly warned that firm voluntarily to eliminate the objectionable parts and to refrain from producing similar films. The Chinese Vice Consul at Los Angeles has also conducted negotiations locally . . . [but no] result has been obtained. It seems that the firm has the deliberate intention of insulting China . . . In addition to discontinuing temporarily the issuance of censorship permits to show its films, the Committee issues this notification to the firm, again instructing it promptly to awake to its error.[101]

In 1937, the Chinese government raised the status of the vice consulate in Los Angeles to that of a full consulate, to boost its authority in the eyes of Hollywood filmmakers (Vice Consul Kiang was promoted to consul general of New York and replaced by a more senior diplomat, Dr. T. K. Chang, who the Chinese authorities saw as someone "of exceptional qualifications to cooperate with American producers in connection with all motion pictures having any relation to China").[102]

As was the case with *Shanghai Express*, Paramount appeased the Chinese censors with an assurance issued by Adolph Zukor, chairman of the board, who wrote on October 28, 1936, "It has always been the policy of this company to respect the sensibilities, characteristics and customs of foreign countries. I wish to give you my definite assurance that this policy will be continued and that so long as I am in charge of this company, I will personally see to it that this policy is maintained and that nothing will be incorporated in any picture which we may produce in the future which will in any way affect adversely the sensibilities of the people of your country and of its government."[103] When Paramount reissued this controversial picture in September 1942, the Chinese consulate general in New York sent an official protest letter to the studio, insisting that "the picture in question has been viewed with great disfavor by the Chinese people and its showing at this time will not contribute to the true understanding of the American people toward the Chinese." Deputy Consul Joseph Ku argued that the rerelease of *The General Died at Dawn* would "undoubtedly do great harm to our common cause" and demanded that the studio "take the appropriate action to remedy the situation."[104]

On November 6, 1942, the Chinese embassy sent a stronger letter of indictment to Lowell Mellett, chief of the Bureau of Motion Pictures, the Office of War Information (OWI), listing their objections in great detail:

1 The picture of Chinese life which it presents is distorted and fantastic.
2 Artistically, it is on a plane with fictitious stories in cheap pulp magazines of the underworld in American cities.
3 The film conveys a picture of Chinese life as dominated by cruel and rapacious warlords. One of the outstanding achievements of the present National Government is the unification of China and the uprooting of local autocracies. This achievement stands to the credit of patriotic, forward-looking and determined Chinese, and not of "soldiers of fortune" from abroad.
4 The portrayal of Chinese character is revolting, and is likely . . . to produce among Americans . . . a reaction of suspicion and disgust. Among Chinese who see the film, it inevitably produces a sense of resentment. For the Chinese people are not fanatical . . . . They are not typically repulsive in appearance. They do not live in an atmosphere of underground mystery.
5 Conversely, there is no portrayal of the positive qualities of Chinese character—ethical sense; loyalty to family, friends and country; humor and good fellowship; tolerance; industry; respect for learning; love of peace, and a deep sense of personal and group obligations . . . . Throughout *The General Died at Dawn*, there is no single portrayal of a really likable or admirable Chinese character.
6 The continued showing of such a film will constitute . . . a hindrance rather than a help to the war effort. Among Americans it will produce no increased understanding of China or the Chinese people; among Chinese who see it, it will produce no increase of goodwill toward the United States.[105]

These damning contentions were corroborated by Earl Minderman, Mellett's right-hand man, who attended a local screening at the Little Theater in the company of Consul T.K. Chang and a Chinese embassy representative. The OWI staff member reported to his chief: "All the Chinese characters in the film are either corrupt, barbarically cruel and fanatical or stupid. The net impression is one of repugnance for China and the Chinese people. The day of the sectional warlords in China has passed and China is now united behind General Chiang Kai-shek to beat the Japanese. At this time when we . . . need all the help that any ally can give us, it is necessary for the American people get a realistic and sympathetic picture of the Chinese people. Anything that creates hatred or distrust of our allies is harmful to the war effort. This picture does that."[106] Wartime propagandists were not the only Americans who found the film unfair and disrespectful to the Chinese. After Paramount's showdown with the Chinese government over *The General Died at Dawn*, Herron conducted many interviews with State Department representatives, private citizens who lived in China for many years, and Chinese government officials in the United States in an attempt to find out "what the answer to our trouble is out there."

In his lengthy letter reporting this research to PCA head Joseph I. Breen, dated April 16, 1937, Herron deplored, "It just seems that there is an overwhelming tendency on the part of our people to perpetuate erroneous conceptions built on mistaken ideas regarding the Chinese people and their customs.... I think our studios have been in operation long enough so that they should have sufficient experience and intelligence in the handling of Chinese situations to cease the silly and asinine depictions of these people, their institutions and customs as is so often done." To illustrate the anachronisms and absurdity of Hollywood's stereotypes of China, the MPPDA foreign manager cited an American expert on China who read the script of *The General Died at Dawn* and found it analogous to "the Chinese of today making a movie with an American theme and centering the action around the speak-easy of the prohibition days in our country, and distorting things so badly as to make it appear to those not familiar with things American that American life generally revolved about the speak-easy." After referring to the studio's previous crisis over *Shanghai Express* and the American legation's diplomatic mediation, which helped lift the ban on all Paramount films, Herron resented that Paramount "went ahead and made *The General Died at Dawn*, having the same types of situations and they got into the same kind of trouble again." The foreign manager opined that, despite the State Department's benevolent intervention that rescued Paramount once again, "we cannot go on forever getting away with murder of this sort" and the government would stop backing the industry at some point if studios continued to deliberately "make pictures of the type that will offend the Chinese."[107]

Herron's unfiltered frustration over studios' unaltered behavior despite their persistent trouble with the Chinese censors is revealing, as it was one of the rare moments that a MPPDA official acknowledged, albeit in a private memo to another industry insider, Hollywood's own responsibility for crises (as opposed to the tendency to blame Chinese hypersensitivity and nationalism or competing media such as newspapers). This frank admission attests to the fact that the hegemonic representational politics of Orientalism and American exceptionalism often overrode the "fundamental rule of merchandising," to borrow Ambassador Johnson's phrase. Despite "a deep dent in the box office receipts for world distribution of any picture that runs counter to the ideas of the Chinese," studios did not cease "the silly and asinine depictions of these people, their institutions and customs," as criticized by Herron.[108] Herron's report is likely the main reason why Breen sent out a cautionary memo about the "Chinese situation" to all major studio heads on May 6, 1937, specifically naming *Shanghai Express* and *The General Died at Dawn* as "the kind of pictures to which the Chinese take violent exception."[109] Paramount's response was defiant. Vice president Henry Hezbrun responded on the same day and complained to Breen, "I think it is unfortunate and unnecessary that Paramount and its films . . . should have been particularly singled out by name . . . as though Paramount had been the only offender and had single-handedly and alone created the difficulties with the Chinese, which are referred to in that communication."[110] This correspondence illustrates that Paramount was more concerned with how their self-image might be perceived by and in relation to other industry leaders than with the Chinese government's reactions to their films or the lessons to be gleaned from such debacles (despite the studio's conciliatory pledge to Chinese officials at the closure of each crisis).

There were, of course, exceptions, such as MGM's *The Good Earth* (1937). This much-admired adaptation of Pearl S. Buck's Pulitzer Prize–winning novel of the same title was produced under an official contract with the Chinese government, which sent two representatives to the Culver City studio to supervise the epic production through the entire three-year period (1934–1937).[111] During the initial script development stage, Vice Consul Kiang collaborated closely with screenwriter Francis Marion for five months in an attempt to eliminate offensive materials (such as opium smoking, foot-binding, banditry, images of squalor, and superstitious practices) from a book that, while well received in the West, was widely considered insulting to members of the Chinese intelligentsia as well as to government officials. This somewhat unprecedented U.S.-China collaboration received a fair amount of positive publicity in the Chinese press and, needless to say, the completed film passed the government censorship review with nary a complaint in sight. As a pet project of MGM's legendary producer Irving Thalberg, driven by a life-draining, spirit-zapping ambition to create the most authentic and superlative depiction of China ever presented on the American screen, *The Good Earth* was indeed a one-of-a-kind, cross-cultural joint venture ahead of its time, something other studios were either not interested in pursuing or capable of duplicating.[112]

In most cases, in the absence of long-term commitment to egalitarian racial, ethnic, and national images, studio filmmakers, executives, and representatives managed diplomatic crises, case by case, during the postproduction stage by appeasing the foreign censors with eliminations of offensive parts and half-hearted conciliatory pledges for future improvement. The almost identical pattern of crises between *Shanghai Express* and *The General Died at Dawn* further underscores the regulatory continuity and limitations of both the SRC and the PCA, staffed by cultural outsiders (Caucasian American writers, educators, publicists, etc.) who deferred to the authority of Chinese diplomatic representatives and State Department officials.[113] In this context, the Chinese government's belief that their national film censorship board was "doing its patriotic duty in seeking to prevent the circulation throughout the world of American films defamatory to China" and that their use of "the few weapons at their disposal, including the banning of all films of an offending company as a means of coercion" was justifiable is not difficult to understand.[114] State Department files on motion pictures in China in the 1930s are steeped in memoranda and consular reports that recount the debates between Chinese officials and American diplomats concerning the role of motion pictures. The former group was convinced that motion pictures should aspire to accuracy and lift up their audiences, while the latter group believed that Hollywood releases should entertain viewers and generate profits for their producers. Chinese officials of the Nanjing censorship board were well aware of the U.S. federal government's inability to exercise any legal restraint over the production of motion pictures and used that knowledge to justify the necessity for strong actions against American films and their producers. Although it lasted less than a decade (1931–1938), the proactive role of the Republic-era Chinese state film censorship board in criticizing Hollywood's racially regressive images and demanding corrections through political and economic negotiations served as a blueprint for today's identity-based media activism, implemented through consumer boycotts, blogs, and hashtag-sprinkled social media movements.

"As Friend to Friend": Sternberg's *Shanghai Gesture* and China's Futile Friendly Persuasion

It is striking to see a major shift in conversation about motion pictures in China in State Department files of the early to mid-1940s. Gone from 1940s documents are such subject headings as "the Chinese Government and the film industry" and "prohibition of exhibition," which are replaced by the new subject "cultural relations, motion pictures." Ironically, the U.S. government during the wartime period adopted a "cultural" view of motion pictures as "an effective means of widening [the] mutual understanding among peoples," mirroring the Nationalist government's stance during the 1930s.[115] Having been recalled to Washington, DC, Willys R. Peck continued to be involved in U.S.-Chinese film affairs, now as a special assistant in the State Department's Division of Cultural Relations. In 1942, the Division collaborated with the War Department (later the Department of Defense) in the distribution of the "Chinese cadet picture" *We Fly for China*. Produced by the Pictorial Section of the War Department's Public Relations Division and cleared by the Military Intelligence Service for nonprofit exhibition in China, this three-reel documentary short depicting the training activities of Chinese student pilots in the United States was available in Chinese narration. Before being widely distributed throughout China, two 35 mm prints of this propaganda short were carried to the mainland in the personal baggage of Dr. Ralph W. Phillips, a technical expert appointed by the State Department.[116] Upon their arrival in Chungqing (then Chungking), the preview prints were screened to high officials, including Chiang Kai-shek, and received enthusiastic approval. The State Department aggressively pushed for the nonprofit showing of both studio-produced short subjects (e.g., MGM's *Profit without Honor*, *Magic Alphabets*, and *One against the World*) as well as industrial films (such as United Steel Corporation's *Steel Man's Servant* and *The Making and Shaping of Steel* and Modern Plastics, Inc.'s *Plastic Age* and *Magic of Modern Plastics*) in China.[117] It also arranged for American engineering professors to take part in campus tours throughout Free China, with the stipulation that they deliver lectures along with screenings of military-industrial complex films.

The State Department developed its own film program independent of the Office of War Information (which produced government propaganda films) and, in 1943, hired H. C. Weng, a local motion picture technician, who assisted with editing, translation, and artwork for its "cultural relations" films.[118] In a report to the State Department, dated January 29, 1943, the American ambassador Clarence E. Gauss stated, "The most fertile field in China for the use of American films having a propaganda value [seems] to be Chungking itself: there is available in that city . . . adequate facilities for the showing of such films to select audiences of representatives of political and economic organizations, and an avid and sympathetic interest in things and events American." Ambassador Gauss shrewdly recommended, "It would seem to be desirable to make provision of propaganda and educational films to be supplemented by a supply of motion picture films of a strictly entertainment nature."[119] In 1944 alone, the State Department made a total of one hundred documentary films available for distribution in China under the program.[120]

While sporadic censorship of commercial films still existed in the relocated wartime capital of Chungqing, where a Film Censorship Bureau was set up under the executive branch (Executive Yuan), the board was incapable of functioning properly due to a lack of basic resources such as a designated screening venue and to the wartime government's more pressing priorities. The only incident in which a particular American film was banned involved one of Hollywood's greatest auteurs, Alfred Hitchcock. As recorded in the aforementioned 1940s files, the master of suspense's 1940 spy thriller *Foreign Correspondent* was prevented from receiving a release by the French censors in Shanghai's International Settlement, not by the Chinese government. It is clear that the Chinese government lost its voice criticizing Hollywood's Chinese stereotypes once it entered into a patron/dependent relationship with the United States during World War II.

Montana Senator Michael J. Mansfield, who was Franklin D. Roosevelt's envoy, met with Chiang Kai-shek three times in late 1944. In the aftermath of those encounters, he listed China's wartime debt to the United States in his report to President Roosevelt dated January 3, 1945:

1 We have performed superhuman feats in getting material . . . to aid China's defense.
2 We are doing a tremendous job in building the Ledo-Burma Road and its auxiliary pipe line.
3 We have carried on operations in the Pacific which were all aimed at weakening China's—and our—enemy, Japan, and which must be included in any reckoning of assistance to our Asiatic ally.
4 We have given China much in the way of financial aid through loans, credits, etc.
5 We have tried to assist in a reorganization of the Chinese Army through developing training schools in this country and China; through detailing liaison personnel to different armies; through better feeding methods; and through the activation of the Chinese-American Composite Wing of the 14th Air Force.[121]

It is no wonder that such lopsided geopolitical power relations and massive institutional/material dependence silenced the Chinese government's cultural dissent over Hollywood's filmic images.

This power differential is likewise demonstrated in the Chinese consular communication with the producers of United Artists' *The Shanghai Gesture* (1941), directed by Josef von Sternberg and based on the 1926 stage play of the same title by John Colton. The sensationalist play revolves around Mother Goddam, a powerful Manchu heroine who owns the world's largest brothel in Shanghai. Twenty years earlier, she had been the local mistress of Sir Guy Charteris, an English businessman, and had given birth to their Eurasian daughter. Betrayed by her white lover, who returned home and married an English woman, the scorned Chinese woman sneaks into Charteris's home when his wife is giving birth to her baby and switches infants (after the English woman dies during childbirth). Sold into prostitution, Mother survives exploitation and rises to power as a wealthy businesswoman of Blood Town, a crime-ridden port on the outskirts of Shanghai. Consumed by her desire for revenge, Mother invites her unsuspecting ex-lover (who has returned to Shanghai with Poppy, their daughter) to a Chinese New Year banquet where Charteris's white daughter, Ni Pau, is sold in an auction to lowlife junkmen as a spectacle to elite guests. Mother reveals the secret of the auctioned virgin's identity, to the wrath of her father. The tables are turned, however, when Mother learns that Poppy, a degenerate drug addict and nymphomaniac, is *her* daughter. Wracked with hysteria, Mother kills Poppy and chants a final lullaby to her dead daughter.

When Universal proposed to adapt Colton's play for the big screen in October 1929, Joy wrote to the studio's head of production, Carl Laemmle Jr., informing him that the story would be "unusable for picture purposes" because of objectionable themes such as prostitution, "miscegenation, illegitimacy, white slavery, murder, and an opportunity to incur ill-will of other countries."[122] Despite this warning, Laemmle hired Colton to develop a Code-conforming script under the revised title *Mother Satan*. The playwright made several major changes to his work (e.g., the main setting is now a casino, not a "bawdy house"; Mother is now Charteris's wife, not a mistress, but their Chinese-law marriage is annulled; Mother is sold for labor, not prostitution; Poppy is addicted to gambling and alcohol instead of drugs and sex). However, none of his multiple drafts received the SRC's approval. Instructed by Hays to "watch out for anything built upon the theme of *The Shanghai Gesture*," Joy continued to dissuade several other companies (including RKO and Warner Bros.) from adapting the risqué play throughout the early 1930s.[123] The shelved project was revived in December 1940 by the Austrian Jewish émigré producer Arnold Pressburger, who chose the controversial material as the subject of his first film in the United States. After all intimations of illicit sexual entanglements were sanitized from the storyline (in accordance with the PCA's advice), Geza Herczeg's first draft script, dated April 12, 1941, was finally green-lighted as meeting "the requirements of the Production Code." The PCA's "first and most important" concern for this script was to do with foreign relations, not sexuality or morality. Breen instructed Pressburger that "it is absolutely essential that you remove from the finished picture anything that might be interpreted as inflammatory anti-Japanese propaganda." The PCA head elaborated that "if your picture has any such flavor, we would not be able to approve it from the standpoint of general industry policy." Specifically, Breen demanded that ethnic or racial slurs such as "Japs" and "monkey thieves" be removed from the script.[124] Anti-German or anti-Japanese representations were suppressed in Hollywood prior to the U.S. entrance into World War II (for both market and political consideration). In light of this policy, Poppy (Gene Tierney)'s unwholesome love interest who gets her addicted to gambling was changed from the Japanese ex-attaché Prince Oshima to the ethnically ambiguous Doctor Omar in a Turkish fez (Victor Mature), who identifies himself as a "thorough mongrel" born to an Armenian father and a half-French mother.[125] On June 21, 1941, the PCA wrote to Pressburger, further cautioning him with these words: "We . . . understand that it is your intention to get competent technical advice from the Chinese angle, so as to avoid anything in the finished picture that might cause offense to that nation, or might cause you difficulty with your release abroad."[126]

Following the PCA's internal regulation protocol, Pressburger sent the script to the Chinese consulate in Los Angeles and encountered Consul T. K. Chang's opposition to multiple storylines. After meeting with Sternberg—the film's director—Consul Chang wrote to Pressburger on August 21, 1941, "In your *Shanghai Gesture*, we regret to note that you should choose to exhibit the underworld activities of the Chinese people alone and neglect the beautiful part of our virtue. As a matter of fact gambling joints in Shanghai have never been owned or operated by Chinese nationals. To impute scandalous acts to a people who in fact never did, is hardly fair to us." The Chinese consul further disapproved of showing a Chinese general as one of the gamblers (on the grounds that such a portrayal is disrespectful to the heroic sacrifice of well-disciplined armed forces in the war of resistance against Japan) as well as the auction of Chinese girls (on the grounds that no such system exists in the country). Consul Chang found the film's ending particularly disturbing: "To slaughter a child at the very hand of her own mother . . . is hardly conceived in good morals, whether it is Shanghai Gesture or Hollywood Gesture. Certainly it is inconceivable in the moral concept of the Chinese people. For ages, we have been taught to revere sacredly the relation between parents and children."[127] Included on an attached list of miscellaneous objections were [1] the introduction of Mother Gin Sling (Goddam in the play) with a gong sound; [2] her talon-like fingernails; [3] three daggers in her hair; [4] a polygamist general referencing his search for a sixth wife; and [5] singsong girls powdered with rice. The list concluded with a more general request: "It is hoped . . . that there will be no mysterious and mythical atmosphere attached to any Chinese character portrayed in the motion picture."[128]

Pressburger accommodated Consul Chang's suggestions selectively, eliminating the general character and modifying Orientalist mise-en-scène, including props. For example, Mother's hair ornaments were transformed from daggers to flower pins and sculptural accessories. However, the producer defended his film from the overall accusation of cultural inauthenticity, insisting in his reply to Consul Chang, "Please do not forget that our film *Shanghai Gesture* is not meant to portray reality, but to display a world of fantasy. This imaginary world has no connection with the realistic aspects of today." Pressburger added, "Both Mr. von Sternberg and I love China. We will certainly see to it that no damage is done to the pro-Chinese sympathies existing in the United States or in any other part of the world."[129] Persistent and determined, the Chinese consul pressed the issue further in his follow-up letter dated August 25, 1941. He began the letter in a diplomatic way, stating, "It is gratifying to note that you are a friend of ours. As friend to friend, I hope I can take the liberty of expressing my views in a frank manner for your sympathetic consideration." Then, Consul Chang argued that while the story was "an imaginative fiction," it was based on "the raw material of realities" and there was "a

FIG. 1.4 Chinese consul T. K. Chang of Los Angeles adamantly opposed the depiction of Mother Gin Sling (right: Ona Munson), a Chinese gambling house owner, and the culturally insensitive plotline involving her filicide of Poppy (left: Gene Tierney) in Sternberg's *The Shanghai Gesture* (United Artists, 1941).

certain local color, descriptive of certain definite people, in a definite place."[130] He forcefully repeated his three main objections: a Chinese national, much less a woman, should not be depicted as the owner of a Shanghai gambling house as it contradicts facts; the scene depicting the auction of women should be eliminated as there is no such system in China; and the scene of the mother slaying her own daughter should be deleted as it is at odds with the Chinese national sentiment. In the final release print, all these objectionable elements were left intact, although the auction scene was presented as a staged spectacle played by hired actors for Mother's banquet guests. As his plead to Pressburger proved to be ineffective, Consul Chang turned to the PCA, forwarding all his correspondences with the producer and enlisting help in "develop[ing] a very cordial friendship between the Chinese people and the industry."[131]

On September 26, 1941, the PCA staff, consisting of Geoffrey Shurlock (Breen's deputy and future successor) and T. A. Lynch, met with Consul Chang to respond to his concerns on behalf of Pressburger and the film's distributor, United Artists. The PCA pointed out to the Chinese consul that "this was one of the few stories laid in China in which the Chinese principal was the heroine, and all the villains were Europeans" and that "it could not really be said to reflect upon the Chinese nation" as the story's setting was "the No-Man's Land of the International Settlement at Shanghai." As for Mother's killing of Poppy, the PCA defended the film's dramatic climax, arguing that "the daughter was to all intents and purposes a European, and not a Chinese girl in any sense, and that the relationship between Mother Gin Sling and the girl could not in any way be considered as representing normal Chinese family relationship."[132] This PCA conference with Consul Chang is uncannily reminiscent of the Washington screening of *Shanghai Express* for Minister Alfred Sze, as discussed earlier in this chapter. In both "explanatory" meetings, American defenders of the industry's interests (be it members of the Bureau of Foreign and Domestic Commerce staff or PCA regulators) used the Eurasian character's mixed identity as an excuse to justify objectionable characterizations and plot elements from the Chinese standpoint.

The PCA did concede to the consul's objection that the scene of the fake sale of caged women "might possibly be distasteful" and pressured Pressburger to rewrite the explanatory dialogue to minimize its offense.[133] In the release print, Mother Gin Sling (Ona Munson) goes out of her way to explain to her banquet guests that the theatrical spectacle of the caged women's auction to junkmen is fake and "staged purely for the tourists" in order to live up to Shanghai's reputation. According to Karen Kuo, this transformation from Mother Goddam's auction of Charteris's white virgin daughter (a character eliminated in the film adaptation) to Mother Gin Sling's mock sale of white and Asian "actresses" in the film neutralizes Colton's anti-Madame Butterfly critique of the West's exploitation of the East through graphic, explicit details of female sexuality and slavery.[134] Although this interpretation might be true from a feminist perspective, given Consul Chang's aversion to the original auction scene, it is difficult to credit it as a more progressive version without considering Chinese national responses.

In her comparative analysis of play and film, Kuo put the blame on the Production Code for "shift[ing] the story from a female-centered critique of race and nationality, to a male-centered narrative."[135] While it is true that the Code played a role in redeeming Charteris (John Huston)'s patriarchy by turning him from a sexual abuser (who sells Mother into prostitution after impregnating her and taking her dowry) to a mistaken husband (who, despite his misunderstanding that Mother is dead, leaves her fortune untouched in her bank account), one should refrain from making a monolithic evaluation that film regulation was responsible for suppressing a more subversive message about race and nationality. Rather, the PCA served as an intermediary between filmmakers and Chinese government representatives, who demanded that additional changes be made to Colton's original storyline, which they saw as contrary to their national interests.

The PCA memorandum uses the phrase, "We analyzed the story at some length," when describing the meeting with Consul Chang. Such clinical defense of contrived narrative logic seems to contradict the Code's reverent spirit of being sensitive to national feelings, or the affective appeal the screen images might have on foreign audiences. Judging from the correspondences among Consul Chang, Pressburger, and Shurlock, one can hardly conclude that

Chinese "feelings" were fully considered and reflected in the process of production. This is not to say that Pressburger and United Artists should have changed the film's script to appease the Chinese consul. The PCA was correct in surmising that, while being "repugnant and shocking to Chinese ideas of family life," the ending could not be changed without losing the crucial climax of the whole story. The problem, however, was the "we-know-better-than-you" approach to cultural representations (which might also be termed "we-have-the-right-to-represent-you-the-way-we-see-fit" defense). Pressburger's final letter to the Chinese consulate, dated September 25, 1941, displayed a barely suppressed air of impatience and cultural entitlement. The letter states, "Please rest assured that the picture will contain nothing which would place the Chinese people in any unfavorable light. On the other hand, you must remember that the film . . . is merely fiction, and not a newsreel or an educational film on China. As I have already told you the picture will mainly serve as entertainment like most of the films shown. As soon as the picture is finished, I will run it for you and you shall judge for yourself."[136] The consulate did not respond to Pressburger this time, nor did it contact the PCA again after the aforementioned conference. Consul Chang must have been resigned to the fact that any further pursuit of his objections would go nowhere except for eliciting more of the same excuses.

Without the national film censorship board's backend bargaining power to put a temporary moratorium on the exhibition of an offending company's entire output in the Chinese market, the Chinese consular pressure turned out to be a futile "friend-to-friend" persuasion in the context of 1941. As will be discussed in the next chapter, the Chinese reps soon found their most loyal and impassioned advocates among OWI film reviewers, who were committed to improving celluloid images of America's wartime allies.[137] Released in a transitional period between the 1938 dissolution of the CMPCC and the 1942 installation of the OWI, *The Shanghai Gesture* is a peculiar East-meets-West film noir that generated 280 pages of internal regulatory documents in the PCA files but remained unmentioned in the 1940s State Department files. The Los Angeles Chinese consul's lone, largely unsuccessful campaign to eliminate culturally inaccurate Chinese images in Sternberg's late-career film is an important reminder that diplomatic niceties in the absence of economic clout could go only so far when negotiating with Hollywood's profit-seeking "dream-makers," despite any professed love for the East Asian country and its people that they so frequently offended.

2

Justified Patricide and (Im)Properly Directed Hatred

Regulating the Representations of Chinese and Japanese in Doolittle Raid Films

The complex, often conflicting relationship of two U.S. regulatory agencies—the motion picture industry's Production Code Administration (1934–1968) and the government's propaganda arm, the Office of War Information (1942–1945)—and their influence on Hollywood's wartime productions are well documented in previous studies by Thomas Doherty and Clayton R. Koppes, among others.[1] In the absence of centralized federal film censorship and under the principle of voluntary self-regulation, wartime motion pictures were subject to "friendly pressures" by internal and external advisory entities (including the PCA and the OWI) and underwent numerous transformations during the production stage before being submitted for official censorship review by local, municipal, state, and foreign boards. While previous scholarship emphasizes the dissonance between the PCA's morality-based control and the OWI's wartime policy-oriented supervision, this study aims to underscore an unexpected "interest convergence" between the industry and the government in creating positive images of Chinese allies in World War II propaganda films. Using Lewis Milestone's Doolittle Raid film *The Purple Heart* (1944) as the central case study, this chapter investigates the complex relationships among film regulation, ethnic representations, and audience reception.

After charting out what I call "Hollywood diplomacy"—a set of regulatory policies regarding diplomatic representations of foreign nationals—from the silent era to World War II, I will use *The Purple Heart* as a metonymic text to showcase competing yet reinforcing impulses of different regulatory organizations, as well as the industry's selective accommodations of such interventions in their construction of screen Orientalism (and its alternatives). Rather than simply reflect cultural fantasies, this wartime film's representations of Chinese and Japanese ethnicities became prickly ideological sites where the commercial interests of Hollywood studios and the political mandates of U.S. foreign policy collided, competed against one another, and were compromised in the process.

This case study will define and demonstrate the mediating capacity of film regulation, not as an obstacle to artists' freedom of expression, but rather as an enforcer of institutional protection, a facilitator of wartime international relations, and a contributor to "political correctness" (or an accidental progenitor of the concept long before it was popularized in the latter part of the twentieth century) regarding images of foreign nationals and racial minorities. Drawing upon archival documents from the PCA and the OWI, I wish to demonstrate that these regulatory agencies each strove to improve the representation of Chinese allies despite the contradictory nature of their suggestions to Hollywood studios. Based on audience reception data compiled by the studio (20th Century-Fox) and the OWI, it also argues that Milestone's film failed to uphold the OWI's progressive policy of "properly directed hatred" by inciting rage against the entire enemy nation (Japan) and its populace rather than its fascist military apparatus. The mixed results of improvements and failures in constructing desirable images of East Asian allies and enemies in *The Purple Heart* attest to the difficulty of overcoming race ideology and ethnic stereotypes in studio system–era motion pictures despite the benevolent intentions of regulatory advisors (both within the industry and without) to curtail foreign offense, increase cultural verisimilitude, and practice good diplomacy for both financial and political reasons.

The Origins of Hollywood Diplomacy in the Silent Era

The origins of Hollywood diplomacy, closely tied to the industry's economic interests in foreign markets, can be traced back to the mid-1910s. Importantly, that was when feature-length narrative cinema became standardized in the American film industry, thanks in part to the pioneering efforts of D. W. Griffith, Cecil B. DeMille, and other filmmakers who sought to "elevate" the motion picture medium as a vehicle for storytelling. In 1915, these artists individually pushed the boundaries of American cinema with technically advanced yet racially regressive silent masterpieces: *The Birth of a Nation* and *The Cheat*. The former, directed by Griffith, not only was notorious for contributing to the resurgence of the Ku Klux Klan but also unwittingly contributed to the emergence of "race movies" in the 1920s, particularly those made by the independent African American filmmaker Oscar Micheaux, who responded to *The Birth of a Nation* with his own masterpiece, *Within Our Gates* (1920), which depicts lynching and interracial rape from the perspective of black victims rather than white perpetrators. The National Association for the Advancement of Colored People (NAACP), a civil rights organization established in 1909, had expanded to 50 branches and 6,000 members by the time of *The Birth of a Nation*'s original release. Members of the NAACP waged a fierce nationwide campaign to ban the film in major cities, such as Los Angeles, New York, and Boston, albeit unsuccessfully.[2] The NAACP's well-publicized demonstrations, however, were a crucial factor in the film's statewide banning in Kansas and Ohio. The Kansas Board of Censorship sided with the NAACP in its ruling to ban Griffith's film because it was judged "historically inaccurate" and "full of racial hatred, promoting the idea that black Americans were the root of many problems in the United States."[3] Just as *The Birth of a Nation* enraged African American audiences, initiating heated national debates about race relations and free speech, *The Cheat* provoked Japanese and Japanese American audiences, and was ultimately forced to adopt diplomatic corrections in the rerelease print.

DeMille's modern melodrama features the charismatic yet cruel villain Hishuru Tori (Sessue Hayakawa), a wealthy merchant of Oriental curios who nearly rapes the socialite heroine Edith Hardy (Fannie Ward) and brands the married woman's shoulder with his signature stamp (the Japanese national symbol of a holy *torii* gate to a Shinto temple) as a sign of ownership. Although Tori outwardly poses as an assimilated, respectable member of the "Long Island smart set," his repressed sadistic side is foreshadowed in the credit sequence, which shows Hayakawa's character in kimono obsessively branding an art object with a brazier of coals and a hot iron. His face looks sinister thanks to the chiaroscuro lighting. Interestingly, in the original script, the Japanese character is introduced in a Western flannel suit, reading a magazine or newspaper and smoking.[4] DeMille penciled in the change that visually codified the character as a Japanese villain, who is associated with traditional symbols such as a kimono and a Shinto gate. It is easy to see why Japanese communities in the United States might have been outraged. Starting in December of 1915, the *Rafu Simpo*, a Japanese newspaper in Los Angeles, ran almost daily protest articles for three months, blaming the Paramount film for "destroy[ing] the truth of the Japanese race" and "caus[ing] anti-Japanese movements," which resulted in the lynching of a Japanese noodle shop owner in front of the Tally Theater in

Los Angeles (where *The Cheat* played).[5] In a manner that anticipates the anti–*Shanghai Express* report in a Chinese newspaper, which I cited in chapter 1, contributors to the *Rafu Simpo* chastised the Japanese-born silent star Hayakawa for playing an evil Japanese villain in an anti-Japanese film and called for the Japanese embassy's intervention. In February 1916, the Japanese Association of Southern California filed a complaint against the exhibition of the film with the Los Angeles City Council, calling for its ban in the city. The Japanese embassy backed the community campaign with an official protest letter to Paramount and DeMille. Although *The Cheat* was not released in Japan, Hayakawa earned notoriety across the Pacific for being an "unforgivable national traitor" who collaborated in Hollywood's "anti-Japanese propaganda."[6] When the film was rereleased in 1918, after the United States entered World War I, fighting on the side of Japan as an allied nation, Tori's ethnicity was changed to Burmese and the character was renamed Haka Arakau in revised intertitles.

One year prior to *The Cheat*'s rerelease, Cecil B. DeMille's elder brother William directed Hayakawa in the World War I espionage drama *The Secret Game* (1917). This time, his character, a Japanese secret agent named Nara-Nara, is introduced in a positive light. As "a patriot of Japan and sincere friend to America," according to one of the film's intertitles, the Japanese spy purchases two miniature flag pins (one American, the other Japanese) from a well-lit souvenir store and proudly wears them side by side on his tuxedo lapel. As Daisuke Miyao points out, "*The Secret Game* was in accordance with the diplomatic discourse that desired Japan to be trustworthy in Asia and the Pacific and to be helpful in American society."[7] The film's contemporaneous reviews likewise emphasized its timeliness. For example, the *Dramatic Mirror*'s film review dated December 8, 1917, observes, "In Paramount's latest release featuring that splendid actor, Sessue Hayakawa, they have fashioned a story that at the present time is bound to have a broad appeal, for it is a romance of the Secret Service."[8] Curiously, this review evaluates Hayakawa's character exclusively in positive terms without mentioning his attempt to force himself on Kitty Little (Florence Vidor), a German spy working as a stenographer in the quartermaster office, who is also being romantically pursued by her boss, Major John Northfield (Jack Holt).

Posing as a curio shop owner who works next to Northfield's office, Nara-Nara has been spying on the officer to uncover the source of leaks of military information to the German enemy. In the process, he discovers Kitty's identity and uses an incriminating letter to blackmail her into sexual subjugation. After being shamed by the German woman, who calls him a traitor to himself, his emperor, and his samurai sword, Nara-Nara awakens to honor and returns the letter to her before leaving to commit suicide. Before he can take his own life, however, he is stabbed to death by an avenging underling of Dr. Ebell Smith (Charles Ogle), the German head spy and Kitty's operator. Earlier, Nara-Nara had assassinated the German spy for both Japan and the United States. The Japanese agent's spirit in kimono, with his sword, rises from the corpse and travels to his parental home in Japan, while a reformed Kitty and her American suitor are united in a romantic embrace. Despite Nara-Nara's bipolar shuttling between two positions—that of a political/military ally and that of a sexual threat to white femininity—Miyao interprets him as a sympathetic character who "sacrifices himself for the good of the German American woman and for a white American family."[9] *The Secret Game* is a contradictory text that pays (contrived) tribute to Japan as a wartime ally without fully discarding Yellow Peril stereotypes of excludable Asian aliens. Notably, Kitty redeems herself and acquires citizenship through marriage despite her treachery, while America's "sincere friend" Nara-Nara has to return home even in death. A similar contradiction can be detected in my subsequent analysis of *The Purple Heart*, a significant yet overlooked Hollywood production in which Chinese figures take the place of Japanese characters as representations of the United States' main Asian ally during the Second World War.

"National Feelings" and Political Mandates: Regulating International Relations from the Pre-Code Era to World War II

As Kerry Segrave observes, "Hollywood had no foreign problem to speak of before World War I because it had no foreign trade to speak of."[10] The situation drastically changed at the end of World War I, when American products largely replaced their key European (French, German, and Italian) competitors in the international film market, constituting 85 percent of all motion pictures shown around the world.[11] As Hollywood's global distribution of its products increased exponentially in the late 1910s and early 1920s, so too did pressures from foreign (Mexican, French, Italian, etc.) governments, which began to turn their attention to representations of their countries and nationals and issued complaints through official channels of political communication, embargos on offensive films and/or their producers, and diplomatic negotiations. In her book *The World According to Hollywood, 1918–1939*, Ruth Vasey argues that the Mexican government's 1922 banning of the entire output of American producers who made films insulting to Mexico was responsible for convincing the industry of the need for regulating their products to satisfy international demand. Among the first board meeting agenda items of the newly formed trade organization the Motion Picture Producers and Distributors of America (MPPDA, now the Motion Picture Association of America) was a resolution to avoid presenting "the Mexican character in a derogatory or objectionable manner."[12]

From its inception, the MPPDA had a Foreign Relations Committee (later the Foreign Department) headed by Will H. Hays's brother-in-law Frederick L. Herron, who was previously a major in the U.S. Army (but commonly called "colonel" by his colleagues) and an officer in the U.S. consular service. Herron served as the MPPDA's foreign manager from 1922 to 1941 and was in charge of maintaining "contacts with the branches of its member companies in foreign nations, officials in those nations who dealt with film imports," and State Department representatives abroad and in Washington, DC.[13] It was Herron's job to solicit the mediation of American and foreign diplomats when the industry's confrontation with foreign interests escalated. In March 1925, the MPPDA established the Department of Public Relations and declared an Open Door policy under which "any group or individual who had suggestions or complaints could lodge them with" the new department, "which acted as the new liaison between the industry and the public."[14] Initially focused on American citizens and organizations, the Open Door was "gradually widened to allow the possibility of access by foreign petitioners."[15] For example, the MPPDA received a letter from the Chen Kwang Theater, a leading exhibitor in Beijing (then Peking), which complained about Mary Pickford's silent comedy *Little Annie Rooney* (1925): "In this play, although the Chinese actor [plays] his part as an honest washer man, his appearance is silly, awkward, and unmannerly, which of course might cause a laughing stock among the foreigners, and on the other hand it would be considered an insult to the Chinese."[16] In the Studio Relations Committee (SRC, 1926–1934)'s meeting on December 14, 1927, which discussed this and other Open Door grievances from China, studio representatives (from Hal Roach Studios, MGM, F.O.B. Studios, Christie Film Company, Harold Lloyd Corporation, Universal, and Educational) concluded that "no pictures with the Chinese actors can be screened in the Chinese cities . . . unless you have cut [the scenes] off," due to the sensitivity of the Chinese market. Unfortunately, this practice could not be applied to *Little Annie Rooney* where "the Chinese actor . . . [was] in such an important position that it would spoil the story and the picture" with the cutting of his role.[17]

Two months earlier, in October 1927, the MPPDA proclaimed the film industry's new moral resolve, "The Don'ts and Be Carefuls," which would be replaced by the more detailed Production Code in 1930. The list includes a self-regulation rule related to international relations, reflecting the caution caused by overseas protests and embargos: "[avoid] picturizing in an unfavorable light another country's religion, history, institutions, prominent people, and citizenry." Article Ten ("National Feelings") of the 1930 Code puts a slightly different spin on the above: "The history, institutions, prominent people and citizenry of other nations shall be represented fairly." As the rationale for this particular application, the Code elaborates: "The just rights, history, and feelings of any nation are entitled to most careful consideration and respectful treatment."[18] Despite the existence of such provisions, it is important to note, as Vasey has pointed out, that "the industry's approach to international distribution involved negative, rather than positive, forms of accommodation."[19]

Although foreign markets accounted for approximately 35 percent of Hollywood's revenues in the 1930s, studios "were not interested in devising ways of making their products more positively attractive to audiences overseas. Even the careful preparation of [films], which had an unusually high dependence on foreign returns, was characterized by a cautious and reductive approach, essentially designed to minimize international offense rather than maximize international appeal."[20] This half-hearted appeasement policy, as opposed to a long-term commitment to equitable representations, brought many headaches to Herron, the SRC's head Jason S. Joy, and his successor, PCA's chief Joseph I. Breen.

Hollywood's foreign stereotypes aroused the State Department's concern as well. On March, 25, 1929, Henry S. Villard, a senior official in the department's Office of the Economic Advisor, observed, "The French are resentful that their nationals are so often pictured as immoral, the Spanish and Italians that they are so frequently villains, the English that they are snobs, etc. The sensitiveness of the Latin temperament to constant tactless allusions of this kind has found vigorous expression on several occasions in Spain, Brazil, Mexico, and Costa Rica."[21] Several Pre-Code (1930–1934) films generated international controversy and diplomatic crises due to such "tactless" ethnic images as criticized by Villard. Howard Hawks's *Scarface* (1932), for example, was met with strong disapproval from Italian ambassador Giacomo de Martino, who wrote to Herron, "This film has produced a very vivacious reaction on the part of Italian-Americans and I have received a number of letters and newspaper clipping showing resentment and indignation."[22] The ambassador went on to observe that "all the heads of the underworld as well as their agents, go-betweens, etc. bear Italian names and are heard to speak more or less with an Italian accent." He further complained that "the whole production gives the unmistakable impression that all the crimes and situations illustrated are absolutely and completely imported from abroad and especially from Italy and that, once such a foreign element eliminated, the problem of American criminality would be solved. In fact, an American official is heard to pronounce the words 'Take them back to Italy.'"[23]

From the earliest days of this film's script stage, the SRC found it problematic that the audience's sympathy was evoked for the criminal, who was depicted as a "home-loving man, good to his mother and protecting his sister."[24] However, a fiercely independent Hughes pushed through production, ignoring the SRC's repeated warnings about the script submitted in May 1931. In an inter-office memo to Hays dated November 3, 1931, the SRC head Colonel Jason S. Joy attested to Hughes's sustained resistance to suggested changes to the rough cut until he flatly informed the producer that "the picture could not play in more than 50% of the English-speaking territory" in its current form.[25] The SRC's grim prediction of market restrictions motivated Hughes to authorize reshooting and to accommodate several regulatory revisions (such as the insertion of a socially conscious anti-gun message to preempt opposition to the gangster genre and an altered ending, which depicts Camonte as a coward begging for mercy). After a special jury of the MPPDA board of directors in New York screened the revised version, it was concluded that the picture was still dangerous and that elements of sympathy for the protagonist needed to be eliminated. The MPPDA hoped that "the ordinary and intelligent person of the audience would leave the theater with . . . no feeling at all that the gangster had been glorified."[26] The film's unorthodox incest subplot (the obsession of Italian gangster hero Tony "Scarface" Camonte [Paul Muni] with his sister Francesca [Ann Dvorak]) was a carefully deliberated outcome of subsequent conferences attended by Hays, Joy, and Hughes in which all parties agreed that several scenes would be added to change "a protective brother-sister relationship to that of jealousy."[27]

In addition to matters regarding crime and morality, the SRC was concerned about Italian representations in *Scarface*. In its script review, dated June 1, 1931, SRC regulator Charleston Simon commented,

> There is present a great deal of Italian atmosphere in the names of the various foods consumed and use of personal names. The mother of the criminal is painted as a grasping virago, distinctly an Italian criminal type mother. All of these presentations would be highly objectionable to millions of Italians in this country. The mother should have been endowed with graceful virtues and the son painted as a black sheep. There was a fine opportunity lost in not having the mother . . . present to the son a dialogue telling him what the Italian race has done for posterity and that, he, Scarface, was bringing odium and shame upon his entire race. This might remove some of the flood of adverse criticism that would otherwise be sure to arise.[28]

Although the mother's role was rewritten to make her a sympathetic figure who was critical of her son's criminality, as predicted by the SRC, *Scarface* was strongly opposed by Italians at home and abroad. The prestigious Roman daily *Il Giornale d'Italia* "urged the film to be banned due to the 'offensive allusions to Italy' contained therein."[29] The oldest Italian American organization, Sons of Italy, sent a protest letter against the film to all state governors, garnering press attention, to the chagrin of many within the MPPDA.[30] Another community group, the Italian Women's Club, demanded that all Italian names be deleted from the film. A Portland theater owner was arrested for showing the film in violation of a local censorship board's ban that resulted from Italian American protests.[31]

Distressed by the "Italian situation," Herron encouraged his colleague Joy to "go to the bat with the studios as strong as [he] possibly can." The Foreign Department manager explained to the SRC head: "We are getting into terribly deep water and the first thing we know we are going to have our product barred from Italy, and instructions from the Foreign Office in Rome will be sent to every country in the world asking their representatives to protest the showing of these different gangster pictures of ours that have Italians in them . . . . I would not be at all surprised, in spite of everything we can do, if United Artists [the distributor of *Scarface*] were banned from distributing their pictures in Italy."[32] As Eric Smoodin concludes in his study of a similar diplomatic crisis with China surrounding Frank Capra's *The Bitter Tea of General Yen* (1933): "Most significant here is . . . that individual Hollywood films did not take shape solely from discussions between the studios and the Hays Office [MPPDA] or from debates between the MPPDA and American censors from various states and localities. Instead, these films also were the product of negotiations between studio officials, the federal government, and foreign governments . . . . The American film industry may have controlled the world market, but the Hollywood studios simply could not impose their will on foreign theaters and viewers."[33]

This principle of the pre-Code era was inherited by Joseph I. Breen, a former journalist and devout Irish Catholic, who headed the PCA (a.k.a. the Breen Office) from 1934 to 1954 and was in charge of cleansing Hollywood products in order to get them ready for external censorship review by 7 state boards, 31 municipal boards, and 200–250 ad hoc local boards, not to mention mostly government-controlled foreign censorship boards.[34] Thomas Doherty, Lea Jacobs, Stephen Prince, and Ruth Vasey, among other film historians, have discussed the productivity of the PCA's in-house regulation in facilitating artistic creativity and nuanced representations of sexuality and violence.[35] One of the most significant and substantive contributions that the PCA made was its effort to ensure diplomatic representations of foreign countries and their nationals (in accordance with the aforementioned "national feelings" provision of the Code) in order to protect the international market and safeguard the industry's overseas reputation. The Breen Office routinely requested filmmakers and studio executives to clear scripts and finished films through official channels of foreign governments, such as embassies and consulates. Oftentimes, Breen himself (who had a brief diplomatic career as vice consul in Jamaica during World War I) served as a middleman in negotiations between studios and foreign consuls based in Los Angeles. While Hollywood's internal censor sometimes found various consular demands unreasonable and difficult, he maintained a realistic view on the matter, stating: "As I view it—we can be 'free, sovereign and independent,' and tell everybody to go to hell, and make all the pictures we want, with Chinese, German, French (or anybody else) characterized in every way possible. On the other hand, if we want to continue to maintain our very lucrative foreign fields, we shall have to be, possibly, less 'free and sovereign—and less independent.'"[36] As Doherty evaluates, "Breen—so far behind the cultural curve on language, sex, and violence—was in perfect synch with the mood on race, religion, and ethnicity."[37] It was the PCA's established practice to request the deletion of derogatory racial and ethnic slurs (such as "nigger," "wop," "chink," "dago," "greaser," etc.). For example, Breen successfully persuaded David O. Selznick to sanitize his script of *Gone with the Wind* (1939) and eliminate the inflammatory word "nigger" unless it was spoken by African American characters.[38]

During the Second World War, the PCA's prerogatives were challenged by the OWI, the Franklin D. Roosevelt administration's propaganda agency, whose national and political agendas often superseded the religious and moral mandates of the Production Code. Eleven days after the Pearl Harbor attack of December 7, 1941, President Roosevelt appointed then-director of Office of Government Reports Lowell Mellett as coordinator of government films and mobilized Hollywood for America's war effort. In April 1942, Mellett set up a Hollywood office headed by Nelson Poynter, liberal publisher of the *St. Petersburg Times*. When the OWI was created by executive order in June 1942 under the directorship of Elmer Davis, a former CBS news analyst, Mellett's office was consolidated as its Bureau of Motion Pictures (BMP). The BMP repeatedly emphasized that its mission was not to censor but to increase the producers' factual understanding of the war and to help shape their efforts toward the winning of the war. Defining its function as purely advisory, the Hollywood office solicited studios to submit treatments, scripts, and rough cuts to be reviewed by OWI film analysts, who in turn provided recommendations based on a vast pool of government war information and area knowledge. In their press release, the BMP insisted: "Our office has no authority and wants none over producers . . . . If our recommendations, documented with facts, make sense they will be followed in the majority of cases because motion picture makers want to win the war just as much as government servants."[39]

In its first annual activities report (May 1942–April 1943), the BMP's Hollywood office testified its successful establishment of collaborative relationships with studios:

> Because of the sincere interest of the motion picture industry in the war effort, producers are increasingly taking the suggestions of this office with great seriousness, revising their treatments, rewriting their scripts, reediting their completed films, and in some cases reshooting certain sequences, in accordance with the suggestions of this Office and the interests of the War Information Program . . . . Most of the studios now have established a procedure whereby every completed treatment and every completed script automatically clears through our office. All of studios at least submit those scripts which present problems from the standpoint of the war . . . . Altogether, since the Hollywood Office opened, we have reviewed a total of 240 feature scripts.[40]

This report suggests that Hollywood tempered its initial mistrust of government intervention and accepted OWI review as an additional step in the self-regulation protocol, supplementing the PCA regime.[41] Considering the difficulty that the PCA's predecessor, the SRC, experienced with recalcitrant producers before the MPPDA made the internal regulator's seal of approval a precondition for distribution and exhibition of studio films, this command of voluntary compliance was no small feat for the BMP without jurisdiction over motion picture business. However, as Clayton R. Koppes points out, the OWI had "more than patriotic suasion at its command" since its Overseas Branch had inter-agency influence over the Office of Censorship in the selection of motion pictures to be granted export licenses, thereby controlling lucrative wartime exhibition outside of the United States.[42] This economic leverage was crucial in strengthening OWI regulation, particularly its role in influencing representations of allies and enemies in wartime Hollywood features. As Koppes and Gregory D. Black state in *Hollywood Goes to War*, "Government and industry discovered that they needed each other; the advancement of political and economic interests went hand-in-hand.... When OWI, like PCA, showed that censorship would be 'smart showmanship,' the industry was only too eager to cooperate."[43]

As Ellen C. Scott points out, because "the OWI was guided by a progressive political interest in the international reputation of the United States... [it] sought to eradicate misinformation about various racial groups, national and international." She goes on to state: "With an eye toward broad international diplomacy, OWI staffers censored Hollywood's racial and national stereotypes."[44] In particular, the OWI discouraged showing allied nationals in "the time-worn stereotypes of the screen" such as "the comic laundryman Chinese, the bearded revolutionary type Russian, and the 'bah jove' Englishman."[45] This OWI policy was in line with the Office of Censorship's stipulation that "derogatory picturization or presentation of nationals of United Nations and of neutral countries is objectionable," indicating that an export license would not be have been granted to ship such material to any country.[46] Albeit deriving from a different agenda (national rather than commercial), the OWI's pursuit of more egalitarian representations of race, ethnicity, and nationality coincided with the Code's call for respecting "national feelings." One of the national groups for which the OWI advocated strongly was America's most privileged Asian ally: the Chinese.

For example, in his October 26, 1942, letter to Paramount producer-director Mark Sandrich about the script of *So Proudly We Hail* (1943), a cinematic tribute to a group of military nurses known as the "angels of Bataan," Nelson Poynter complained:

> A condescending attitude toward our Chinese allies is evident. Only two Chinese are shown, both in rather menial positions. And one of them says to

> an American: 'Horrible as it is, I still must say I'm glad you and your country are in it—because now we shall all be free'. This recurring tendency among Americans to aggrandize the role that America is going to play in winning the war must be hard for China, who has fought so long and lost so much, to take. Instead of picturing ourselves always in the role of Lady Bountiful to the world, perhaps we should take a look at how much we owe to our fighting allies.[47]

This sentiment is echoed in a condensed version of the *Government Information Manual* dated April 29, 1943, and circulated among writers, directors, and producers. The pamphlet cautions studios against showing "Americans single-handedly licking the whole Axis" and encourages them to remember that "the [contributions] made by the British, the Russian, and the Chinese . . . have been so much greater than that of the United States to date." It goes on to instruct Hollywood filmmakers to emphasize that "our allies are courageous and valiant people . . . . Our allies are human beings like ourselves . . . . Despite superficial differences of language and custom, essentially we are all alike."[48]

"Our Kind of People": Displaced Japanese Atrocities and Permitted Chinese Patricide

Produced and co-written by the studio head of 20th Century-Fox, Darryl F. Zanuck, who had just returned from his service for the U.S. Army Signal Corps as a colonel, *The Purple Heart* is an imaginary account of what might have happened to eight American fliers who were captured by Japanese troops in China following their mission in the Doolittle Raid of Tokyo (April 18, 1942), the first U.S. airstrike in response to Pearl Harbor. They were part of eighty volunteer crewmen of sixteen B-25 "Mitchell" bombers deployed in attacking military and industrial targets in Tokyo, Yokohama, Nagoya, Kobe, and Osaka. At the dawn of mission day, the U.S. navy's aircraft carrier *Hornet* with B-25s was sighted by *Nitto Maru*, an enemy picket boat, which sent a radio warning to Tokyo before being destroyed by an American attack. This incident forced the early launch of bombers 800 miles from the Japanese coast, instead of the planned 400-mile distance. After the mission, none of the planes could reach designated allied airfields in China due to low fuel and stormy weather. One headed to the closer Soviet Union and fifteen reached the eastern Chinese coast, where the crews either crash-landed or bailed out. Out of eighty airmen, sixty-nine escaped capture or death thanks to Chinese allies who helped bring them to safety. One died during the bailout and two aircraft (with ten men) went missing. It was not until October of that year that the Japanese radio announced having tried eight captured raiders (out of the missing ten, minus two casualties of the crash landing) for war crimes and sentencing all involved to death.

Out of the eight prisoners, Lt. Dean E. Hallmark, Lt. William G. Farrow, and Sgt. Harold A. Spatz (two pilots and a gunner) were executed in Shanghai on October 15, 1942. The death sentence for the remaining five was commuted to life imprisonment.[49] Out of those individuals, Lt. Robert J. Meder died in captivity. After surviving three and a half years as POWs, the surviving four (Lt. George Barr, Lt. Robert L. Hite, Lt. Chase J. Nielsen, and Cpl. Jacob D. DeShazer) were repatriated following the end of the war. In the powerful denouement of *The Purple Heart*, a fictional account released during the war before details about the fates of the captured aviators were known at home, all of their screen surrogates choose honorable death over a treacherous bargain with the Japanese prosecution and march out of the court as proud Americans.

Reputed by historians as the most socially conscious of all moguls during the studio system era, Zanuck was a gambler who was not afraid of tackling sensitive topics, from mob lynching in William A. Wellman's *The Ox-Bow Incident* (1943) to Northern anti-Semitism in Elia Kazan's *Gentlemen's Agreement* (1947) to Southern racism and segregation in Elia Kazan's *Pinky* (1949). Even for Zanuck, *The Purple Heart* was a risky project: it went into production while the State Department's ban on pictures depicting Japanese atrocities against American prisoners was in effect. The prohibition was aimed at preventing retaliation against American POWs in Japanese camps. Despite this official ban, low-budget pictures such as RKO's *Behind the Rising Sun* (1943)—a follow-up project bringing together director Edward Dmytryk and writer Emmet Lavery, who had just completed another sensationalist exploitation picture on Axis atrocities, *Hitler's Children* (1943)—broached the subject of Japanese brutality against Chinese women and children as well as American civilians in China during the Sino-Japanese War.

Although *Behind the Rising Sun* was not in direct violation of the ban on showing atrocities against POWs, the OWI was still critical of "scenes of outrageous Japanese brutality" that might prompt "the emotional reaction of hatred . . . against the Japanese" instead of an intellectual assessment of the Japanese fascist system, which turns a Cornell-educated youth with Western ideals (Taro Seki, played by yellowfaced Tom Neal) into a hardened officer who callously watches baby killings and falsely denounces his American friends as spies.[50] The ban on "atrocity pictures" was lifted in January 1944, when the government released to the public details of Japanese atrocities against Bataan prisoners in 1942.[51] Although the OWI and the War Department (later known as the Department of Defense) still did not encourage Hollywood producers to make atrocity pictures, the subject was allowed as long as studios limited themselves to depictions of reported atrocities.[52] The timing of policy change could not have been more fortuitous for Zanuck, who had greenlighted the production in the fall of 1943 without knowing when his company would be able to release the completed film to exhibitors. In his interview with

Erskine Johnson of *Los Angeles Daily News*, Zanuck dubs *The Purple Heart* "the biggest gamble I've ever taken." The risk-taking mogul elaborates: "I was ready to keep the picture on the shelf, unreleased, until the government changed its policy . . . . The picture has never been on the release schedule. I was prepared to keep it on the shelf for two years if necessary."[53]

The government ban on atrocity pictures, still in effect during the film's production, might explain the special care given to the treatment of Japanese torture in *The Purple Heart*. Between show trial sessions, the prisoners are taken, one by one, to an offscreen interrogation room where unseen torture takes place. What the audience is allowed to see is its aftereffect on each prisoner: one returns unconscious and is carried on a stretcher; another is shown with his broken arm bandaged; and yet another has had his throat so burned that he is unable to speak or drink tea. The most impactful and lengthy offscreen torture scene is the first one, involving a physically fit football player named Sergeant Jan Skvoznik (Kevin O'Shea). His fellow inmates are anxiously waiting in the prison cell, wondering what is being done to him and assuring themselves that the enemy won't be able to break him. One prisoner says, "He is strong as an ox. He worked as an iron puddler every summer alongside his father." Another exclaims, "Boy, was he tough on a football field." A third adds, "The best game he ever played, he played with three broken ribs. They won't get anything out of him. He'll take all they've got." The group pep talk is interrupted by a wake-up call: a long offscreen scream of excruciating pain from a distance, instilling fear and uncertainty in the minds of fellow prisoners awaiting their turn to be called. Skvoznik's fate is withheld for another seven minutes of screen time, until the next courtroom scene, which takes place the following morning. Despite the court-appointed Japanese defense counsel's request to excuse the sick prisoner from testifying, General Mitsubi Ito (Richard Loo), a sadistic army intelligence officer, summons him to the witness stand. The courtroom door opens and the shadow of an upright figure approaches only to reveal a startling sight: despite his motor skills, Skvoznik is in a semi-vegetative state, twitching his head involuntarily and looking blankly ahead. The camera slow pans to show closeup reaction shots of his seven colleagues, whose faces register shock and silent rage.

Skvoznik's torture scene supports Stephen Prince's argument that "sound gave filmmakers [the new ability] to aesthetically stylize acts of cruelty and violence and to make these vivid and disturbing at a new and evocative sensory level."[54] In their preview print assessment, the OWI offered praise: "The atrocities have been played down to a minimum of sensationalism and emphasis has been placed on the theme of strength and courage of people who are fighting Fascism, exemplified by the eight American fliers."[55] What the OWI underestimated is the power of "the sound of pain" in "augment[ing] a viewer's impression of the overall level of violence" occurring offscreen and the effectiveness

FIG. 2.1 Having sunk into a semi-vegetative state due to offscreen Japanese torture, Sergeant Jan Skvoznik (left: Kevin O'Shea) is summoned to the witness stand by General Mitsubi Ito (right: Richard Loo), a sadistic army intelligence officer in Lewis Milestone's *The Purple Heart* (20th Century-Fox, 1944).

of such a disciplined, economic approach in provoking intense spectatorial reactions as will be discussed in the subsequent section about the film's reception.[56] Along with the sounds of pain and suffering, *The Purple Heart* adopts the visual code of what Prince calls "spatial displacement" in order to reconcile the Code's prohibition of "repellent subjects" ("brutality and possible gruesomeness") as well as the government's ban on showing Japanese atrocities against American POWs. Prince defines the strategy in this way: "Rather than directly showing a beating, stabbing, shooting, or the bloody results of these acts, a filmmaker using spatial displacement will cut away either to a new scene or to some other object or character in the vicinity of violence that has been suppressed."[57]

While torture takes place offscreen, the camera focuses on a different space, the jail where fellow prisoners discuss Skvoznik's physical strength and, after hearing his scream, confess doubts about their own ability to resist torture. Instead of cutting to the interrogation room to show the aftermath of torture and the Japanese handling of Skvoznik's brutalized body, the film introduces a distracting narrative event: General Mitsubi visits the cell at night and spies on Captain Harvey Ross (Dana Andrews), the leader of the squadron, who is murmuring in his sleep. On the soundtrack, we hear Ross's dream as an aural flashback of the order he was given before the mission: "If any of you are forced down, destroy your ship at once. We don't want to take any chance on the Japs tracing you back to this carrier. Whatever the cost, protect the *Hornet*." The captain wakes up in time without unconsciously disclosing military secrets to his captor through sleep talking. Before the courtroom scene in which the condition of Skvoznik is revealed, there is another cutaway to a Swiss Red Cross representative (Torben Meyer), who is unsuccessfully trying to cable Washington to get help for the American prisoners (his communique is censored and discarded). It is notable that *The Purple Heart* employs both spatial and temporal displacement in handling sensitive torture scenes. The two inserted actions—General Mitsubi's act of spying on Captain Ross and the Red Cross official's quibble with a Japanese bureaucrat over the censored cable—push narrative time forward without showing the immediate aftermath of brutal torture, which was presented obliquely through spatial displacement. It is not until the next morning, at least a half day later, that the audience is allowed to see the tortured subject, who by that time has been cleaned up by the Japanese, despite his visible internal damage onscreen.

General Mitsubi's attempt to question a non-responsive Skovznik (who can barely mumble his own name) is interrupted, first by two fellow airmen who burst into an angry demonstration and are carried out of the courtroom after being knocked on the heads by guards. When the general tries to resume the questioning of his witness, it is disturbed again, this time by news of the fall of Corregidor—information that arrives as a note to the presiding judge. The victory is publicly announced to the court, which erupts in euphoric celebration. With no explanatory dialogue, Japanese army and naval officers in attendance burst into an impromptu sword dance, moving rigidly like synchronized automatons. This brief scene juxtaposes the individuality of the five remaining defendants (whose reactions are shown in close-ups, one by one)—minus Skovznik, who is still on the witness stand, and the two men outside the room—with the machine-like collectivity of the Japanese enemies, whose faces, in contrast, are obscured in fragmented shots. Bookended with a medium shot of all five Americans gazing at the offscreen foreground is a rapid montage of twelve shots lasting ten seconds in total. In a medium low-angle shot, the bottom half of a line of five officers in light army uniforms (on the right side of the frame) is shown pulling out their swords. A cut to the first prisoner's face in a close-up, looking up, is followed with an eyeline match—a third shot showing five blades lifted up by white gloved hands on the far right side of the frame. Then comes a cut to the second prisoner's close-up as he looks down. Next we see a second line of five naval officers in decorated dark uniforms who pull their blades simultaneously. A close-up of Captain Ross's face follows, and from that point the scene is cut into the following units:

> five blades being raised by gloved hands;
> a reaction shot of the fourth flier's face;
> the first group of five soldiers turning around (their backs are toward the camera and their swords are held up by both hands across their torsos);
> a final closeup reaction shot;
> five naval officers repeating the action/positioning of their army colleagues;
> a shot of the bottom half of the naval officers' bodies with their feet jumping up and down as if dancing.

By intercutting individual close-ups of five raiders' tense, concerned faces with medium shots of the same number of blades being drawn and lifted as part of an intimidating, impersonal group action, the elliptical montage (reminiscent of Sergei Eisenstein's dialectical montage of the 1920s) implies the violence of beheading in the visual code of what Prince calls "metonymic displacement." This code can be defined as "the occlusive or evasive composition [that] contains some object or action that stands in for the violence that is occurring out of view," in this case, outside of the diegetic world of film narrative.[58]

Notably, one month after *The Purple Heart*'s original release, in April 1944, the shocking photograph of blinded and kneeling Australian commando Leonard Siffleet (positioned in the foreground of the image, to the left) about to be beheaded by a Japanese naval officer (Chikao Yasuno) wielding his execution sword (in the right middle ground), with Japanese and native onlookers (in the background), on the Aitape Beach in Papua New Guinea on October 24, 1943, was shown in various newspapers and *Life* magazine.[59] An enlarged newspaper front page with this iconic image also features in the opening scene of the War Department's orientation film *Know Your Enemy: Japan* (1945). That film, directed by Frank Capra, associates the enemy with barbarism, inhumanity, and cruelty. Although the photograph of the atrocity was not yet available for public viewing during *The Purple Heart*'s production (which occurred concurrently with Sergeant Siffleet's execution) and its first-run release in March 1944, the imagery of Japanese beheadings of POWs had already been planted in the American public's collective mind by the government's report on Bataan atrocities. A joint report by the army and the navy, dated January 28, 1944, was summarized by the Associated Press in the following way: "Compiled from the sworn statements of officers who survived the starvation and torture and escaped, it catalogued the infamy of a brutal enemy, and wrote in shocking terms the code of the Japanese warrior—to subject 36,000 gallant soldiers to deliberate starvation, to shoot in cold blood the thirsty who seek water, to watch

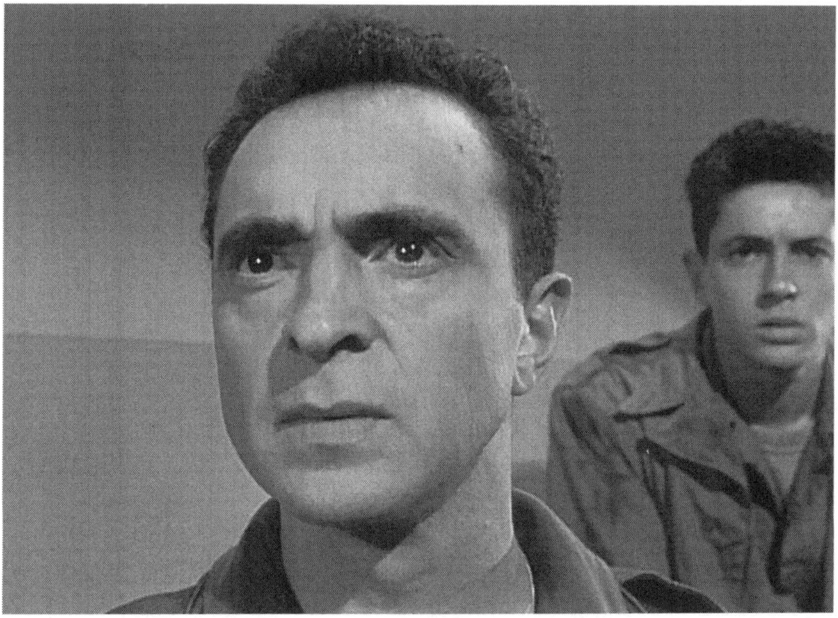

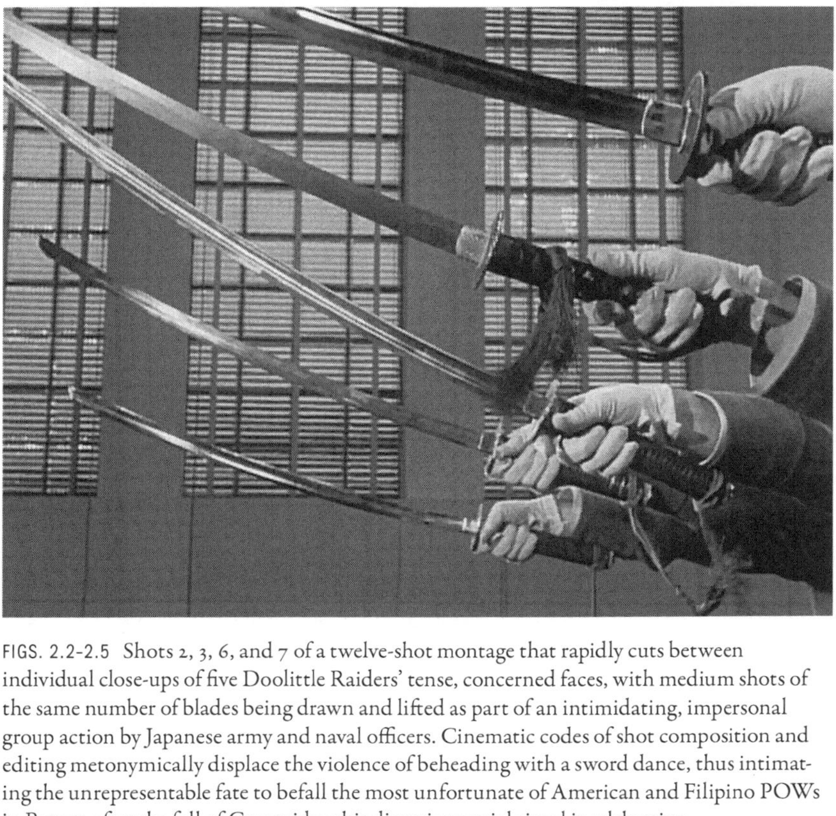

FIGS. 2.2–2.5 Shots 2, 3, 6, and 7 of a twelve-shot montage that rapidly cuts between individual close-ups of five Doolittle Raiders' tense, concerned faces, with medium shots of the same number of blades being drawn and lifted as part of an intimidating, impersonal group action by Japanese army and naval officers. Cinematic codes of shot composition and editing metonymically displace the violence of beheading with a sword dance, thus intimating the unrepresentable fate to befall the most unfortunate of American and Filipino POWs in Bataan after the fall of Corregidor this diegetic martial ritual is celebrating.

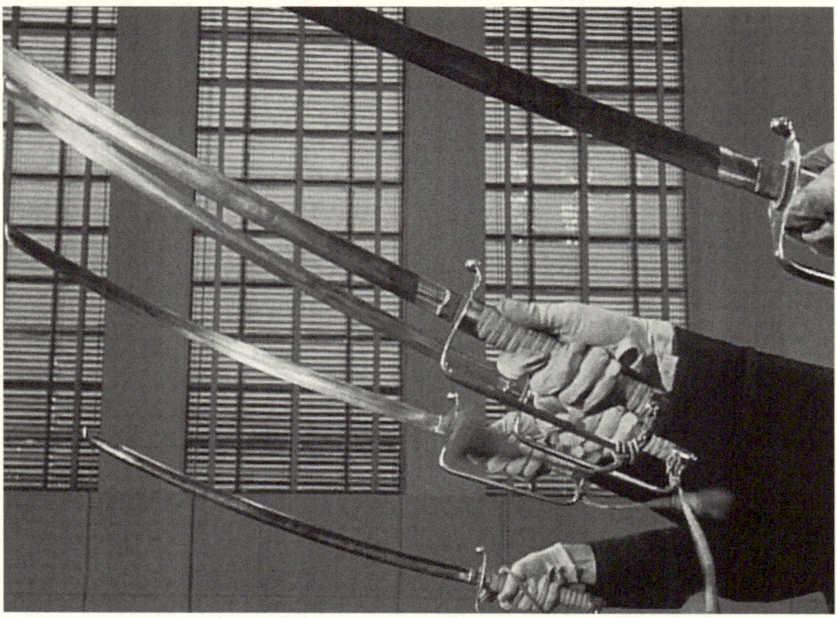

FIGS. 2.2–2.5 Continued

sick men writhe and deny them medicine, to horsewhip those who help their fallen comrades, to beat men with two-by-fours, to *behead* those who try to escape, and to bury tortured men alive."[60]

Instead of capturing the Japanese dance spectacle in long shot, director Lewis Milestone deliberately shifts the audience's attention to lifted sword blades in fragmented medium shots intercut with close-ups of each American captive's head. Cinematic codes of shot composition and editing metonymically displace beheading with dance, thus intimating the unrepresentable violence to befall the most unfortunate of American and Filipino POWs in Bataan after the fall of Corregidor, which this diegetic martial dance is celebrating. This is not to say that *The Purple Heart*, through such strategies of spatial, temporal, or metonymic displacement (which evoke, rather than represent, Japanese atrocities), could have been released during the period of the government ban on atrocity pictures. As Prince points out, displacement of violence in Classical Hollywood cinema "does not create serious narrative ambiguities" for the viewer, who "understands its operation and those things it implicitly references." However, such displacement works indexically and bespeaks "the presence of the system of film censorship and regulation governing screen content of this period."[61] For *The Purple Heart*, that system expands to include the Production Code, the OWI's information manual, and the State Department's ban on atrocity pictures. Although Zanuck did not expect to release the film until the government policy had been changed, the ongoing ban during the production must have influenced how Milestone and his crew deigned to depict, or rather evade depiction of, Japanese atrocities onscreen. Along with the ally's racial, ethnic, and national images, violence and atrocities committed by the enemy were another area of convergence where the PCA's goals and the government's interests dovetailed. The above textual examples from *The Purple Heart* attest to the positive effects of regulatory guidance on the latter subject, and hint at the "poetry of the indirect" or the "eloquence of expression that splatter effects often degrade," as evidenced by Angelina Jolie's *Unbroken* (2014), a contemporary torture-porn version of Japanese mistreatment of American POWs that exhibits a lack of such things.[62]

Interestingly, during the film's production between September 1943 and February 1944, the plotline that received the most vocal opposition from the OWI was not the treatment of Japanese torture but the inclusion of a Chinese puppet governor who betrays the American fliers and hands them over to Japanese authorities. One scene in particular that generated censorship discussions revolves around the murder of the traitorous governor by his own son, a young patriot named Moy. His assassination occurs publicly, in the courtroom where the American airmen are being tried. The PCA objected to the portrayal of patricide for violating the Production Code, which explicitly prohibits depictions of revenge killings in a modern setting. In a letter dated October 14,

1943, Breen offered Colonel Joy, former SRC head and director of public relations at 20th Century-Fox, his usual advice regarding diplomatic protocols: "We urge upon you the advisability of consulting with Chinese authorities [regarding] elements that concern China." Then, he went on to voice his disapproval of the murder scene in the shooting script, stating: "The action of Moy in killing his father is unacceptable, as a murder of revenge. In this connection, see likewise the condoning of the act by the Americans."[63]

The BMP, in contrast, extolled the scene as a fitting tribute to the courage of Chinese allies fighting for freedom. In a letter dated October 21, 1943, OWI analyst Warren H. Pierce gave a positive review to the studio publicist Colonel Joy, indicating that "this picture very well can be one of the greatest of all war films. We are tremendously enthusiastic over it. It should be the best contribution toward a general understanding of our Japanese enemy yet turned out by the industry."[64] However, the government propagandist added a caveat: "There is only one possibly problem from our standpoint . . . . That is the episode involving the Chinese quisling. I think this could be completely resolved by two small interpolations. First, it might be made more clear that the fliers who were betrayed by the quisling crashed in occupied China. Second, I think that Moy might be built up a little bit so that he is not only an individual hero, but more specifically a representative of the young Chinese who are fighting for freedom."[65] In an attached script review, the OWI offered a radically different evaluation of Moy's patricide from the PCA's: "Moy's action avenges not only the Chinese people, but her allies, the American fliers. Following through in this connection, the American fliers rise as Moy is dragged out, in tribute to a man. Perhaps this gesture could also specifically be made as a tribute to our China ally, indicating that they feel Moy, rather than Yuen Chiu Ling [Moy's father], represents China."[66]

The finished film supports the government's view on the scene. After the puppet governor (H. T. Tsiang) is called to the witness stand and lies that the bailed-out raiders were boastful of having mowed down children with machine guns and destroying hospitals and temples, General Mitsubi corroborates the first witness's perjury with false newsreel footage, which is presented as evidence of civilian casualties caused by the Doolittle Raid.[67] The motion picture screening is stopped and courtroom lights are turned back on when a shrill scream in the dark startles the diegetic audience. The camera cuts to a medium shot of Moy (Benson Fong), who stands up to display his knife, a murder weapon, while his father's lifeless corpse falls to the edge of the bench on the right side of the frame. The young Chinese declares to the judge (Peter Chong), "This, at least, Excellency, is the truth." Then, he casts his gaze toward the defendants' stand and tells the offscreen Americans, "I am a solider of China. My father has answered to his ancestors for your betrayal." As a Japanese solider arrests the Chinese man and escorts him out of the court at the judge's order, Captain Ross

FIG. 2.6 To the Office of War Information's delight, Moy Ling (left: Benson Fong) publicly assassinates his father (right: H. T. Tsiang), a collaborator with the Japanese, in order to avenge both the Chinese people and the American fliers.

issues a command to his group: "Stand up, fellas, for a man." With a polite bow, Moy reciprocates the respect that the standing raiders show to him during his exit. Captain Ross's group reencounters Moy Ling across the bars when the latter is temporarily put in a jail cell adjacent to theirs. Ross proposes to "elect him an honorable member of [their] squadron," to which his men respond with enthusiastic "ayes." The camera cuts back and forth between a close-up of Moy in his cell and a reaction shot of the airmen, who silently listen to their neighbor's confession. He mutters: "I wish to explain why I did not act before I did. It required much time to decide to kill my own father." This intimate emotional exchange is cut short when a couple of Japanese soldiers open Moy's cell and take him away for his execution. After saying goodbye to the brave Chinese youth passing through the corridor in front of their cell door, Ross whispers in sincerity to a fellow inmate next to him: "I'd have him on my team any time."

20th Century-Fox accommodated OWI recommendations in a moderate way. As Eleanor Berneis, an OWI analyst who saw the preview print, writes, "Following suggestions of this office . . . the part of Moy, the quisling's son, has been built up to some extent in the film to show his comradeship with the American fliers. They now vote him an honorable member of their squadron."[68]

Even with this alteration, the OWI felt that the finished film was not entirely fair to Chinese allies who had made personal sacrifices to save the Doolittle raiders. Its preview feedback includes an additional recommendation for the studio: "The addition of a line when the fliers are preparing to bail out, for example, would make it clear that there is a great difference between bailing out over friendly Free China and Japanese-occupied China. It is urged that this point be clarified, in fairness to the innumerous Chinese who risked their lives to give vital assistance in escorting many of the Tokyo raiders to safety."[69] The dialogue in the bailout scene of the released print still makes the difference between free vs. occupied China ambiguous. When his navigator informs him that they are over China, Lieutenant Vincent (Don "Red" Barry), second-in-command, cynically replies: "Splendid. That narrows things down considerably." However, as Captain Ross gives bailout instructions to his crew, he insinuates the possibility of landing in an enemy-held territory by saying that "she [the plane] mustn't fall into Japanese hands." It would have broken the illusion of drama had the captain given a gratuitous lecture on Chinese geography and Japanese occupation at this crucial juncture of action. In other words, studios took the OWI's advice selectively, just as they did with the PCA's, and strove to make realistic accommodations without compromising narrative causality and dramatic flow. Like the PCA, the OWI was malleable and was willing to compromise. Despite their reservation about the Chinese traitor, the agency highly recommended *The Purple Heart* for "special distribution in liberated areas."[70]

For another Doolittle Raid film released by MGM in the same year, Mervyn LeRoy's *Thirty Seconds over Tokyo* (1944) (which was based on Captain Ted W. Lawson's memoir of the same title), the aforementioned OWI reviewer, Berneis, made the following suggestion for script revisions: "From the standpoint of this office, it would be possible to improve this valuable script by adding to it some dialogue or action which would show that the gratitude is not all one-sided—from the Chinese to the Americans .... It would be most appropriate for the Americans to show some realization of the fact that the bombing mission they have accomplished, while it is important, is only one great exploit against the Japanese, whereas China has been giving everything she had, including millions of lives, for five years."[71] After watching the preview print, another analyst, William S. Cunningham, pointed out an understated yet effective alteration that MGM made to accommodate the OWI recommendation: "The only suggestion made by this office, that the picture could be improved by showing the gratitude is not all one-sided ... has been followed to some extent .... This does not seem to be over-done and in one speech the hero gives credit to the Chinese soldiers and says something to the effect that he and many other Americans will be in China to fight alongside them because 'You're our kind of people.'"[72] These documents indicate that BMP staff were capable of appreciating subtle, nuanced modifications of scripts that studios accommodated without overhauling narrative or characterizations for propaganda purposes. After all, it was the OWI's philosophy to avoid the excesses of the Committee on Public Information's World War I propaganda and infuse Hollywood entertainment "with a memorable yet subtle propaganda theme" so that the public would not be conscious of being propagandized.[73]

Although the OWI intervened to reinforce the role of Moy as a tribute to Chinese allies in *The Purple Heart*, the nonwhite character remains marginalized in the racial hierarchy of Classical Hollywood cinema. After bonding with the all-white American heroes in two scenes, Moy is prematurely eradicated from the narrative forty minutes into the film. Incidentally, the Chinese American actor who played Moy Ling (Benson Fong) also played Dr. Chung in *Thirty Seconds over Tokyo*, a character who saves Van Johnson's Captain Lawson (and to whom Lawson says "You're our kind of people" as a farewell).[74] Despite their brief screen time, both of Fong's supporting characters play a significant symbolic role, in terms of personifying the wartime Sino-American alliance. As a representative of a new, modern China, Moy—like Dr. Chung in *Thirty Seconds over Tokyo*—is dressed in a Western suit and tie and speaks perfect English, unlike his father, in a traditional Mandarin gown, who speaks with exaggerated accent. The father-son relationship is depicted as being undemocratic and oppressive, as suggested by the two characters' dialogue (in untranslated Chinese) in the scene in which the son tries to stop his father from testifying against the fliers. In the revised script dated October 14, 1943, their argument is translated in English. The father angrily responds, "Silence, unrespectful one!" to his son's plea, "Please, honorable father! Don't do this."[75]

The use of untranslated Mandarin and Japanese in the film deserves attention. While Mandarin is spoken by Chinese American actors (Benson Fong and H. T. Tsiang) with greater cultural verisimilitude, heavily accented Japanese is awkwardly uttered by Chinese-born Peter Chong (Judge Toyama) and Hawaiian-Chinese American Richard Loo (General Mitsubi), who, like so many other persons of color in Hollywood during the studio system era, were forced to perform cross-ethnic roles (during the Second World War, this was due to the internment of Japanese American actors and extras on the West Coast).[76] It should be said, though, that in terms of casting these Asian roles *The Purple Heart* was ahead of its time, as it is thankfully devoid of the kind of stomach-churning yellowface performances that feature in many other productions of that era, such as *China Girl* (1943), *China Sky* (1944), and *Dragon Seed* (1944). Philip Ahn, a Korean American actor who played a bit part as a Japanese sailor, credited its director and producer, saying, "The change came during the war years when Milestone called me in to do a screen test for *The Purple Heart*. He wanted to prove to Darryl Zanuck that Orientals could act and that the key Japanese roles should be played by Orientals: Richard Loo,

FIG. 2.7 Ted Lawson (right: Van Johnson) bids farewell, with the tribute "You're our kind of people," to Dr. Chung (left: Benson Fong) in Meryvn LeRoy's *Thirty Seconds over Tokyo* (Metro-Goldwyn-Mayer, 1944).

myself, and others. Zanuck enthusiastically bought the idea after seeing the test and it was the turning point. Oriental actors started getting the big Oriental roles."[77]

In 1946, Milestone wrote a letter to California representative Helen Gahagan Douglas, petitioning her to sponsor a private bill for Tsiang, an immigrant writer and political radical from New York, who was detained on Ellis Island in 1940–1941 for a visa problem, to protect him from the immigration authorities. The filmmaker justified his request, saying, "I am the first director who ventured to use Orientals in playing major Oriental parts in a picture. There are very few Chinese actors in the country. Mr. Tsiang is one of the very few who had made the grade . . . . During the war period, the alien (Tsiang) took part in the production of films which were of great service as morale builders, both on the field and on the home front."[78] Tsiang's on/offscreen duplicity in *The Purple Heart*—a collaborator who poses as an ally to stranded raiders in the narrative and a patriotic immigrant who played a traitor in a morale-boosting wartime propaganda picture—is emblematic of the representational ambivalence of Oriental characters, a facet of ethnic performativity that had persisted since the silent era (as demonstrated in my earlier analysis of the World War I film *The Secret Game*). It is ironic that Tsiang, a cosmopolitan proletarian artist critical of Chinese cultural nationalism and conservatism, embodies feudal China in *The Purple Heart*, whereas there is something subversive about his hammy, over-the-top performance as a betrayer of the Americans given his socialist literary philosophy, nine-month detention on Ellis Island, and subjection to FBI investigation during the McCarthy era.[79]

As Warren I. Cohen explains, the period of 1900–1950 was an "era of paternalism" in Sino-American relations. Following the "era of deference" (1784–1841) and the "era of contempt" (1841–1900) and preceding the "era of fear" (1950–1971), this period was "an era of great concern over issues that related to China" for many Americans. For government officials, "China was a geopolitical concern," while for "missionaries and foundations, China was a world concern, a beleaguered country that could benefit from American spiritual, technological, educational, or medical aid."[80] To extend this metaphor of paternalism toward China into the arena of filmic representation, one can argue that Moy rejects his biological, cultural father in favor of an ideological, political father that is the United States. A cinematic vision of Westernized China "killing" its feudal "father" (both literally and symbolically) is not inconsistent with the Nationalist (Kuomintang) government's aggressive modernization and nation-building project during the Nanjing decade (1927–1937). Under the leadership of Generalissimo Chiang Kai-shek, the Nationalists along with Western advisors strove to modernize the country's military, finance, transportation, and communications infrastructure. Education was reformed, superstitions were tempered, and certain feudal customs, such as the practice of breast- and foot-binding, were abolished. The urban middle class quickly adopted Western lifestyles and ideas. The state-controlled Chinese National Board of Film Censors (later the Central Motion Picture Censorship Committee) suppressed superstitious genres such as ghost and martial arts films and banned several of Hollywood's warlord films that exploited China as a backward, Orientalist backdrop, as discussed in chapter 1.

On the other hand, regardless of its motive, patricide is practically unimaginable in the context of traditional Chinese culture. As mentioned in chapter 1, Consul T. K. Chang vehemently opposed the Chinese mother's filicide in *The Shanghai Gesture* (1941) for cultural reasons. The Chinese consul elaborated, "For ages we have been taught to revere sacredly the relation between parents and children. So sacred we hold this tradition that either in literature or in the conventions of dramatic stage there has never occurred such a violence [the killing of a child by a parent, vice versa]; if it occurred at all, it was invariably rescued by divine intervention."[81] Although the Western literary tradition of patricide dates back to Greek mythology, such as the story of Oedipus, it is an unlikely subject (even more so than filicide) for the Chinese. During the Qing dynasty (1644–1911), patricide was punished by dismemberment, the most severe form of capital punishment, attesting to the extent of its moral taboo in Chinese society.[82] From a cultural perspective, glorifying Moy's patricide as a proper tribute to the Chinese ally is absurd, a myopic interpretation that is inherently American. Rather, the act can be better read as a powerful symbol for Moy's Americanization/Westernization and his no-looking-back severance from Chinese cultural tradition.

If we shift our focus to the question of narrative rationale or verisimilitude, publicly staged patricide might still come across as a contrived, implausible plot device, regardless of its cultural implications. As Kate Cameron complains in her *New York Daily News* review of March 9, 1944, "Except for a highly melodramatic and completely Hollywoodian touch, the trials are presented with the starkness of a documentary film. But the murder of the Chinese informer by his son destroys the realism of the courtroom scenes."[83] Nevertheless, the assassination scene is loosely based on a real-life event reported in Captain Lawson's aforementioned memoir: "[Lt. William G.] Farrow . . . had horrible luck. He got through the bombing, made his getaway, reached China, and then had the terrible break of landing near a village controlled by a Japanese puppet governor. The loyal Chinese of the village immediately got in touch with Chungking. The Chinese Government attempted to bribe the puppet and get Farrow and the boys. But the puppet finally turned them over to the Japanese. The puppet was assassinated shortly thereafter, the Chinese said."[84] Owen Lattimore, U.S. advisor to Chiang Kai-shek and director of OWI Pacific Operations, cited the above passage as proof of the factual nature of the quisling incident when Chinese authorities raised a preemptive objection to the film over the plotline.[85] Transforming the identity of the puppet governor's assassin into his own son was a dramatic necessity, as *The Purple Heart* is a courtroom drama with only two main settings (the court and the prison). It heightened the melodramatic effect of Hollywood narrative while strengthening the state-sanctioned message about the loyal Chinese who would go as far as committing patricide to avenge the betrayal of American allies.

In compliance with OWI policy, the studio made a further effort to curtail the Japanese judge's offensive comments about the Chinese ally. In the shooting script, the judge addresses the court after the murder and Moy's exit: "The court regrets this interruption and especially deplores its nature. The Chinese are treacherous people. Try as we will to enlighten and guide them—they remain barbarians who will strike down even their own flesh and blood, if the price is high enough. It is the opinion of this court that the honorable Yuen Chiu Ling was killed by a paid assassin—fortunately not before he could testify."[86] The final incriminating line for the murder motive is cut in the finished film. The diegesis makes it clear that Moy's patricide is neither personal nor mercenary but political and collective, thus transcending the traditional notion of individualized morality. While privileging the OWI's interpretation of patricide as a justified, commendable act admired by American characters, the studio wisely struck a balance between morality and politics by upholding the Production Code through the punishment of Moy for his offense.

"Properly Directed Hatred"? The Reception of *The Purple Heart*

In addition to honoring allies, Hollywood producers were pressed to exercise caution in depicting enemies in accordance with the OWI's wartime policy of "properly directed hatred." Government bureaucrats urged film producers *not* to direct ill feelings toward fascist leaders or the people of the Axis nations but to the doctrine of fascism, militarism, and force.[87] The aforementioned 1943 *Government Information Manual* elaborates: "Don't characterize the enemy in such personalities as Hitler, Goebbels, Goering, Mussolini, Tojo or Yamashita, to the extent that the public will believe that if a handful of enemy leaders are eliminated, the Axis powers can then be trusted."[88] At the same time, the OWI cautioned filmmakers *not* to "inspire hatred for the whole German, Japanese, and Italian people," as the majority of them "are probably the unfortunate tools of their masters." The OWI further discouraged racializing enemies with such derogatory epithets as "little brown men," "yellow rats," "slant-eyed," and "monkeys." The *Government Information Manual* reminds Hollywood producers that "this is not a racial war. Many millions of our allies belong to the brown and yellow races and such references are offensive to them. Moreover name-calling is an ineffective weapon at best."[89] As Doherty points out, "The OWI wanted an ideology, not an individual, to be the Hollywood villain, a policy good in theory but bad as theater.... The OWI harbored a deep suspicion of the American tendency to perceive political problems in personal terms.... Just as the OWI doted on collective villainy, it preferred group heroism."[90] Albeit well-intended and progressive, the policy was easier said than done in the context of Hollywood's melodramatic, black-and-white moral universe.

The OWI praised the overall representation of the Japanese enemy in *The Purple Heart*. Its script review, dated October 13, 1943, assessed: "The screenplay gives an excellent picture of Japanese fascism at work. The wide divergence between their way and ours is graphically brought out in the courtroom procedure, the characterizations of the Japanese officials, and the methods they use against the Americans."[91] The film indeed conforms to the OWI directive to show that "the enemy is powerful, ruthless, and cunning" instead of underestimating or belittling him.[92] The chief antagonist, General Mitsubi, is a resourceful, capable army interrogator who not only guesses correctly that the bombers came from an ocean carrier but also knows how to wage psychological warfare on his prisoners. Along with coercion and (offscreen) torture, he resorts to cunning wit and tempts the fliers with offers of the dismissal of murder charges, fair treatment as POWs, and access to the Red Cross, in exchange for military intelligence. However, the film strips any signs of humanity from Japanese characters (who are either sadistic and brutal or calculating and mechanical) and portrays the entire populace of Japan as belligerent hatemongers, violating the OWI's policy. For example, in his private conversation with Captain Ross, General Mitsubi fanatically declares that "Japan is united in this war through emperor worship and hate. Hate for all foreigners, white or otherwise!"

Contemporaneous reception casts further doubt on the film's compatibility with the "properly directly hatred" policy. As elaborated in the studio booklet, "*The Purple Heart* was produced for a purpose . . . to awaken the American public to a full realization of the nature of our enemy in the East . . . to remind the American public of the brutality, fanaticism and barbaric war the Japanese waged in the Pacific. A further purpose of the film was to immortalize the American solider as typified by those gallant Americans who were captured by the Japs, tried and convicted on the charge of murder in a Tokyo court. It is evident that the film accomplished its purpose. This booklet presents the tribute of an aroused America."[93] Quoted in the booklet are several critics' responses, which attest to the film's success in inciting intense hatred for the Japanese enemy:

> "Will arouse moviegoers to a cold, passionate fury!" (Andrew R. Kelley, *Washington News*)
>
> "A damning indictment of Jap atrocities! Stirring its audiences so deeply every member becomes a missionary!" (Alton Cook, *New York World-Telegram*)
>
> "Will make good red American blood surge with pride . . . boil in furious resentment!" (A. De Bernardi Jr., *Denver Post*)
>
> "A blockbuster loaded with righteous wrath against the Japs! This one hurts!" (Leo Miller, *Bridgeport [CT] Herald*)
>
> "Rousing! You want to go out and skin a Jap alive. A necessity for Americans. Will jolt you right where you live!" (Vincent Townsend, *Birmingham News*)
>
> "If you think you hate the Japs, see *The Purple Heart*. Fired audiences to a pitch of indignation. Cried to be made and 20th has done a wonderful job!" (Harrison Carroll, *Los Angeles Evening Herald-Express*)

Louella O. Parsons's *Los Angeles Examiner* review of the film, dated March 10, 1944, is further evidence of *improperly* directed hatred by a passionate moviegoer: "If nothing else wakes us out of our apathy to the danger of the Japs, *The Purple Heart* will do it. I defy anyone to see this picture and not want to go out and kill, single-handed, every Jap."[94] A similar destructive spectatorial rage is expressed by Lee Mortimer in his article for *New York Mirror* dated March 9, 1944: "After seeing *The Purple Heart*, one conclusion is inescapable: either we destroy the mad Japanese warrior caste, or they destroy us."[95] As James Lindsley reports in his *Hollywood Citizen-News* article dated February 3, 1944, these hateful responses were intended by the film's producer: "The picture is *Purple Heart*, which Zanuck, production chief at 20th Century-Fox, frankly hopes will harden American hatred of the Japanese solider into implacability, while instilling in the American mind a weighted respect for the little brown man's fighting prowess."[96]

Overseas reception data gathered by the OWI's Overseas Branch corroborates the stateside critics' responses to Milestone's film. The OWI did a focus group study of twenty-two audience members (of varied ethnicities including Turkish, Czech, Italian, Greek, British, Yugoslav, Armenian, Spanish, and Hungarian) who saw *The Purple Heart* at the OWI theater in Istanbul on January 18 and 19, 1945. Under the title "Motion Picture Reactions—Turkey: Turkish Responses to *The Purple Heart*," the report summarizes its findings: "The film . . . appears to have been successful in conveying its propaganda point, if we consider this to have been the heroism and moral strength of American soldiers as compared to the brutality and treachery of the Japanese . . . . Many of the members of the audience felt the emotional impact of the film very strongly. A few believed that release of the sustained tension should have been provided by showing some acts of punishment or revenge against the Japanese."[97] Some of the vengeful responses against the Japanese noted in the report include: "I felt like piercing the eyes of the Japanese"; "Only the end should have been different and should have shown us some American bombardments of Japan to satisfy us"; "Whoever has seen this film of the torture of men by apes dressed as generals and admirals with decorations down to their knees, needs for psychological release a film showing these brave aviators throwing heavy caliber bombs on the capital of these inhuman creatures."[98]

The above-quoted reception data compiled by both the studio and the OWI clearly suggests that hatred was misdirected to the entire Japanese nation and people rather than the militaristic system of Japan. This failure, from the OWI's standpoint, was already foreseen by Lillian R. Bergquist, whose script review reads: "Although it clearly contributes to our understanding of the Japanese enemy, it fails to make anywhere the important distinction between the Japanese militarists and the Japanese people, a distinction called for by our government's information policy."[99] The OWI analyst, however, was not oblivious to the difficulty of making such a distinction in commercial Hollywood entertainment. Bergquist advised: "Obviously, this cannot be the main point of the story. It would be helpful, however, if somewhere in the script, some hint of this viewpoint could be expressed."[100]

Koppes and Black provide a rationale for the failure to uphold the "properly directed hatred" policy in *The Purple Heart*: "The agency had tried to soften racial propaganda in 1942. But by 1944 the emotional impact of the Japanese treatment of American POWs was being felt. The popular conception of the Japanese as inhuman beasts was too ingrained to counter, and too convenient a propaganda tool to abandon."[101] However, even in 1944, it was possible to inject a subtle message that differentiates Japanese militarists and Japanese civilians; penned by Dalton Trumbo, a leftist screenwriter who would be blacklisted in 1947 as one of the infamous "Hollywood Ten," *Thirty Seconds over Tokyo*—released eight months after *The Purple Heart*—does exactly that. On the deck of *Hornet* at nighttime, Ted Lawson confides to his friend Bob Gray (Robert Mitchum) confusion about his feelings toward the Japanese: "My mother had a Jap gardener once. He seemed like a nice little guy." Bob replies: "You know—I don't hate Japs yet. It's a funny thing. I don't like 'em—but I don't hate 'em." Our hero agrees: "I guess I don't either. You get kind of mixed up." However, he ultimately justifies his upcoming mission: "I don't pretend to like the idea of killing a bunch of people—but it's a case of drop a bomb on them or pretty soon they'll be dropping one on Ellen [his wife]."

Koppes and Black give sole authorship of the scene to Trumbo, stating: "While OWI wanted this type of presentation, the real credit must go to Dalton Trumbo. He deplored racism in American films and kept *Thirty Seconds over Tokyo* free from the usual 'hate the Japs' material that dominated American war films."[102] However, as film historian Thomas Schatz reminds us, "The quality and artistry of [studio system era] films were the product not simply of individual human expression, but of a melding of institutional forces. In each case the 'style' of a writer, director, star—or even a cinematographer, art director, or costume designer—fused with the studio's production operations and management structure, its resources and talent pool, its narrative traditions and market strategy."[103] In this complex gestalt of the collaborative system (under the tight management of strong-willed production chiefs such as Harry Cohn, Louis B. Mayer, Jack Warner, Darryl F. Zanuck, and others) it is nearly impossible to single out any individuals as sole "authors" of studio films. In his recent study *Hollywood's Censor: Joseph I. Breen and the Production Code Administration*, Doherty expands Schatz's understanding of the studio system to include the titular regulator as coauthor who "stamped his vision on Hollywood cinema" between 1934 and 1954 "more than any actor, director, or producer."[104] Particularly, regarding sensitive themes such as gender, sexuality, race, and ethnicity, it would be naive to assume that personal visions of individual writers, directors, or producers could pass unfiltered through the rigorous regulatory system (both within the industry and without) or that their visions were not influenced by codes of regulation to begin with. Although written by Trumbo, the following passage from his preface to MGM's *Thirty Seconds over Tokyo* script could have been easily derived from one of copious OWI memos to studios, complicating the question of authorship: "Those scenes portraying the devotion and courage of the Chinese people as they smuggle scores of American airmen to safety will, we hope, constitute a genuine contribution to relations between the American people and their courageous Chinese allies."[105]

In their analysis of the representation of the enemy in wartime Hollywood cinema, Koppes and Black argue that "the movies, despite OWI's efforts, for the most part reinforced an interpretation of Japan that gave the Pacific war its particular savagery."[106] As the authors correctly evaluate, the OWI "had failed to convince Hollywood that the Japanese could be shown as something more than a 'buck-toothed little Jap'" despite their belief that "the enemy should be portrayed in terms of fascism rather than racism."[107] The OWI documents cited in this essay demonstrate that the agency's priority was to curtail the negative representation of allies rather than push for the sympathetic representation of non-fascists in enemy nations. In their final correspondence with 20th Century-Fox regarding *The Purple Heart*, dated February 29, 1944, the OWI steadfastly restates its commitment to improving images of Chinese allies: "Our only suggestion would be that it would have been a stronger film from our point of view if it had been more clearly shown that the Chinese quisling is an exception to the many millions of Chinese who are fighting the Japanese."[108]

The OWI view that *The Purple Heart* could have done more to acknowledge Chinese allies was vindicated by the Chinese embassy's reaction to the released film in the following month. In a March 21, 1944, letter to William S. Cunningham, the acting chief of the Los Angeles Overseas Bureau's Motion Picture Division, Randolph Sailer from the China section of the OWI Far East Division reported that "some of the Chinese Embassy people feel very badly over the film . . . on the ground that while the betrayal of the fliers by a Chinese is shown, no mention is made of the many thousand Chinese reported killed by the Japanese because of the fliers, and that in other cases the fliers were helped to American bases even though large money rewards had been offered by the Japanese for their betrayal."[109] An estimated 250,000 Chinese lives were lost as a result of Japanese reprisals following the Doolittle Raid. Chiang Kai-shek cabled to Washington: "After they had been caught unaware by the falling of American bombs on Tokyo, Japanese troops attacked the coastal areas of China, where many of the fliers had landed. These Japanese troops slaughtered every man, woman and child in those areas."[110] The Chinese villagers who had rescued and aided the Doolittle raiders paid a high price for their goodwill. As Reverend Charles L. Meeus, a Belgian-born naturalized Chinese citizen reports, "Little did the Doolittle men realize . . . that those same little gifts, which they gave their rescuers in grateful acknowledgment of their hospitality—the parachutes, gloves, nickels, and dimes—would, a few weeks later, become the telltale evidence of their presence and lead to the torture and death of their friends."[111]

In his memoir, Captain Lawson deferentially describes Dr. Chen (the real-life model for Dr. Chung in MGM's adaptation), a Chinese physician who helped save his life after the raid: "He was the most loyal man I ever met. There wasn't anything he wouldn't or didn't do for us. . . . He waited on us night and day, never complaining. He never got or wanted a penny. Later on, in a letter to the War Department, after it asked us to supply a list of Chinese who had helped us, I tried hard to express my gratitude and respect for Dr. C. But when I wrote the letter there were no right words to put down."[112] Given the considerable debt that Lawson and other fliers owed to their Chinese benefactors (who risked their own lives to save those of strangers from another country) and the loss of a quarter million Chinese lives caused indirectly by the raid, it is hard not to sympathize with the disappointment that Chinese embassy staff members felt when *The Purple Heart* fell short of honoring the monumental sacrifice that was made for the Doolittle airmen, despite the OWI's concerted efforts to guide the studio in the right direction.

As evidenced by archival documents quoted in this chapter, the PCA and the OWI represented divergent ideological views and conflicting agendas. The former was headed by the religiously devout conservative Breen, whose mission was to preempt costly postproduction changes requested by external censorship boards by monitoring moral content of motion pictures during the production stage. The latter was staffed with liberal New Dealers whose objective was to persuade film producers to modify celluloid images of allies and enemies in accordance with Washington's war aims. As Schatz argues, "The PCA's extreme conservatism and obsessive concerns over moral and sexual issues was fundamentally at odds . . . with the OWI's ethos of 'mild social democracy and liberal internationalist foreign policy.'"[113] However, their interests surprisingly converged when it came to images of foreign nationals and racial minorities during wartime. Of course, this does not mean that the PCA's policy regarding its concerns about *all* racial minorities was progressive and protective at all times. As Ellen C. Scott points out, the PCA (like its predecessor the SRC) has also attempted to repress images of lynching, miscegenation, and social inequality, thus further marginalizing African Americans on the silver screen.[114] In principle, Hollywood's internal regulators were finically motivated to mitigate offensive stereotypes of race, ethnicity, and nationality to protect the studios' interests in international markets and support Washington's foreign relations. In other words, images of minorities *mattered* as long as they might pose diplomatic barriers to market access.

The OWI's motivation was not altruistic or ideologically pure either. The war information agency pushed for more respectable images of people of color because it would benefit U.S. war efforts to counterprogram Axis propaganda against American racism, to bolster the morale of minority soldiers and workers, and to pay lip (or more accurately, reel) service to non-European allies. For example, in its feedback on an early script of *The Red Dragon* (then titled *Charlie Chan in Mexico*) dated August 1945, the OWI cautioned the Poverty Row studio Monogram about two interrelated yet distinct concerns of race: civil rights (African Americans) and foreign relations (the Chinese). For the former, the government agency was upfront about its propaganda agenda: "We hope Birmingham [a black character eliminated in the final print]'s stereotyped Negro comedy characterization will not be taken by overseas audiences as an indication of American ridicule of a racial minority group."[115] For the latter, the OWI was concerned that "the characterization of Charlie Chan is a questionable depiction of a national of a friendly nation—a characterization which has been protested by the Chinese."[116]

While neither the PCA nor the OWI were entirely successful in eliminating racial and ethnic stereotypes from Hollywood productions, the two organizations joined forces in gently nudging producers in a progressive direction in pursuit of their own converging interests. In this respect, the censorship dilemma over *The Purple Heart* is particularly rich and complicated, as both agencies' recommendations could be vindicated from different perspectives. The PCA's prohibition of patricidal images is "correct" from a Confucian perspective of traditional Chinese morality, while the OWI's support for patriotic images of New China is "correct" from a political/diplomatic perspective of contemporaneous Sino-American relations. Albeit contradictory and oppositional on the surface, both interpretations advocated positive Chinese images from alternate viewpoints. *The Purple Heart* challenges a simplistic race-based reading of Orientalist stereotypes, as both the PCA and the OWI made strategic regulatory interventions, urging producers to seek technical advice from Chinese authorities and to eliminate or counterbalance negative images of the Chinese.

3

Beyond the Propaganda Model

The Pentagon as a Technical Advisor for Brainwashing Films of the Cold War Era

In *The Hollywood War Machine: U.S. Militarism and Popular Culture*, Carl Boggs and Tom Pollard persuasively critique the American media industry's collusion in advancing militaristic and imperialist agendas of the United States government through glorifying spectacles of violence and bloodshed across multiple platforms (including cinema, television, and video games). Distinguishing this phenomenon from official propaganda of past totalitarian regimes such as Nazi Germany, the authors label it "'propaganda' of a different sort, more integrally merged with the larger popular and political cultures" and responsible for the "very solidity of mass consensus behind U.S. militarism."[1] Boggs and Pollard's premise coincides with Edward S. Herman and Noam Chomsky's "propaganda model" thesis put forth in their coauthored book *Manufacturing Consent: The Political Economy of Mass Media*. According to Herman and Chomsky:

> In countries where the levers of power are in the hands of a state bureaucracy, the monopolistic control over the media . . . makes it clear that the media serve the ends of a dominant elite. It is much more difficult to see a propaganda

> system at work when the media are private and formal censorship is absent. This is especially true when the media actively compete, periodically attack and expose corporate and governmental malfeasance, and aggressively portray themselves as spokesmen for free speech and the general community interest. What is not evident . . . is the limited nature of such critiques, as well as the huge inequality in command of resources . . . . A propaganda model focuses on this inequality of wealth and power and its multilevel effects on mass-media interests and choices. It traces the routes by which money and power are able to filter out news fit to print, marginalize dissent, and allow the government and dominant private interests to get their messages across to the public.[2]

Applying Herman and Chomsky's news media–focused theory to Hollywood's war-themed films, Boggs and Pollard make the case that "in lending the studios military facilities, men, and equipment, as well as logistic support, Washington was able to exercise rather strict control over filmmaking, always vigilant regarding any deviations from established military codes and norms. It was a [symbiotic] relationship that worked splendidly for both sides."[3] In *Operation Hollywood*, David L. Robb elaborates this idea, saying, "This collaboration works because the Pentagon has what Hollywood wants—access to billions of dollars-worth of sophisticated military hardware to put into movies; and Hollywood has what the Pentagon wants—access to the eyeballs of millions of viewers and potential recruits."[4]

This chapter sets out to challenge the idea that the Pentagon has exerted ideological control over Hollywood's productions in exchange for material and logistic support by allowing filmmakers to access military bases, equipment, personnel, and stock footage. After the creation of the Motion Picture Section of the Pictorial Branch within its Office of Public Information (OPI) in 1949, the Department of Defense (DoD) served as a liaison between Hollywood producers seeking military assistance and the individual services (army, navy, air force, marine corps, coast guard, and national guard). As Lawrence H. Suid points out, "In this capacity, the office could recommend that a service provide assistance, could help with negotiations between a filmmaker and a service, or could refuse to approve cooperation on a film that did not serve the best interests of the armed forces."[5] Not unlike the Office of War Information (OWI) during the Second World War, the DoD had a moderate degree of negotiation muscle as individual filmmakers were obliged to submit their scripts and preview prints in exchange for technical advice and material assistance. However, like the OWI, the DoD had no means of penalizing producers for neglecting its suggestions, although it had the option of declining an acknowledgment in the credits and disassociating itself from completed films. Because of the fractured nature of military branches, the DoD did not even have the authority to supervise the collaboration process between filmmakers and the armed services after approving projects. As Suid states, "Consequently, throughout the 1950s each service had virtually a blank check to provide assistance . . . . Filmmakers received as much help on any movie as a service's public affairs office in Washington and its commanders in the field decided served its best interest."[6]

Defense contractor–turned–studio mogul Howard Hughes' RKO production *One Minute to Zero* (1952), which was initiated at the request of the air force to showcase the kind of close air support that its fighter planes were providing to ground troops in Korea, is an illustrative example of the limited influence that the military had on Hollywood producers. Hughes was granted access to Camp Carson and Peterson Field near Colorado Springs for the shooting of ground and aerial sequences for three months. Formations of Mustang fighter planes and F-80 jets were culled from Buckley Field in Denver and Peterson Field to appear in the film. Lieutenant Colonel Stanley Paul Latiolais, the director of combat operations for the Fifth Air Force in Korea, and Captain Edward R. Harrison of the army served as the film's technical advisors. In addition, 100,000 feet of actual combat footage filmed by army and air force cameramen were put at RKO's disposal to reinforce on-the-spot recordings shot by a second unit in Japan and Korea. According to the studio publicity handbook, "Thousands of foot soldiers, hundreds of tanks and other pieces of mobile equipment and scores of planes, including jets, bombers and helicopters, were involved in the film."[7] After receiving full cooperation of unprecedented scope and scale from the army and the air force, Hughes refused to eliminate an objectionable scene that was absent from the approved script but added in the completed print. In this climactic scene, the all-American war hero played by Robert Mitchum orders an artillery attack on a group of Korean refugees infiltrated by communist guerrillas.

In July 1952, the Pentagon instructed all public affairs offices of the armed services not to endorse *One Minute to Zero*, and the film was released without the acknowledgment of all-out support it garnered from the Pentagon, the army, and the air force.[8] The Department of Army (DA) publicly issued a statement explaining that "the picture has a sequence which has been objected to by the Army and the Defense Departments and which the studio has declined to correct. Accordingly this picture does not have final approval from Defense or Army."[9] It was the first major studio film made with DoD and DA cooperation and then denied approval after production.

From a different regulatory perspective, Joseph I. Breen of the Production Code Administration (PCA) made impassioned pleas to the studio, demanding the elimination of derogatory images of allies in a fashion reminiscent of the OWI's practices during the previous war as detailed in chapter 2. In his letter to RKO dated July 11, 1951, Hollywood's internal regulator reiterates this point multiple times: "At the outset, we wish to recommend that, in view of the critical international situation, some sort of technical advice be obtained with regards the portrayal of the South Koreans in this story." Breen continues to advise the studio that "we feel quite sure that the reference to the backwardness of the Koreans . . . should be eliminated. Having in mind a fair representation of these people, we feel that this could not be approved in the finish picture." He further objects that "it is our opinion that [an American character's] derogatory reference to the Korean Army is unacceptable and should be eliminated."[10]

Archival evidence suggests that it is incorrect to assume that the Pentagon's approval for scripts was a precondition for any type of military support for film productions. After reviewing the final script of 20th Century-Fox's submarine drama *Hell and High Water* (1954), shot in CinemaScope and produced by World War II veteran-turned-maverick director Samuel Fuller, the DoD's OPI concluded that the project did not qualify "for official cooperation" because it appeared to have "no significance or public informational value to the Department of Defense or to the U.S. Navy."[11] Regardless, the office green-lighted the studio's use of a nonoperational, training submarine at Terminal Island, San Pedro, as a prop for background and interior filming. Lieutenant Colonel Clair E. Towne of the Motion Picture Section of the Pictorial Branch extended a further courtesy to 20th Century-Fox with no strings attached: "Some of the minor items of equipment if available locally, and surplus to the needs of the command concerned, and if unobtainable from any commercial source, and absolutely essential to the production, might also be arranged for."[12] This goodwill gesture belies the stereotypical caricature of Pentagon liaison officers as arbitrary propagandists who "use threats or rewards to shape films to advance a particular sanitized view" and the military as a creator of "tailored historical accounts" achieved through "withholding important resources."[13]

It should be noted, however, that the DoD had more than an altruistic reason to be gracious toward Hollywood, which made significant contributions to the war efforts (both World War II and the Korean War) by collaborating with the Army Signal Corps training film program and "gifting" 16 mm prints of motion pictures and short subjects for showings in overseas military camps, posts, and stations. Under the "film gift service," between 1941 and 1952, major studios provided complimentary prints of 43,306 features and 33,236 short subjects, valued at $38.5 million. They were shipped to entertain American troops in every corner of the world, from lonely posts in the South Pacific and Africa to war zones in Europe and Asia. Hollywood's gifts to armed forces represented 80 percent of the overseas recreation program and were widely touted by generals and admirals as "the number one morale factor in the service."[14] Given the military's dependence on the film industry's generosity in keeping their soldiers entertained and encouraged, it is no surprise that the Pentagon was willing to reciprocate with occasional rentals of their surplus equipment to producers even when their films did not qualify for official cooperation.

In addition to registering the institutional difficulty for any federal agency to enforce its desired messages on Hollywood filmmakers with no means of controlling the private industry's distribution and exhibition sectors, it is worth examining the precise nature of technical advice that the DoD provided in response to submitted scripts in order to test whether or not the propaganda model was at work. With this goal in mind, this chapter will investigate the DoD input in the making of Cold War brainwashing films, drawing upon the archival documents in the DoD Film Collection housed at the Georgetown University Special Collections Research Center. Two main case studies—MGM's *Prisoner of War* (1954) and Columbia's *The Bamboo Prison* (1954)—should be contextualized as productions of the Joseph McCarthy era, when Washington's influence on Hollywood was at its most forceful and direct. Out of a dozen files on Cold War–themed productions set in 1950s Korea and/or Japan that I reviewed at Georgetown University, I selected these two Korean War films as central case studies because their files are inclusive of materials that shed light on general policies and procedures of the Pentagon's collaboration with studios.[15] *Prisoner of War* in particular is a productive text to investigate as there is a voluminous paper trail on its production at the Academy of Motion Picture Arts and Sciences' Margaret Herrick Library. In the following pages, I will put Hollywood's archive in dialogue with the DoD papers in order to reconstruct a full account of the film's regulation history.

In 1947, the House Un-American Activities Committee (HUAC) opened a series of hearings on the alleged communist infiltration in the film industry and cited for contempt of Congress ten "unfriendly witnesses" (a group of left-wing screenwriters and directors today famously known as the "Hollywood Ten") who refused to testify. The members of the Association of Motion Picture Producers issued the Waldorf Statement in November of that year, committing to dismiss the Hollywood Ten and not to reemploy them, as well as to purge any subversive or disloyal elements from the industry. This signaled the beginning of Hollywood's dark period of blacklisting, which continued until the early 1960s. HUAC returned for a second round of hearings in 1951, and by the end of that year, more than 300 writers, actors, directors, and other creative personnel with alleged communist ties had been blacklisted. The culture of fear, paranoia, and mistrust continued to plague Hollywood as private Red hunters and the extrajudicial "clearance" system (which coerced the accused to publicly repent "political sins" of the past and name names of "fellow travelers" as proof of rehabilitation) replaced official congressional investigations.[16] As film historian David A. Cook states, "Everyone was scared of the government and of everyone else, and the industry tacitly imposed a form of self-censorship more repressive and sterile than anything HUAC could have devised . . . . Safety, caution, and respectability were the watchwords of the studio chiefs, and controversial or even serious subject matter was avoided at all costs."[17] Studios were all too eager to play safe with escapist genres such as the Western, the musical, biblical epics, and science fiction in order to evade governmental scrutiny on subversive motion picture content. Given this repressive climate, the themes of communist brainwashing of American POWs and their collaboration with the enemy during the Korean War in this chapter's case studies were sensitive, risky subjects, to say the least.

The archival documents quoted throughout the chapter will demonstrate that Pentagon-sponsored technical advising on Hollywood's anti-communist films cannot simply be reduced to a propaganda model aimed at force-feeding the governmental ideology and interests to the public, even though the above-mentioned historical context might lead one to assume so. Undoubtedly, anti-communism is a political slant found in some of the advisory comments provided by military script reviewers, who had firsthand negative encounters with communist enemies in Korea. However, the primary impulse of military technical advising was to strive for realism and authenticity often lacking in Hollywood's fanciful scripts penned by screenwriters with no experience of combat or incarceration, not to mention any close contact with Cold War enemies. Along with experts (e.g., historians, linguists, scientists, doctors, lawyers, and diplomats), the military was one of the many technical advisors that Hollywood employed to enhance the verisimilitude of its productions in specialized areas. The fact that the Pentagon and the armed services are public institutions and that they provide their assistance free of charge in return for potential publicity and recruitment distinguish them from fee-based, profit-seeking technical advisors.[18] However, it is ultimately producers who decide whether to accept or reject suggestions of any technical advisors. Therefore, the Pentagon's involvement in Hollywood filmmaking, through script consultation and print preview, during the Cold War era should not be misconstrued as an example of the propaganda model as defined by Herman and Chomsky or a form of government censorship. The relationship between Hollywood and the military was reciprocal, as the Pentagon and the armed services were dependent on the willing cooperation of individual filmmakers, who were free to adopt their advice selectively.

Russian Camp Masters and Traitors-as-Heroes: The Question of Authenticity in MGM's *Prisoner of War*

Often dubbed the "forgotten war" in the popular vernacular of keywords and catchphrases, the Korean War was not simply forgotten but intentionally repressed in American popular culture because it was "the counterpoint to the patriotic memories of World War II."[19] One of the most ignominious and repressed memories of the Korean War is the defection of twenty-one American GIs in the 1953 Operation Big Switch (POW exchange) and alleged wholesale

American POW collaboration.[20] According to government statistics, out of 7,140 American POWs, 2,701 died in captivity.[21] Having survived torture, death marches, starvation, lack of medical care, and indoctrination by their North Korean and Chinese captors, 4,000-odd surviving POWs were repatriated to the cold, unreceptive bosom of the government and citizenry. Starting with their sea voyage back home, the returnees were subjected to strenuous, repeated debriefing interrogations during which they were pressured to inform on fellow prisoners. Although only 14 out of 565 men charged with misconduct faced actual court-martial (10 of them were convicted), many repatriates continued to experience harassment from FBI agents and military interrogators for years after they resumed civilian life.[22]

The news media sensationalized Korean War POW stories with such headlines as "Cowardice in Korea" (*Time*, November 2, 1953), "Brain-Washed Korean POWs" (*Scholastic*, May 12, 1954), "Brainwashing: Time for a Policy" (*Atlantic*, April 1955), and "Why POWs Collaborate" (*Science*, May 11, 1957).[23] In his much-quoted book *In Every War but One*, journalist Eugene Kinkead argues that U.S. servicemen had never been so dishonorable in any war before Korea, where "one out of every three American prisoners was guilty of some sort of collaboration with the enemy . . . [and] one man in every seven . . . was guilty of serious collaboration."[24] Although more objective studies subsequently revealed that the behavior of the Korean War POWs was no worse than that of American captives during previous wars, this unfortunate group was an all-too-easy scapegoat of the Red Scare and McCarthyism in 1950s America. The popular media (film and television) contributed to perpetuating the distorted images of treacherous Korean War captives—weak, pampered victims of "momism" and brainwashing.[25] First coined by intelligence agent-turned-journalist Edward Hunter in 1950, the term "brainwashing" originally referred to "reeducational" practices in Red China and was subsequently applied to describe the status of Korean War POWs exposed to intense indoctrination programs by communist captors. Captain Gene N. Lam, a battalion surgeon who was captured in December 1950 and interned in Camp Five, defined the experience in this way: "About mid-May of 1951 . . . our 'education' began. From dawn until dark we were forced to undergo Communist indoctrination by English-speaking comrades. Marx, Engels, Lenin, and Stalin were our diet for the next ten months. We were the first American POWs who were forced to undergo so-called 'brainwashing.'"[26]

As Charles S. Young points out, unlike scores of World War II and Vietnam War films that pay tribute to the brave escape efforts and heroic adventures of American POWs, a smattering of Korean War POW films, including *Prisoner of War*, *The Bamboo Prison*, *The Rack* (1956), *Time Limit* (1957), *The Manchurian Candidate* (1962), and *Sergeant Ryker* (1968), confront the grim subjects of collaboration, informing, and betrayal, which are "fixtures of real incarceration [but almost] invisible in prison camp adventures."[27] However, another historian, Susan L. Carruthers, observes that "all the films were concerned to demonstrate America's POWs to best advantage, even when the critical mood was in fact turning against the 'turncoats' and degenerate collaborators."[28] Labeling *Prisoner of War* and *The Bamboo Prison*—the first two Korean War POW films in which collaboration with the enemy is depicted as a mere ruse for undercover intelligence officers—as the "most blatant cinematic attempts at redemption," Carruthers argues that these films reflect the political zeitgeist of the time by destabilizing "any sense that heroes and villains could be straightforwardly distinguished."[29]

In the first scene of *Prisoner of War*, Captain Webb Sloane (Ronald Reagan) reports to his commanding officer, Major O. D. Halle (Henry Morgan), and is given a new assignment: to voluntarily become a prisoner of war in order to document evidence against North Korea for violating the Geneva Convention in the treatment of American POWs. Sloane parachutes into enemy territory and infiltrates a column of exhausted, starving prisoners marching a great distance in the cold. When the group finally arrives in the camp, their number has dwindled from 718 to 211 during the death march, which lasted for days. The camp is run by two North Korean officers, Colonel Kim Doo Yi (Leonard Strong) and Captain Lang Hyun Choi (Rollin Yoriyama), who are joined by their Russian advisors from Moscow, Colonel Nikita I. Biroshilov (Oscar Homolka) and Lieutenant Georgi Robovnik (Stephen Bekassy). The Russians teach North Koreans how to break the spirit of American POWs with Pavlovian techniques of reward and punishment. As the master brainwasher, Biroshilov coerces pilots to read false confessions of germ warfare in front of the camera and breaks down uncooperative prisoners with gruesome torture and mock executions. One by one they beg to sign an affidavit refuting maltreatment of POWs at the hands of communist captors. He also recruits a handful of "pros" (a shortened term for "progressives," or collaborators), including Sloane and Jesse Threadman (Dewey Martin), and uses them to monitor fellow prisoners. Corporal Joseph Stanton (Steve Forrest) is an arch-"reactionary" who remains resistant in the face of stressed positions, exposure to elements, starvation, dehydration, and repeated threats to life. He ends up kidnapping and murdering Biroshilov after the Russian orders Stanton's pet dog to be slain as punishment for his recalcitrance.

Kim vows to avenge the death of the Russian advisor but receives an order to improve the standard of living in the camp and compile a list of twenty prisoners to be repatriated in a POW exchange. The North Korean commander stipulates that Threadman and another pro, a few wounded, and a few reactionaries (such as Stanton) be added to balance the list. He also instructs that Sloane and the remaining pros be sent to Russia to further their education. Later, Sloane discovers that Threadman has switched their spots and is headed for Russia in his place. In a brief private moment of farewell, Threadman reveals himself to be a fellow agent and informs Sloane that he is going to Russia on a new mission. In front of the truck for repatriating prisoners, Stanton derogatorily calls Sloane a "commie buzzard" only to learn his lesson when the latter hands him his missing dog tag—incriminating evidence for Biroshilov's murder. When another prisoner behind them disparages Sloane, Stanton intervenes and barks at him, "Don't talk unless you know what you are talking about." Then, Stanton goes on to badmouth Threadman, who is mounting another truck (bound for Russia) across the yard. Sloane gives him another sobering lesson: "Don't talk unless you know what you are talking about. Two minutes ago, you were saying the same thing about me." In disbelief, Stanton murmurs, "Jesse, God help him," before accepting Sloane's helping hand and getting on the truck headed for freedom.

The DoD Film Collection file on *Prisoners of War* shows that MGM started preparing a script "dealing with the treatment of the American prisoners of war by the Communists" as early as August 1953, one month after the Korean War ended in a stalemate.[30] MGM representatives contacted both the DA's Los Angeles Information Office and the DoD's OPI, seeking assistance for research and production. In his November 3, 1953, memo to the DA's

FIG. 3.1 Toward the end of Andrew Marton's *Prisoner of War* (Metro-Goldwyn-Mayer, 1954), Jesse Threadman (right: Dewey Martin) reveals himself to be a fellow agent and informs Webb Sloane (left: Ronald Reagan) that he is going to Russia on a new mission.

chief of information in the Public Information Division, Clair Towne of the DoD's Motion Picture Section acknowledged that until very recently Universal Pictures had a priority on a Korean War POW story but the studio abandoned the production. MGM's project of the same subject (which was proposed later than Universal's) was now to be given the DoD's consideration for military cooperation. Requesting the DA's comments, recommendations, and objections on MGM's submitted screenplay, Towne clarified that the DoD would handle "coordination with other agencies of the government as may be made necessary because of the significance of the story."[31] To the Pentagon's dismay, the DA's Los Angeles office of the chief of information sent an unauthorized, premature report to the studio three weeks later, informing MGM that both the "Department of Psychological Warfare and the Intelligence Department are deep into the matter of MGM making the POW story. Both departments are working hard on details concerning present peace negotiations and repatriation of POWs from either side. The departments want to be sure whatever is done picture-wise, there will be nothing that might tend to upset the apple cart as far as U.S. policies and negotiations are concerned. The departments feel that [the] MGM story must undergo some major changes before approval can be given."[32]

Startled by the army's suggestion of a red flag, MGM's executive committee called an emergency meeting to discuss possible actions to be taken should the DoD turn down their request for cooperation. In their internal memorandum on the subject, the DoD expressed resentment over the DA's action:

> Our own preliminary estimate of the situation . . . was that there was a lot of good in the project and as usual there were some things which would give us trouble. However, it is not our policy to allow rumblings of possible trouble to get to studio until we have had an opportunity to make a careful and objective evaluation of all angles and to rationalize all aspects so that our comments and recommendations will make sense to the studio and our objections will be recognized and action taken accordingly. . . . To indicate that Psy War and G-2 are interested in this script is to discuss aspects of our internal operations which are not the province of the studio to know. Such reports go far beyond the mission of the Los Angeles Information Office and serve only to confuse established channels of communications and to break down our excellent relations with the studios.[33]

These reports underscore the DoD's challenges in coordinating communications between studios and the armed services, whose own publicity arms could send mixed messages directly to producers. They also define the DoD's important yet limited role as a collector/consolidator/editor of comments and recommendations from various military branches (rather than a sinister backstage censor leveraging military resources as bargaining chips to pull studio strings).

Despite the initial hiccup in the process of coordination with the Army, on November 20, 1953, Towne forwarded to MGM a streamlined list of revisions and adjustments that the army and the DoD desired "for the purpose of improving [the film's] overall accuracy and authenticity" before approving full cooperation. There are six main items on this list, which can be summarized thusly:

1. The opening surrender scene should be rewritten to show that "our men were out of ammunition, over-burdened with casualties, tried to escape, but the overwhelming force of the Communist were too much for them."
2. It is suggested that the film make it ambiguous which agency sent Webb Sloane to North Korea as "implications that indicate that the U.S. Army [G-2] deliberately sent agents into North Korea hit a very sensitive area."
3. The portrayal of Sloane's collaboration should be handled more carefully as "it would not serve the interest of our country to indicate that writing [procommunist] letters and making [propaganda] broadcasts from the prison camps was instigated by agents from our side."
4. The Russian characters—Col. Biroshilov and Lt. Robovnik—should be Chinese as "there is no evidence that Russians ever acted in the capacity in which they are illustrated in this story."
5. The plotline of progressives as intelligence operatives might give the false impression that "all men who were progressives or who were considered in that category may likewise be heroes" and "all returned prisoners in this category might use the story to further their own end." It is suggested that Jesse, once established as an agent, not remain with the progressives since the scene "would not serve the best interests of our personnel still in Communists' hands."
6. It is suggested that references to Japanese atrocities against American POWs during World War II be eliminated in consideration of Japan's current status as a U.S. ally against communism. Instead, Sloane could be made a former liaison officer with the Russians (a former ally) who witnessed their mistreatment of POWs and brainwashing technique.[34]

The DoD's memo singled out that the opening surrender scene, the identity of Russian advisors, and references to the Japanese maltreatment of American POWs were "of greater importance" than the other problems. In the final print, the surrender scene is eliminated altogether. As suggested by the DA and the DoD, Sloane is introduced as a former liaison officer who observed the

Russian treatment of German POWs during World War II, and G-2's name is not directly mentioned in relation to the agency behind Sloane's secret missions. However, Biroshilov and Robovnik remain Russian characters, and Threadman stays with the pros at the end. Sloane still makes propagandistic speeches in radio broadcasts but manages to embed code words intended for Major Halle and intelligence officers back home. In other words, MGM selectively accommodated suggestions made by the army and the DoD, a common studio practice of handling advisory comments from various regulatory entities including the PCA and the OWI, as examined in the previous chapter. Although a military technical advisor (Captain Robert H. Wise, who was interned in a North Korean camp for nearly three years) provided insights during the production, MGM's finished film was denied official endorsement from the DoD and the DA.

The DoD's internal memorandum dated February 11, 1954, indicates that G-2 was strongly against the film and the Psychological Warfare Division wanted no DoD connection to it.[35] Seven days later, the DA sent out a memo to all its headquarters, informing them that "cooperation or participation in exhibition of [MGM's *Prisoner of War*] at premieres and subsequent showings is not authorized. Limited cooperation was provided MGM during the production of this picture by DoD but certain major changes suggested by [DoD] and DA were not made by the studio; consequently, it is felt that cooperation in the exhibition of *Prisoner of War* is not justified."[36] According to a report by *Variety* on May 24, 1953, the DoD's withdrawal of endorsement (and denial of promotional courtesy for Pentagon-assisted films, such as the symbolic presence of bands and military police honor guards at premieres) took the studio by surprise, particularly since it "has the full approval of the Prisoner of War Association, a group of some 11,000 members with chapters in 43 cities."[37] In his interview with the *New York Times*, screenwriter Allen Rivkin argued, "The Defense Department withdrew approval at the last minute because the Army's Adjutant General's Office requested it in order to strengthen its stand in the court-martial of former American POWs who falsely confessed germ warfare in Korea."[38] In another interview, the film's director, Andrew Marton, claimed, "The Army was probably secretly pleased with the film, but their approval of it would place them in an untenable position, because they are investing soldiers who were treated understandably in the picture."[39] Neither of these claims are supported by archival documents in the DoD Film Collection, although these factors may have been discussed at the Pentagon without leaving a paper trail. Publicly, the DoD simply responded that the film "was too fictional" and "was not an accurate portrayal of events."[40]

In the Andrew Marton Papers housed at the Academy of Motion Picture Arts and Sciences' Margaret Herrick Library is an MGM interoffice memo, dated November 24, 1953, with an attachment of all the comments from the various agencies of the military establishment submitted to the DA in regard to *Prisoner of War*'s script (this document is different from the correspondences/memoranda found in the DoD Film Collection and is presumed to have been handed over to the studio by the DA's Los Angeles Information Office). The DA memo attests to the overall concern of military elites regarding the film's seemingly confusing message about communism. One reviewer notes, "In addition to the general lack of realism, many subtle lines reflecting the Communistic point of view were written into the script. The resultant impression, I feel certain to any viewer to this film . . . especially in a foreign audience, would be one of discounting the distorted POW life picture, as incredulous, through so many falsifications and thus being impressed by only a few of the subtleties which are strictly Communistic." Another reviewer expresses a similar view, stating, "It is our feeling that in spite of our conviction of MGM's most loyal and patriotic motives in wishing to make this picture, this screenplay is going to require certain major revisions in order not to be considered by many people as a subtle vehicle for conveying the Communist 'party line.' Specifically, we feel that Webb's purveying of the Communist line . . . for the purpose of re-ingratiating himself with [captors] is psychologically wrong, bad and must be changed."[41]

Some comments are minutely technical and concerned with fact-checking. For example, one reads, "North Koreans always are addressed by rank, the Chinese as Comrade," while another notes that, "because of the hunger drive, which began almost immediately, the men's conversation, even on the march north, was devoted almost exclusively to good foods." Other comments include the following:

> "The soup here should not be soybean and rice. Millet and cracked corn were exclusively the foods served during the week and rice was issued for one meal on Sunday";
>
> "Don't use rank in Commie speech";
>
> "This story has a setting compatible with no prisoner camp that ever existed in North Korea . . . . These missionaries and diplomats were never at Pyoktang, the supposed setting of this story";
>
> "The language and grammar used by the Chinese and other Communistic personnel is much too perfect. Their English is very broken and very colorful";
>
> "Make reference to 'lotebooks' as Chinese called 'notebooks.'"[42]

Other comments criticize the implausibility of certain plot points:

> "The sequence on the capture of Biroshilov is ridiculous. Were there no Red guards . . . ? This is 'B' picture stuff, not MGM . . . . After Biroshilov is killed

> there would have been a reign of terror in the whole camp. Many innocent men would have paid for this. The segregation of Whites and Negroes seems an absurd penalty, and pointless, unless it is meant to show that Communists preach race equality but don't practice it. This needs much more thought and work."[43]

MGM undoubtedly benefited from military specialists' technical expertise and made improvements on their script based on some of their reasonable advice. By the studio's own account, they accommodated 80 percent of the suggestions made by the DA and the DoD.[44] For example, the unwarranted announcement of segregation between white and black soldiers as a reaction to Biroshilov's murder is deleted from a revised script resubmitted to the DoD on November 23, 1953. In the original script, dated October 30, 1955, Captain Lang announces, "Effective immediately, all members of the Negro race will be separated from sharing barracks with members of the White race." American POWs boo and protest, "You're kidding.... What're you trying to do, start a riot?" Joe Stanton raises a hand and asks permission to ask a question, which Lang grants. The "reactionary" prisoner reasons that "we're all prisoners together." "We fought together," he says, "regardless of race, color, creed or religion. What is to be gained for Socialism by this move?" The communist comrade retorts, "They do not let you live together in America. Why should we here?"[45] While this passage of dialogue presents a fascinating ideological debate over race between Americans and their communist captors, its placement right after Stanton's murder of Biroshilov and the North Korean commander's order of criminal investigation is baffling and illogical. Moreover, it justifies a shared concern of some army script reviewers who saw the MGM production as "a subtle vehicle for conveying the Communist 'party line'" by calling attention to racial segregation and discrimination in the United States. In the finished film, this gratuitous segregation announcement is replaced by Lang's delivery of an envelope with an order from Pyongyang that prepares the camp for an impending exchange of sick and wounded prisoners. Colonel Kim opens the envelope and reads his instructions: "Increase rations of food, clothing, medical supplies. Relax all pressures. Make camp as pleasant as possible."

The *Prisoner of War* case study illustrates different interpretations of authenticity and realism among Hollywood producers and DoD and DA officials. Although the latter found a plethora of inaccuracy, fabrications, and distortions in the MGM script, it was written after Allen Rivkin interviewed the first group of fifty-eight repatriated prisoners who arrived in San Francisco in August 1953. In the *Prisoner of War* file of the Turner/MGM Script Collection at the Margaret Herrick Library is Rivkin's sixty-seven page compilation of these interviews under the title of "The P.O.W. Story," dated August 23, 1953. These firsthand accounts of returned POWs significantly influenced story development. For example, Rivkin took the story of Harold Dunn of Baldwinsville, New York, who was the only son of a widowed mother and had been in the army for six years. He was injured and captured by the enemy in November 1950 and spent thirty-three months in Camp Five. There, he became a progressive and voluntarily went to indoctrination lectures even after communist captors stopped requiring them of POWs. He gave the following reasons for being attracted to communist ideology: "Nobody ever told me why I was in Korea. I got a mother to take care of. The Army told me, when I enlisted in 1947, that I could be stationed near home where I could see her and take care of her. That was so, until they sent me over there. What was I doing so far away from her, I kept asking myself. . . . When the Chinese told us we were war-mongers, it made sense."[46] In *Prisoner of War*, Threadman repeats Dunn's story of his mother almost verbatim when he first approaches Colonel Biroshilov and tries to convince him that he is willing to collaborate.

In a temporary complete script dated November 17, 1953, Sloane gives a propaganda speech on film, which is a word-for-word plagiarism of a speech that a North Korean prison official gave to progressive POWs in Camp Five the day before they were to be repatriated (which is quoted in Rivkin's "The P.O.W. Story"): "Do what appears best for the cause of peace. Some of you might want to join the Communist Party. If that's too much, you can join progressive organizations. If that's too much, you can speak for peace. If that's too much, then for God's sake don't, at least, go against peace."[47] This pacifist speech was dropped in the finished film and replaced by a condemnation of U.S. germ warfare: "Let's stop this useless Korean war which is killing so many innocent civilians with this horrible germ warfare my country is using." This fabricated accusation is denounced by diegetic audiences (fellow prisoners) who are watching Sloane's filmed speech in the camp's makeshift theater. The angry American POWs destroy the projector and screen and begin to riot (an inciting event that leads to the brutal torture and mock executions of "reactionaries"). This change was presumably made in response to the DA's feedback cited in the aforementioned MGM interoffice memo, in which a couple of military reviewers expressed concern about the film's subtle conveyance of "the Communistic point of view" or "Communist 'party line.'"[48]

Prisoner of War is a contradictory text whose gritty realism in torture scenes is undermined by the implausible narrative premise of turncoats-as-spies and gross caricatures of North Korean and Russian communists. Contemporaneous audiences and reviewers were not blind to this contradiction. In the Andrew Marton Papers at the Margaret Herrick Library can be found MGM's audience research report on the survey results of 310 test viewers of *Prisoner of War*. Some audience members acknowledged the film's brutal realism in such comments as "Torture scenes so realistic, they're hard to take"; "The horror scenes were too realistic"; "It was too brutally true and will tear the heart out of any

FIG. 3.2 In an attempt to appease Pentagon script reviewers, MGM modified Sloane's filmed propaganda speech from a pacifist plead of the "Communist point of view" to a condemnation of U.S. biological warfare, a false accusation that incites a prisoner riot.

others like myself who have dear ones missing still"; and "It's enough to kill any mother who has a son in Korea." Other viewers pointed out the film's exaggerations, inauthenticity, and message-heavy indelicacies, as evidenced by such comments as "I am becoming allergic to propaganda and this was a little heavy"; "Picture became a comedy through depiction of Russian and Korean stereotype at such an exaggerated degree"; "Cut phony shots of camp which is shown several times too many!"; and "Should be barred! Fairy tale." An audience member who identified himself as a seventeen-year-old was particularly harsh in his criticism of the film's overall insensitivity and fakeness, saying, "The picture disgusted me with . . . such illiterate atrocities as you Beverly Hills war correspondents could think up. You'd think the War Department paid you to create such trash. I've seen people in as much pain as the tortures you have shown but never have they looked so fake as your powder puff actors."[49]

Contrary to this young viewer's assumption, the DoD (formerly the War Department) not only offered no funding for the picture but also dissociated itself from it when it was released. In his brief review of the film for the *Saturday Review*, Arthur Knight reports, "There was a newspaper note recently that *Prisoner of War* . . . had incurred the wrath of our Department of Defense as a 'distortion' of the atrocities committed in Communist POW camps during the

Korean War. Distortion or not (the writer, Allen Rivkin, claims full documentation on the authenticity of the incidents shown), the picture is so loaded with tendentious dialogue, shock effects, and stock characterizations that it fails to convince even on its own terms."[50] For screenwriter Rivkin and MGM Studios, incorporating selected testimonies of Korean War POWs into dialogue and narrative merited their claim to the film's authenticity. For Pentagon and army technical advisors, the Hollywood script was problematic as not only did it get wrong the everyday details (e.g., food, speech patterns, salutations, captor-captive relations) of North Korean camps, but it also distorted the bigger picture of war in its portrayal of Russian officers.

A Covert Soviet Mission in Korea and Russian Images in Hollywood from the 1930s to the 1960s

The DoD's list of recommended revisions, dated November 20, 1953, emphasizes the importance of adhering to known facts of the Russian role in Korea:

> If Russians are to exist in the story they should be illustrated as we know they functioned in Korea. There could be a military advisor with the unit which captured the prisoners and on the Death March. The prisoners could pass the quite famous Russian attack unit located north of Pyongyang. Russian interrogator teams might draw prisoners from the compound. Here much color might be presented by portraying the very famous 350 lb. woman Russian interrogator, who used to use two chairs to sit on. If a Russian is to be associated with a study program and with camp administration, as such his presence would not be known in the camp. He might be portrayed in the background directing the whole prisoner of war policy in Peking [Beijing].[51]

This advice seems politically prudent and diplomatically sound, given the official secrecy surrounding Russian involvement in Korea. Although the Soviet Union provided weapons, supplies, advisors, air cover, and diplomatic strategies to its allies in North Korea and China, the leaders of the communist nation never officially admitted its military intervention.

Kathryn Weathersby's study based on new evidence from the Soviet Foreign Policy Archive (open to researchers in 1992, one year after the fall of the Soviet Union) suggests that the "North Korean invasion of South Korea in June 1950 was not the result of Soviet determination to expand the territory under its control," as it was interpreted by the Truman administration, which sent U.S. ground troops in an effort to contain the spread of communism in Asia.[52] From 1945 to early 1950, as pointed out by Weathersby, the Soviet aim in Korea was to maintain a "balance of power" by "prolonging the division of the country, retaining effective control of the northern half."[53] North Korean leader Kim

Il Sung had a different idea. He repeatedly pressured Moscow to support his military campaign to reunify his country, which had been arbitrarily divided along the thirty-eighth parallel by two superpowers at the end of World War II. In the spring of 1950, Joseph Stalin reluctantly approved Kim's plan and provided military equipment and supplies, only after being persuaded that the United States would not intervene. Fearful of a direct military conflict with the United States, the Soviet Union refused to send military forces to defend its client state North Korea after U.S. troops were deployed to invaded South Korea. It was not until after the Chinese entrance to the war (in October 1950) that the Soviet Union started to provide air cover for Chinese troops under the Sino-Soviet treaty of alliance.

By April 1951, the Soviet Union had sent 150 planes along with bombers and deployed two antiaircraft divisions. Approximately 72,000 rotating Soviet personnel served in Korea.[54] However, Soviet aircraft and equipment were disguised with Chinese or North Korean insignia. The Russian pilots wore Chinese uniforms, carried forged identification in case they were captured, and were even ordered to speak Korean or Chinese in their radio communication. This extraordinary secrecy could be maintained thanks in part to an American complicity in silence. As Lester H. Brune explains, "Stalin's secret measures were successful only because U.S. authorities knew but did not publicize Soviet involvement . . . the Truman administration feared that any disclosure of Soviet combat fighters in Korea would cause the American public to demand war against the Soviet Union, which could precipitate another world war. Later, President Eisenhower agreed with this policy, and the Soviet involvement never became a U.S. media event."[55] Exceptions of this media silence are a handful of Korean War films, such as *Prisoner of War*, *The Bamboo Prison*, and *The Manchurian Candidate*, in which Russians or their proxies are openly shown as torturers/brainwashers of American POWs. From the perspective of the DoD and the DA, MGM's finished film was unfit for full cooperation and official credits because it failed to correct this misrepresentation of Russians, which was both fallacious (no Russians were in POW camps, as military advisors had informed the studio) and undiplomatic (the Russian military operation in Korea was not to be publicized, according to both superpowers' policy).

Classical Hollywood's portrayal of Russians is a fascinating subject in its own right. In the 1930s, American motion pictures were barred from the Soviet market, allowing Hollywood producers to exploit Russian villains freely, without fear of economic repercussions, unlike the Mexican, Italian, and Chinese cases. As Ruth Vasey puts it, "In dollars and cents, Russian indignation was cheap [and the] Russification of the villain was becoming a more or less routine practice, in the interests of avoiding offense to other Europeans."[56] In 1930s comedies, Russians "not only behaved liked deranged lunatics but—even worse perhaps—had no sense of humor, wit, or style," as exemplified by a disheveled, eccentric Bolshevik vagabond who chastises a fashionable, wealthy French widow for squandering a fortune on an expensive handbag in Ernst Lubitsch's *Trouble in Paradise* (1932).[57] Although Franklin D. Roosevelt officially recognized the Soviet Union and reestablished diplomatic relations in November 1933, ending sixteen years of non-engagement, the American public's suspicion of communism (coupled with Hollywood's lack of market concern) undoubtedly contributed to unsympathetic images of Russians before World War II. Despite the Production Code's respect for "national feelings" of foreign governments and their citizens, the PCA was "consistently opposed to treatments it deemed favorable to USSR" since its inception in 1934.[58] At the same time, Hollywood remained silent about the horrors of Stalin's murderous dictatorship, except in a light comedy mode as in Lubitsch's *Ninotchka* (1939), in which Greta Garbo's titular character, a devoted communist bureaucrat from Moscow, reports to her Three Stooges–like bumbling comrades in Paris with deadpan seriousness, "The last mass trials were a great success—there are going to be fewer but better Russians."

Once the United States became the Soviet Union's ally against Nazi Germany in World War II, Hollywood's relationship with Russia underwent an about-face. Pressured by the OWI to increase the visibility of Russian allies and to counter the anti-communist propaganda of the Nazis, studios produced a cycle of pro-Russian films, including Warner Bros.' *Mission to Moscow* (1943), RKO's *The North Star* (1943), United Artists' *Three Russian Girls* (1943), and MGM's *Song of Russia* (1944). Joseph I. Breen, the PCA's anti-communist head, found himself in a precarious position when being forced to issue a seal of approval to Jack L. Warner, a pro-Roosevelt studio chief, for *Mission to Moscow*. This screen adaptation of Ambassador Joseph E. Davies's book was the most notorious American apology for Moscow show trials against Stalin's political foes. The internal censor reluctantly approved the picture but only after sending a warning to Warner, "You understand, of course, there is another 'school of thought' which seems to hold very definite views that are in sharp conflict with views enunciated in this script . . . and it is not unlikely that, when your picture is put into general release, considerable protest will be voiced against the sentiments as now set forth in your manuscript."[59] And of course, Breen was right. On May 6, 1943, John Dewey, a renowned philosopher, and Suzanne La Follette, a Guggenheim fellow, who were, respectively, chairman and secretary of the Dewey Commission (which conducted an independent inquiry into the Moscow trials of 1936–1937), jointly wrote to the editor of the *New York Times*. They denounced *Mission for Moscow* as "the first instance in our country of totalitarian propaganda for mass consumption—a propaganda which falsifies history through distortion, omission, or pure invention of facts, and whose effect can only be to confuse the public in its thought and in its loyalties."[60] Although its reviewers praised

Warner Bros.' film as "one of the finest contributions to the war information program" and "a most convincing means of helping Americans to understand their Russian allies," the OWI received a score of protest letters from outraged citizens urging the government agency to stop the studio from disseminating the "vicious falsification of recent history" for "political expediency . . . or as an useful adjunct of diplomatic policy."[61] Lowell Mellett, chief of the OWI's Bureau of Motion Picture, responded with the following standard legal statement: "I can only tell you that there is no authority under which this or any other Federal office can force its views on the producers of motion pictures [who] enjoy the same freedom of expression that is guaranteed to the press and other media of public opinion."[62] That freedom of expression, however, did not protect the film's screenwriter, Howard Koch, from being blacklisted in 1951, after the HUAC concluded its investigation into his participation in the making of "communist propaganda."

Burnt by the fiasco of wartime pro-Russian films and unable to predict future U.S. foreign policy decisions (given the mutability of allies and enemies in a short period of time), 1950s Hollywood adopted an evasive approach to Russian representations and was happy to escape to an earlier historical period, that of czarist Russia before the 1917 Revolution. As Harlow Robinson explains, "That Russia could be contained and admired from a distance [and] was more palatable to Hollywood producers than the real scary Russia of the Cold War era."[63] Examples include literary epics adapted from Russian classics by Leo Tolstoy and Fyodor Dostoyevsky, such as Paramount's Italian coproduction *War and Peace* (1956) and MGM's *The Brothers Karamazov* (1958). As a nuclear superpower perceived as a national security threat, however, Russia nevertheless had a pervasive allegorical presence in 1950s invasion paranoia narratives, as evidenced by the political thriller *Invasion U.S.A.* (1952) and the science fiction film *Invasion of the Body Snatchers* (1956). The burden of explicit national images was conveniently lifted in these examples by displacing Russians with communist invaders of an unnamed country (in the former film) and alien "pod people" (in the latter). Obscuring the national origins of foreign settings and characters as a means of avoiding diplomatic trouble was Hollywood's established self-regulatory practice from the 1930s on. As Ruth Vasey elaborates, "The effect was to remove these generic foreigners from the geopolitical sphere altogether and to give them citizenship of Hollywood's mythical kingdoms."[64]

As observed by Cyndy Hendershot, in the early 1960s "images of China as demonic Red force began to supplant postwar images of a brutal and monstrous Russia" as the Kennedy administration took a conciliatory approach to the Soviet regime of Nikita Khrushchev, Stalin's successor who pursued a policy of "de-Stalinization" and peaceful coexistence with the West.[65] It is worth comparing and contrasting the introduction of Russians in *Prisoner of War* and

The Manchurian Candidate to understand the subtle political transformations occurring from 1954 to 1962—changes that were registered and reflected in the Korean War POW film subgenre. Both films ascribe so-called brainwashing to a Russian origin: the Nobel Prize–winning scientist Ivan Pavlov's experiments on involuntary reflex conditioning.

Twelve minutes into *Prisoner of War*, Colonel Biroshilov greets his North Korean comrades in the camp's administration office and offers them help with "any details of the prisoners' daily life." When Colonel Kim complains, "These Americans, Comrade, those already in the camp, in spite of what we do, still have an enormous spirit," Biroshilov gives a little lecture to his North Korean counterpart as if he were a college professor testing his student: "As you know, there was in our Motherland one of the great scientists of the world, Ivan Petrovich Pavlov. Professor Pavlov, he gained renown for his experiments with dogs and rats. This technique was called . . . ?" As if conditioned himself to dutifully answer, Kim responds, "Conditioned reflex. When a rat went through the wrong door, he got an electronic shock. When he went through the right door, he got a bit of cheese." Biroshilov gleefully nods and explains, "Exactly. We, in our work in political security, are adapting Pavlov's techniques to the fullest. In fact, we are going beyond Pavlov because we are dealing with a higher organism—man." The North Korean colonel asks with skepticism, "Will this work with Americans, Comrade?" to which his Russian advisor gives an assurance, "It will work with anybody."

In an earlier script dated December 10, 1953, Biroshilov goes further to share more details of his Pavlovian planning: "We punish resistance with torture, starvation, threats of death. We reward those who cooperate with extra food and better treatment. As a matter of fact, the Pavlov method works better with men than with rats. Because men can talk, we can make them say anything we want. We can disturb man's sense of values. Reduce him to a status lower than animals."[66] Although Biroshilov clarifies his advisory capacity to North Korean officials in the introduction scene ("Of course, you are in charge. We are merely your guests"), the Russian colonel is depicted as the de facto boss who calls the shots. He personally handles the most grueling prisoner interrogations, like those of Stanton's, and offers leniency to tortured rioters—after two days and two nights of outdoor sun treatment (whereby they are forced to lie in shallow graves half-naked with no water or food)—in exchange for collaboration, while the nominal camp commander Kim is standing next to Biroshilov as a silent spectator. The heavy-handed caricatures of Russian and North Korean villains undermine the realism of brutal torture scenes and distract the audience from the serious human rights violations and war crimes depicted in the picture. As one *Variety* reviewer put it, "Interrogation lectures by Russian and North Korean officers, played by Oscar Homolka [Colonel Biroshilov] and Leonard Strong [Colonel Kim], are so broad as to be almost

FIG. 3.3 Russian advisor Colonel Nikita I. Biroshilov (right: Oscar Homolka) teaches North Korean camp commander Colonel Kim Doo Yi (left: Leonard Strong) how to break the spirit of American POWs with Pavlovian techniques of reward and punishment.

comic opera. A particular offender is Homolka, who gives an opera bouffe flavor to his Russian character."[67]

In *Brainwashing: The Story of the Men Who Defied It*, Edward Hunter makes an explicit connection between Chinese communist practices of brainwashing and Pavlovian experiments on reflex conditioning. According to Hunter, "The Chinese as a race are undergoing mind treatment inside a Great Pavlovian Wall.... They are undergoing what the disciples of Pavlov callously term 'mental hygiene'.... A saturation treatment is being given to communist society. The routine of each day and night is so arranged that the people simply cannot escape from the sight and sound of communist propaganda pressures."[68] In another book on the same subject, *Brain-Washing in Red China*, Hunter distinguishes "brain-washing" (indoctrination) from a more sinister and complicated concept: that of "brain-changing," which involves "emptying [one's] mind of old ideas and recollections" and "filling these gaps in memory" with "the ideas which the authorities want this person to 'remember'" through the aid of "hypnotism and drugs."[69] Although Hunter admitted that "China evidently was not so 'advanced' as yet" as to use the brain-changing process, the hypothetical concept was fictionalized as a Chinese practice against American POWs in the far-fetched, science fiction–like premise of Richard

Condon's novel *The Manchurian Candidate* and its screen adaptation distributed by United Artists.[70]

In the film's famously disorienting, 360-degree pan shot—a nightmare sequence occurring after ten drugged, hypnotized POWs are captured in Korea and flown to Manchuria for three-day intensive brainwashing sessions—shows the scientific experiment subjects in front of Chinese and Russian military and intelligence officers sitting in an amphitheater. The stage looks like a sterile, white laboratory curiously decorated with oversized portraits of Stalin and Mao and a large red star in the background. Unlike in *Prisoner of War*, it is a *Chinese* brainwashing expert, Dr. Yen Lo (played by ethnically ambiguous Khigh Dhiegh, who is of Anglo-Egyptian-Sudanese ancestry), who is in charge and behind the lectern, delivering a lecture to his Soviet counterparts in the diegetic audience. It is notable that Yen's professional credentials are indebted to the Russian scientific tradition of Pavlov: he later identifies his association as the Pavlov Institute and, in the amphitheater scene, cites Pavlovian behavioral therapist Andrew Salter's book *Conditioned Reflex Therapy* as a source for his technique. As the scientist's verbose speech becomes ever more laden with academic jargon, a Russian agent grows impatient and disparagingly comments, "My dear Yen. As you grow older, you grow more long-winded. Can't we get to the point?" The Chinese man outwits the agent and shows him the upper hand, reversing the power dynamic between Russians and their Asian allies as shown in *Prisoner of War*: "I apologize, my dear Dimitri. I keep forgetting that you are a young country and your attention span is limited."

To demonstrate his theory that the hypnotized subject can kill with no moral repulsion or feeling of remorse (or "those uniquely American symptoms—fear and guilt," as the character puts it in a later scene), Yen instructs Sergeant Raymond Shaw (Laurence Harvey), who is being transformed into a killing machine for the purposes of assassinating a U.S. presidential nominee (so that Shaw's stepfather, a McCarthy-like demagogue senator running as vice president, can galvanize voters and take over the White House as a Soviet mole), to strangle and shoot in cold blood two of his platoon buddies. Cyndy Hendershot notes that, in the film's nightmare flashbacks, in contrast to the more reserved (and possibly more humane) Russians, who remain complicit yet distant observers of brainwashing, Yen is portrayed as a whimsical villain who derives "great pleasure out of the process" of conditioning Shaw to commit senseless murders.[71] The diabolical Chinese doctor, who is later described as "that Chinese cat . . . smiling like Fu Manchu" by the platoon leader, Major Bennett Marco (Frank Sinatra), is the only communist in the packed amphitheater who grins, laughs, and jokes throughout the terrifying experiment. As Hendershot concludes, "*The Manchurian Candidate* suggests that the Chinese are more amoral and cruel than are the Soviets," signaling a major shift in the portrayal of communist enemies in the 1960s.[72]

FIG. 3.4 Dr. Yen Lo (left: Khigh Dhiegh), a diabolic Chinese brainwashing expert, instructs a drugged and hypnotized Sergeant Raymond Shaw (right: Laurence Harvey) to strangle his combat buddy in John Frankenheimer's *The Manchurian Candidate* (United Artists, 1962).

Prisoner of War is a rare film that openly depicts Russians as brainwashers and torturers in North Korean camps. Unlike their cinematic compatriots in the 1930s, Russian villains during the 1950s and 1960s became a thorny subject for Hollywood from a political standpoint, as the Eisenhower and Kennedy administrations sought to improve relations with the Soviet Union in the aftermath of the Korean War and the Cuban Missile Crisis, respectively, to avert another global conflict. This diplomatic imperative led studios to take more indirect, safer routes by exploiting the fear of ideological others in an allegorical fashion and conflating the Red Scare and the Yellow Peril by demonizing the Chinese in place of Russians. The DoD of the Cold War era promulgated its own version of the OWI's World War II policy of "properly directed hatred" when it came to images of the enemy. Not unlike the case of 20th Century-Fox's *The Purple Heart* (1944) and its representation of Japanese characters and customs (discussed in depth in the previous chapter), MGM's film apparently elicited rage toward the Russian enemy among audience members. In the above-quoted MGM audience research report, a number of the respondents singled out Stanton's torturing and killing of Colonel Biroshilov as their favorite scene. Taking into consideration the fact that Russian and U.S. forces never engaged one another directly in Korea except for covert air combat, this spectatorial animosity was misdirected and illegitimate from the perspective of Washington's decision makers. In the context of Classical Hollywood, however, and given the narrative formulas so central to the standardized motion picture output of the studios, the archvillain would need to be a worthy match for the hero in terms of prowess, charisma, and intelligence. According to the racial politics of 1950s Hollywood, this meant that the antagonist should be a white male, matching the race and gender of the protagonist. Authenticity aside, MGM refused to accept the DoD's suggestion and make Biroshilov (played by Austrian actor Oscar Homolka, who was often typecast as a communist spy or a KGB officer) a Chinese in order to not downgrade the respectability of their chief antagonist.

In a way, the Hollywood studio took its cue from returned POWs themselves in discounting the Chinese as an unworthy adversary. Among the testimonies compiled in Rivkin's "The P.O.W. Story" are alarmingly racist comments about Chinese camp officials in North Korea. According to Captain James Curry, a thirty-two-year-old officer, "If our Americans had one year of high school they could out-think, out-reason and out-react any of the Chinese fellows with college degrees."[73] Private First Class Roosevelt A. Lunn opined, "The Chinese, they are more barbaric than the Koreans. You can't call the Chinese a member of the civilized world at all. They're like animals. But they're human enough to be sadistic. How that fat little Chinaman loved to beat us!"[74] In eliminating the Chinese altogether and depicting North Koreans as subordinates to powerful Russians, MGM distorted history in what critics might call a typical "Hollywood way." In reality, as historian William Stueck points out, "Of the great powers, the Soviet Union clearly was the prime loser by virtue of the Korean War," which "contributed enormously to the international prestige of the new China [and] led to North Korea's development as a distinct identity" independent of its two competing allies.[75]

From *The Steel Helmet* to *The Bamboo Prison*: The DoD's Responses to Controversies

In December 1954, seven months after MGM released *Prisoner of War*, Columbia Pictures circulated another Korean War POW film with a similar theme, *The Bamboo Prison*, produced by Bryan Foy and directed by Lewis Seiler. Like its MGM counterpart, Columbia's motion picture features a "progressive" hero who turns out be a government agent (Sergeant John Rand, played by Robert Francis) on a mission to gather intelligence about missing Americans for leverage in peace talks with the communist side. Rand seduces—and later genuinely falls in love with—the Russian ballerina wife (Dianne Foster) of the camp's brainwashing expert from Moscow, an American newspaperman-turned-defector named Clayton (Murray Matheson), to access confidential documents. Mirroring Rand's charade is that of Father Francis Dolan (E. G. Marshall), a communist mole who poses as a Catholic priest and spies on fellow prisoners on behalf of Chinese captors. Just like Jesse in *Prisoner of War*, a character who falsely defects to Russia, after the armistice is signed, Rand chooses to go to communist China (in lieu of repatriation to America) in order to continue his espionage mission. In his book-length overview of Korean War films, Robert J. Lentz evaluates *The Bamboo Prison* more favorably than *Prisoner of War*, stating that the former is not only "a slightly more serious and believable glimpse of P.O.W. life" but it also draws attention to "the larger issue of global communism" by depicting the Chinese and Russians, rather than North Koreans, as villains.[76]

DoD and DA reviewers did not share this charitable view of Columbia's project at the time of its production. On February 18, 1954, J. Raymond Bell of Columbia Pictures Corporation sent a copy of *The Bamboo Prison*'s final-draft script (then titled *Those Reported Missing*) to Donald Baruch, chief of the Motion Picture Section of the DoD's OPI. The studio's representative clarified that "this picture is being made without any request for official cooperation." The only thing that Columbia was requesting was military-owned stock footage for a few scenes involving U.S. bombings of Korea and the Freedom Village, Panmunjom, at the border of the two Koreas, where prisoner exchanges took place. Bell emphasized that the new film would "highlight communist atrocities and expose the manner in which the communists infiltrate prisoner camps for their own propaganda purposes."[77] Despite the studio's assumption that the government would be favorable to such a scenario, the opposite was true. On March 2, 1954, Patrick Welch, chief of the DA Public Information Division, sent his office's recommendations to the DoD after reviewing Columbia's script. Identifying the script as "a travesty on a national problem of very grave importance," the DA recommended that "the studio be encouraged to delay the production in order to consider changes and suggestions which DA would like to make in order to assure that this production will be authentic, realistic, and afforded a treatment which a subject of such grave national importance deserves."[78] The following day, Baruch informed Bell that the script "in its present form does not qualify for [the DoD's] cooperation and we do not feel justified in extending the courtesy of releasing stock footage under the circumstances" because it would imply "a form of cooperation and approval."[79]

Three years earlier, the DoD gave clearance to writer-director Samuel Fuller to use up to 1,000 feet of army-owned unclassified, unedited stock footage of combat actions (e.g., artillery firing, tank operations, infantry move) from the Long Island Signal Corps Photo Center in *The Steel Helmet* (1951), a low-budget Korean War film independently produced by Lippert Pictures. After reviewing Fuller's rough cut, the DoD disqualified the project for official cooperation on the grounds that it contained no public informational value and declined the filmmaker's offer of courtesy credit. This decision to allow Fuller to use military motion picture footage in an officially unapproved film turned out to be a publicity fiasco for the DoD. Despite its overall anti-communist message, *The Steel Helmet* was vehemently attacked by Victor Riesel, a syndicated labor columnist. Drawing the critic's ire was a scene in which the antihero, Sergeant Zack (Gene Evans), kills an unarmed North Korean prisoner in retaliation for the death of a young South Korean orphan boy, who has been shot down by a communist sniper. Riesel made the case that the film could serve as "communist propaganda" by citing the *Daily Worker*, the official newspaper of the Communist Party USA, which identified *The Steel Helmet* as a "further proof of the savagery of the U.S. war against the Korean people." Furthermore, the communist newspaper (inaccurately) reported that Fuller's film was approved by the DoD.[80] Critic Westford Pedravy alleged that Fuller "was secretly financed by the Reds" and called for the Pentagon's investigation.[81]

During the film's production, the PCA attempted to preempt several potential problems from the standpoint of race, religion, and foreign relations. In October 1950, the self-regulation agency raised objections to Fuller's script regarding [1] the use of the derisive epithet "gook" to refer to Koreans throughout the script; [2] the use of a Buddhist temple as the film's main setting, where excessive destruction of sacred artifacts of worship takes place; [3] Zack's murder of a North Korean prisoner, which would have been in violation of the Geneva Convention; and [4] several unfavorable references to the Japanese people, America's Cold War ally.[82] As discussed in this book's Introduction, in a story conference with Fuller's assistant on October 19, PCA staffer Morris Murphy went on record to express the overall regulatory concern that "in view of the critical war situation in the Far East . . . this story, even in those parts which do not specifically violate the [Production] Code, could cause serious damage to the international relations of the United States, as well as serious embarrassment to the motion picture industry" and urged extreme care in the portrayal of North Koreans. The PCA opined that, while "none of us could say what might be the desired relation between our government and the people of North Korea" at the time of the film's release, "*The Steel Helmet* could cause serious embarrassment to our State Department at a later date."[83]

Considering that this view was expressed just a few weeks after the Truman administration ordered U.S. troops to Korea (on June 30, 1950), it is remarkable how the industry saw itself as a responsible player in the shaping of U.S. foreign policy at this juncture of history (an attitude that contrasts sharply with Sony Pictures' handling of the North Korean crisis in 2014, a subject that I will return to in this book's final chapter). Fuller's team conceded that the expression "gook" would be spoken only once by an American character (and then used by a South Korean boy with reference to North Koreans) and that Zack would be reprimanded more severely for killing an unarmed prisoner.[84] In the release print, Zack's commanding officer, Lieutenant Driscoll (Steve Brodie), emphatically denounces the unauthorized shooting with a moralizing speech: "It's good that this army isn't made of fatheaded snobs like you that think this war's run by idiots. Just because those little rats kill our prisoners is no reason we have to do the same thing. . . . You're no solider. You're just a big, dumb, stupid, selfish, fatheaded sergeant." When Fuller was summoned to the Pentagon and questioned by twenty officers about the controversial scene, the World War II veteran defended his script, telling them, "I fought a war. Things like that happen! And you know it!" He even got his old company commander, now a brigadier general, on the phone to confirm the fact that prisoners did get shot by American troops.[85]

In a letter to the Motion Picture Association of America (MPAA)'s branch in Washington, dated February 1, 1951, the DoD's Motion Picture Section articulated its position about the controversy as follows:

> Department of Defense has neither the power nor the desire to interfere with private enterprise. If the producer of *The Steel Helmet* was to produce his picture without the assistance of the Department, our objections could be considered only in the light of their being constructive comment, and could in no way operate to prevent the production of the picture . . . . The picture was produced without cooperation of the Department of Defense or any of the Services, and without approval either actual or implied, on either the script or the finished picture, or on the premiere and/or subsequent showings . . . . We did, however . . . allow the producer to use a few hundred feet of stock material that has previously been cleared for newsreel, television, and other pictorial use. It was specifically understood that this act did not constitute approval of the picture.[86]

From the DoD's perspective, their friendly, uncredited assistance to independent film producers had backfired and got the government organization mired in the blame game with the film industry. Concerned about the scene depicting the killing of a POW, a prudent Joseph Breen (of the PCA) had instructed Fuller to telegraph the DoD and extract a "definite statement from the Army" authorizing the use of military footage in his film. In his report to the parental trade organization (MPAA)'s Washington staff, Breen reasoned, "Because it has always been our understanding that the Army will not lend, or give, footage for inclusion in any motion picture which they have not approved, we were inclined to . . . presume that the Army's willingness to give [Fuller] stock footage carried with it, if not the *approval*, at least the suggestion that the Army had no *objection* to the film."[87] The Pentagon's own internal screening (with twenty-five responsible officers and high-ranking civilians selected from the DoD and DA) concluded that "if *The Steel Helmet* was subtle communistic propaganda, it was too subtle for any ordinary person to see," and the DoD decided not to withdraw the film from military-controlled theaters in camps, posts, and stations. Still, in light of that controversy it is not surprising that the organization denied similar footage assistance to the producers of Columbia's *The Bamboo Prison*.[88]

In his follow-up letter to the DoD, dated March 5, 1954, Welch criticized *The Bamboo Prison* for being "capricious and irrational fiction and fantasy."[89] The DA's chief of public information saw the film "actually promot[ing] the Communist philosophy in some areas" by depicting American collaborators (including the main architect of the "brainwashing" program) profit from their betrayal and "live in luxury." After correcting a geographical implausibility of the film's setting (Pyongyang, where regular prisoner camps did not exist), Welch elaborates, "Even more imaginary is the writer's idea that the room-monitors ['progressives'] were allowed the luxury of a bed or delectable tidbits of broiled pork—such things were not even available for most of the Communist soldiers to say nothing of the so-called 'progressives.'" The DA expressed its commitment to collaboration with Columbia in developing an "accurate treatment" of the subject that is also "artistically satisfying and profitable for the studio."[90] As one of the "Little Three" minor studios known for lower-budget B movies—as opposed to the "Big Five" majors (Paramount, MGM, 20th Century-Fox, Warner Bros., RKO), which employed higher-value production lines—Columbia declined to delay their motion picture for the sake of technical accuracy and military assistance. In the aforementioned letter to Columbia, the DoD indicated that, in order to qualify for official cooperation, the studio would have to make changes to a few plotlines, including the "establishment of one of the remaining prisoners as an agent; Russian part as portrayed in the affairs of the prisoners; and the Russian girl coming to the U.S. Forces for apparent asylum."[91] Such drastic overhaul of narrative would have postponed the film's production considerably. Columbia decided to opt out of any obligation by simply forgoing the use of military footage. Despite the amiable relationship between the DoD and Columbia over the project (after the production was completed, the studio voluntarily sent a review copy to the Pentagon as a courtesy), external censorship pressures burdened the government organization when *The Bamboo Prison*, like *The Steel Helmet*, agitated cultural watchdogs upon its original release. A particularly loud voice of dissent came from Catholics, who found the imposter Father Dolan degrading to the memory of Father Emil J. Kapaun, a priest who died in captivity in Korea and was posthumously awarded the Legion of Merit. Selfless and compassionate, Kapaun "literally worked himself sick" (to quote a witness) in taking care of fellow prisoners and was left to die by Chinese captors who resented his leadership. This plotline was first opposed by Breen's PCA, which urged Columbia, "It will be essential that competent technical advice be obtained, in connection with the scenes dealing with the Communist posing as a Catholic priest. Care should be taken to avoid anything which might prove objectionable to religious minded members of our audiences."[92]

This friendly advice turned out to be prophetic. Senator Carl Hayden forwarded to the DoD a complaint letter from one of his Arizona constituents, a high school teacher named E. A. Wheat, who demanded that the senator use his "strongest influence [to] have this most un-American practice corrected . . . and to have Columbia Pictures publicly reprimanded."[93] The DoD replied to Senator Hayden, confirming that the film was made without any military cooperation due to the fact that the studio's schedule could not accommodate the extensive rewriting required for government assistance.[94] The alleged anti-Catholic representation likewise offended a columnist named Dale Francis, who attacked *The Bamboo Prison* in the December 12, 1954, issue of *Our Sunday Visitor*. His column prompted more than 10,000 Catholic readers to send protest letters to Columbia Pictures. The producer, Bryan Foy, who was a Catholic himself, defended his film from the religious backlash, pointing out that it was made with the technical advice of Monsignor John J. Devlin of the Catholic Church.[95]

The more painful headache for both Columbia Pictures and the DoD derived from the Memphis Board of Film Censors, among the toughest and most notorious of the thirty-one municipal film censorship boards, headed by the insurance executive–turned–draconian censor Lloyd T. Binford (who served as chairman of the board from 1927 to 1955). Owing to the Mississippi native's predilection for banning films for a variety of capricious reasons (from Ingrid Bergman's out-of-wedlock pregnancy and Charlie Chaplin's alleged communist sympathies to depictions of train robberies and juvenile

FIG. 3.5 The unholy portrayal of Father Francis Dolan (left: E. G. Marshall), a communist mole who poses as a Catholic priest, drew the ire of Catholics, who sent more than 10,000 protest letters to Columbia Pictures, the distributor of Lewis Seiler's *The Bamboo Prison* (1954).

delinquency in Westerns and themes of integration and racial mixing in musicals and comedies), the term "Binfordized" became a popular industry shorthand for stringent censorship or the outright banning of motion pictures.[96] The sensational publicity generated in the wake of Memphis's banning of *The Bamboo Prison* (on the grounds that the Korean War POW film was "unpatriotic") was an appropriate sendoff to the octogenarian censor in the twilight days of his career (Binford died in 1956, one year after his retirement). B. F. Edwards, one of the three women (of the five-member board) who voted to ban Columbia's film, told *Variety*: "We ladies found it . . . inimical to public welfare . . . . At the end the star (Robert Francis) denounced the U.S. . . . . It was most unpatriotic. He (Francis) said he didn't believe in democracy. I don't think it would be a good picture for young people to see."[97] Alongside this interview, the February 1, 1955, issue of *Variety* included an editor's note, which states, "The ladies got lost somewhere in the plot turns of *Bamboo Prison* . . . . Character played by Robert Francis is a U.S. Army Intelligence plant who . . . merely pretends to his captors he's a Communist . . . . he elects to remain in Red hands so he can go on spying for the U.S."[98] Just over two months after the original ban, on April 5, 1955, the Memphis Board of Film Censors reversed its decision and approved *The Bamboo Prison*'s exhibition as Columbia Pictures was preparing to file a lawsuit against the board that week.

Cornered by Columbia's threat of litigation, Binford turned to the DoD and tried to borrow the Pentagon's authority to justify his board's decision to ban *The Bamboo Prison* in Memphis. Before raising the white flag and reversing the ban, on March 23, 1955, Binford wrote to C. Herschel Schooley, the DoD's public information director, in an attempt to verify a newspaper report that referred to the government's disapproval of Columbia's film:

> The Memphis Board of Censors unanimously decided that there were several reasons why *Bamboo Prison* could not be approved . . . for it appears that the Department of Defense clearly informed Columbia Pictures that the script for *Bamboo Prison* was unacceptable, and "Columbia refused to even discuss the Government's objection." Hence, insomuch as "with full knowledge that the Defense Department had said the script required many changes, Foy deliberately went ahead and produced the script he had been told by his own Nation's officials was unacceptable." If the above is true, I am confident you will approve the action of the Memphis Board of Censors in declining approval without further information from you and the Department of Defense.[99]

In their response to Binford dated March 30, 1955, the DoD explained the protocol of military-industry cooperation on a voluntary, nonobligatory basis and even shared its correspondences with Columbia Pictures regarding *The Bamboo Prison*:

> Department of Defense extends cooperation on the production of motion pictures in accordance with a basic policy.... This policy is in no way a form of censorship. There is no requirement or obligation on the part of a motion picture producer or company to submit a script concerning the Army, Navy, Air Force or Marine Corps for our review unless some military assistance, unattainable through commercial channels, is desired. Mr. Foy found he needs a small account of stock motion picture footage from the Armed Services film libraries. We believe the best way to explain our reaction and set the records straight would be for you to read our letter after reviewing the script.[100]

Furthermore, the DoD forwarded their correspondences with Binford to J. Raymond Bell of Columbia Pictures for two-way transparency. In his letter to Baruch, dated March 25, 1955, Bell grumbled at the public ignorance about the exact nature of the Pentagon's involvement in commercial filmmaking: "While you and I know the procedures involved in obtaining Pentagon cooperation, and while you and I know that any company can make any kind of picture it wants without either submitting scripts, or having voluntarily done so, not being required to follow suggestions or recommendations, the public and Mr. Binford do not know these things. [MGM] made [*Prisoner of War*] which follows a theme parallel to ours, and while you did not cooperate, neither did you stigmatize that production."[101] These words still ring true, as the Pentagon's technical advising continues to be conflated with official government censorship in both the popular imagination and academic scholarship. The DoD's correspondences with studios and its internal memos, extensively cited in this chapter, disprove such a simplified assumption.

The Baruch Factor: Putting a Human Face on Pentagon Regulations

In the early 1960s, under the initiative of Assistant Secretary of Defense for Public Affairs Arthur Sylvester, the Pentagon revisited its process of cooperation with the film industry in the wake of increased public scrutiny for the utilization of U.S. servicemen and military resources in assisting Hollywood productions at a time of security crisis. This was in part a response to controversy that arose after the DoD assigned a large number of troops and plenty of equipment for simulating the D-Day landing in Normandy for 20th Century Fox's World War II epic *The Longest Day* (1962) during the Berlin Crisis of 1961 (caused by the Soviet Union's ultimatum to block Western access to Berlin). Republican lawmakers attacked the Kennedy administration for allowing the military to serve the entertainment industry in the midst of a global Cold War crisis. Although the DoD did not retreat from its commitment to aid the film's production, the number of troops assigned to the project was cut from 700 to 250.[102] Sylvester's resolve to tighten Pentagon control over military assistance to commercial filmmaking hardened after a sailor on leave lost his life while preparing explosives on the set of *No Man Is an Island* (1962), a WWII combat picture produced with limited navy assistance. A frustrated assistant secretary of defense declared in 1942 that the U.S. military "can't be rented by anyone. They are not going to be turned over to motion pictures indiscriminately."[103]

In January 1964, the DoD issued new regulations governing military assistance to Hollywood, with a clearer delineation of qualifications and basis for cooperation and stricter requirements for submitting a detailed list of desired resources and precise service dates. In Pentagon parlance, "the production, program, project or assistance will benefit the DoD or otherwise be in the national interests" based on two criteria: "authenticity of the portrayal of military operations, or historical incidents, persons, or places depicting a true interpretation of military life" and "compliance with accepted standards of dignity and propriety in the industry."[104] The 1964 directive also mandates that "diversion of equipment, personnel, and material resources from normal military locations or operations . . . shall be held to a minimum and without interference with military operations" to preempt another controversial situation like *The Longest Day*.[105] As Suid points out, while Sylvester's new set of regulations had little effect in changing operational dynamics of military-industry cooperation on location, it may have contributed to "Hollywood's turning away from its reliance with the military services" and catering to "America's changing attitudes toward the armed forces" with antimilitary, antiwar sentiments in war films.[106]

In his 1973 oral history interview with Suid for the John F. Kennedy Presidential Library, Sylvester calls Donald Baruch "a weak fellow who wants to ride with everybody and has been in bed with the motion picture people . . . . he's been for years with these people and their representative in the Pentagon, in effect, and not the Pentagon's representative to them."[107] While it may not be fair to take the assistant secretary's subjective evaluation of his former underling at face value, there is some truth in Baruch's special allegiance to the entertainment business. Born into a prestigious South Carolina family of financiers, statesmen, and diplomats, the Pentagon regulator started his career in Broadway and Hollywood in the 1930s (producing four off-Broadway plays and working at Hal Roach Studios and MGM Studios) before moving to Washington, where he produced training films as an army/air force public information officer during World War II. Given his familiarity and connections with the film industry, it is no surprise that he was appointed as chief of the new Motion Picture Section of the DoD's OPI in 1949.

In the aforementioned interview, Sylvester confides that the DoD "created an Audio-Visual Department and took it away from Baruch as a sole arbiter . . . and put it . . . in a larger division."[108] While Baruch remained as the DoD's chief liaison with Hollywood until his retirement in 1989, the OPI's media branches were reorganized in the 1960s with the express goal of restraining his autonomy in handling Hollywood affairs and subjecting him to the authority of the Office of Assistant Secretary of Defense for Public Affairs. This obscure anecdote in history is an important reminder that the human agency of individual regulators should be taken into consideration when analyzing institutional policy. As Sylvester aptly put it, "of course you can write all the directives in the world you want. It goes to the people who administer them. Now if Mr. Baruch or whoever else . . . wants to close eyes and let things go, he can."[109] The Baruch office's benevolence toward the film industry in the 1950s, as attested by this chapter's case studies, should be understood in this personal, as much as geopolitical, context.

There are further complications in defining the role of Pentagon technical advising in today's blockbuster context, as Hollywood producers are under increased pressure to get their scripts approved so that they can access free military resources and lower production costs. In an age when special effects–driven blockbuster movies cost an average of $200 million to produce, the budgetary concern of studios is far more significant than it was for producing low-budget, black-and-white action movies in the 1950s (such as *Prisoner of War* and *The Bamboo Prison*). For example, through the DoD's military assistance, Warner Bros. could save $1 million in producing the Superman movie *Man of Steel* (2013) with a $225 million price tag.[110] This economic leverage has empowered Phil Strub, a former navy videographer, who succeeded Baruch in 1989 as the DoD's film industry liaison under the new title director of entertainment media. In a 2011 interview, Strub referred to the relationship between the Pentagon and Hollywood as "a mutual exploitation," adding that "we're after military portrayal, and they're after our equipment."[111] With the end of the U.S. military draft system in 1973, the Pentagon has faced a greater need to "exploit" its role as a technical advisor to Hollywood for the purpose of recruiting and retaining career soldiers. On July 8, 1993, in a letter to Bruce Hendrix, senior vice president of Walt Disney Company, Strub expressed concern about the portrayal of "a distinctly inaccurate, unpleasant way of life in the Navy" in the script of *Countermeasures* and listed three criteria of the DoD's support: [1] "feasible, authentic depictions" of the military; [2] public informational value regarding the military; and [3] helpfulness for military recruiting and retention.[112] This added third criterion (which did not exist in the 1964 directive) undoubtedly compromises the DoD's professed pursuit of realism in technical advising. As David Robb cynically pointed out, "*Apocalypse Now* was viewed as 'not realistic' because of negative scenes about Vietnam . . . while the producers of the recent film *Windtalkers* yielded to Pentagon demands of script changes [because] many of these historical accounts [of Navajo "code talkers" during World War II] showed the military in less than a flattering light."[113]

While it is true that the DoD openly pursued positive images of the military and service personnel in both classical and contemporary Hollywood films (as is the case with any other technical advisors representing various vocations, such as medicine, law, religion, academia, etc.), its claim to authenticity cannot be entirely discredited as a ruse for self-serving propaganda or a recruitment ploy. On *Armed with Science*, the official DoD science blog page, Phil Strub contributed an article aptly entitled "Pentagon's Entertainment Office Brings Military Science to Hollywood." In this short blog entry, dated May 20, 2010, Strub explains the DoD's role as a technical advisor to contemporary Hollywood productions:

> Despite the sophistication of special effects, computer generated graphics, and other technologies, filmmakers still very much want U.S. military production support—even though it comes with strings attached. For example, along with their "wish lists" for military support, filmmakers must also send us the scripts. These ultimately have to present a reasonably realistic portrayal of the military. . . . If filmmakers are willing to negotiate with us to resolve our script concerns, usually we'll reach an agreement. If not, filmmakers are free to press on without military assistance, and they often do. Filmmakers are notorious for claiming to be sticklers about realism. But, in practice, realism is quickly reduced or tossed aside altogether when they think it interferes with drama and action.[114]

In the process of challenging Hollywood's geopolitical fabrications for the purpose of "drama and action" (such as fictional Russian torturers and the myth of "progressives" as undercover agents in Korean War brainwashing films), the DoD's technical advising has often generated productive dialogue with studios and filmmakers on matters of great national import, even when it failed to persuade the profit-driven commercial industry to implement desired changes.

Part II

The War on Terror, Contemporary Hollywood, and Its Global Discontents

4

From *Die Another Day* to "Another Day"

The Anti-007 Movement, Pan-Asian Nationalism, and Protests as Censorship

Produced in the wake of George W. Bush's January 2002 State of the Union speech designating North Korea as part of the "axis of evil," *Die Another Day* (2002)—the twentieth film in the perennial James Bond franchise—reflects the contemporary political zeitgeist in a way that few blockbusters in recent memory have. The film begins with British super agent 007 (Pierce Brosnan) surfing onto a beach in North Korea, where he battles a megalomaniacal colonel who, harnessing the destructive power of the sun, seeks world domination. With the latest technology at his disposal, Bond—though imprisoned and tortured by his captors—inevitably emerges victorious at the end, sending a reassuring message to audiences that real-life dictator Kim Jong-il's threats to the West can be easily surmounted. Though the explosive action darts around the globe, from Cuba to England to Iceland, much of the narrative is geographically, politically, and thematically focused on the Korean peninsula—one of the last frontiers of the Cold War.

As a U.K./U.S. coproduction, *Die Another Day* can be seen as an outgrowth of global capitalism and what Toby Miller and others call the "new international division of cultural labor."[1] The film was produced by Brits (Anthony

Waye, along with his American partner Barbara Broccoli), directed by a New Zealander (Lee Tamahori), and shot in Pinewood Studios, London, as well as on location in Wales, Hawaii, Spain, and Iceland, rather than in Hollywood. The multiethnic/multinational cast includes Pierce Brosnan (Irish British); Halle Berry (African American); Judi Dench, John Cleese, Rosamund Pike, and Toby Stephens (all English); Rick Yune and Will Yun Lee (both Korean American); Kenneth Tsang (Hong Kong Chinese); and Emilio Echevarría (Mexican). Two major Hollywood studios—MGM and 20th Century-Fox—were respectively responsible for the production and international distribution of *Die Another Day*, whose overhead cost reportedly climbed as high as $150 million. Twenty multinational corporate sponsors, including Ford, Omega, British Airways, Visa, Revlon, Philips Electronics, and Sony, spent more than $120 million on ads and cross-promotions highlighting the fortieth-anniversary 007 adventure (which self-reflexively pays homage to its predecessors through intertextual quotations and allusions). The exploits of Her Majesty's Secret Intelligence Service (SIS or MI6) were likewise endorsed by Queen Elizabeth II herself, who sponsored a royal charity premiere in London's Albert Hall on November 18, 2002.

Later that month, *Die Another Day* opened with great fanfare in theaters around the world. Headlines across North America and Europe trumpeted this latest entry in the Bond franchise as a box office champion, having successfully outsold its chief nemesis, *Harry Potter and the Chamber of Secrets* (2002). It subsequently became the biggest Bond film to date, grossing $400 billion worldwide as of March 2003.[2] In marked contrast to world audiences' celebratory reception, Koreans voiced their criticisms against the film's foregrounding of North Korea as a high-tech rogue state and its problematic portrayal of South Korea as a provincial backdrop under U.S. military control. *Die Another Day* generated fierce protests in South Korea for what was perceived to be an insult to national pride and a distortion of reality. Culminating with a sex scene set in a Buddhist temple, the film offended a diverse cross-section of Koreans, from leftist students to spiritual and religious leaders. Anti-007 boycotts intensified as part of a general anti-American movement triggered by the acquittal of two U.S. soldiers whose armored vehicle accidentally ran over and killed two Korean schoolgirls in June 2002.

This chapter examines the ways in which the discourses surrounding the 007 controversy link the issue of representation (post–Cold War Orientalism in Euro-American coproductions) with that of politics (pan-Asian nationalism and anti-imperial "culture wars") in the global context of cultural production, distribution, and reception. Despite the geographical and temporal specificity of the anti-007 movement in South Korea, acts of inter-Korea cultural resistance can be recuperated within the larger sphere of regional nationalism precisely because of the interchangeability of different Asian ethnicities, locations, and icons in hegemonic Western texts like *Die Another Day*. In the pages that follow, I apply a two-pronged interpretation of the term "nationalism," first to a South Korean context and then to a broader pan-Asian context. My second use of the term borrows from Louis L. Snyder's concept of "macro-nationalism," a "super-territorial imperative" pertaining to various pan-movements based on linguistic, ethnic, religious, cultural, or continental ties, such as pan-Slavism, pan-Europeanism, pan-Islamism, pan-Arabism, pan-Africanism, pan-Americanism, and so on.[3] I will, however, differentiate my usage of Asian nationalism or pan-Asianism from that of Snyder, who emphasizes the racial factors behind the movement.[4] My focus resides in the cultural solidarity among Asian people from different national and ethnic backgrounds, united in their collective opposition to the hegemony of globalized Hollywood and its perpetuation of stereotypical Oriental imagery. This solidarity entails not only a disavowal of racist portrayals of Asians in Hollywood films but also a shift of spectatorial loyalty to local productions or regional films, as evidenced by the recent craze for South Korean cinema in pan-Asian markets.

Moreover, such recuperation of national/regional boycotts of hegemonic or imperialist cultural productions gives us an opportunity to understand the complex relationship between film censorship and consumer protests in a global context. As Charles Lyons states,

> In the context of film production, distribution, and exhibition, the word *censorship* is certainly not monolithic. It refers to a set of practices by institutions or groups, either prior to or following a film's release, the result of which is the removal of a word, a scene, or an entire film from the marketplace. The most obvious forms of film censorship are actions by federal, state, and municipal governments and the mechanisms of self-regulation established by the motion picture industry itself. A third kind of censorship occurs as a result of group protests. Not all protests lead to censorship; many are primarily a means of publicizing a group's complaint. But when, as a result of street protests, a movie is reedited or pulled from theaters, such protests can be said to result in censorship.[5]

As a result of prerelease online protests against Korean representations in *Die Another Day*, the film was "censored" for the regional market: the Korean dialogue spoken by British actor Toby Stephens (playing a racially transformed North Korean colonel disguised as a Caucasian businessman) was dubbed by a native speaker, and the film's Korean title was changed to *Another Day* in an effort to downplay the two onscreen deaths of the North Korean villain. The negative online publicity doomed the film's box office potential even before protestors in major cities around the nation (Seoul, Busan, Daegu, Gwangju, etc.) picketed theaters playing this "anti-Korean" film. Most theaters reduced the number of showings or canceled them early due to low audience turnout and public pressure.[6]

As a "third kind of censorship," such media advocacy of ordinary citizens and consumers opens up a dialogical space that has been referred to by Heather Hendershot as "competing censorships." The media scholar elaborates, "It is precisely because the United States does not have official state censorship and is not overtly fascistic that censorship can thrive here. Censorship can never be challenged within a system where it is insufficiently acknowledged. Admitting censorship's prevalence does not have to make one into a despairing cynic. Rather, acknowledging the pervasiveness of censorious impulses—from the left, right, center, and every other direction—enables critical thought, discussion, and activism."[7] The power of activism lies not in its ability to bring radical change to representational politics of oligopolistic media giants but in its ability to attract the public's attention to the hegemony, inequality, and inauthenticity manifested in their mainstream productions and call for collective action (boycotts, picketing, etc.). As Ellen C. Scott argues in her survey of the National Association for Advancement of the Colored People (NAACP)'s film activism during the Classical Hollywood period, "While Black activists could not control Hollywood's production of Black images, they could influence the film's reception—and sometimes local censorship. With varying levels of success, activists wielded this control as an ideological wedge against various kinds of image-bound inequality, often through careful and poignant readings of a film's social value and historical weight."[8]

The anti-007 movement in South Korea represents an opportune confluence of "competing censorships" (adding international voices to existing debates about Hollywood representations of sex, violence, and race) and what Jiyeon Kang calls the "new democratic sensibilities" of a country that experienced decades of political repression under dictatorial military regimes (1961–1988).[9] With nearly 60 percent of its population having access to high-speed internet by 2002 (becoming one of the most wired countries in the world), South Korea saw the rise of a new youth protest culture that merged online activism with the practice of street candlelight vigils (*ch'oppul siwi*). Young Korean internet users (or "netizens," as locals call them) were early adopters of what Zeynep Tufekci calls the "digitally networked public sphere," which harnessed the power of digital technology and social media as an enabler of prodemocracy street protests during the Arab Spring of 2011–2012.[10] As Kang notes, "When the first candlelight protests appeared in 2002, participants and observers alike compared it to the anti-American activism of the 1980s, implicitly characterizing the then-new format of vigils as radical activism."[11] Although the anti-007 movement was not an official part of candlelight vigils protesting against the U.S. military responsible for the deaths of two schoolgirls, the periods of the two movements were consecutive (November–December for vigils and

December–January for boycotts) and they were connected in the spirit of anti-Americanism and shared tactics of youth-oriented networked dissent. This does not mean that the discourses of censorship generated from this media activism were inherently positive and progressive because of their affiliation with "new democratic sensibilities" of post-authoritarian South Korea and its counter-hegemonic, anti-imperialist rhetoric. Rather, the movement epitomizes the "paradox of protest" that continues to resonate with film regulation scholars. As eloquently put forth by Lyons, the paradox can be summed up in this manner: "Take away our right to protest against something, especially a piece of art that may offend our sensibilities, and you radically limit one of our most cherished and democratic freedoms—the right to dissent. But permit protest and you give life to the possibility of censorship by political pressure."[12]

Cold War Heroes and Villains in the World of James Bond

Before discussing the controversy swirling around *Die Another Day* in the context of post–Cold War Asia,[13] it will be useful to examine the genealogy of Cold War themes in the James Bond series, the longest-running film franchise in history. While the connection between British author Ian Fleming's 007 fiction and the Cold War seems self-evident, it is worth pointing out that the film versions took a slightly different path from their original sources. The first Bond novel by Fleming, *Casino Royale*, was published in 1953, the final year of the Korean War. Although this fratricidal clash replaced a direct military confrontation between two nuclear superpowers (the United States and the Soviet Union), the fear of communist expansion in Asia and Europe reinforced a "Cold War consensus" sweeping through the West. As James Chapman has noted, James Bond was "a product of the historical and ideological conditions of the Cold War," and Bond's enemy was not "just a country (Russia) but an ideology (communism) that presented a very real threat to the 'free' West."[14] Out of seven Bond stories written in the 1950s (*Casino Royale*, *Live and Let Die* [1954], *Moonraker* [1955], *Diamonds Are Forever* [1956], *From Russia, with Love* [1957], *Dr. No* [1958], and *Goldfinger* [1959]), all but one of the villains therein are employed by the Russian government or its espionage agency SMERSH (an anagram of *Smiert Spionam* or "Death to Spies"). Referring to the cinematic adaptations of Fleming's novels, Klaus Dodds argues that "one of the reasons for the enduring appeal of Bond is the connection to the geopolitics of the Cold War and the use of place-based imagery to convey intrigue, mystery, and danger." According to Dodds, "the places depicted in the James Bond films . . . actively contribute to the geo-graphing of the Cold War as a series of Manichean struggles between good and evil," just as North Korea functions in *Die Another Day*.[15]

Many commentators have observed that the film adaptations, undertaken by North American producers Albert R. Broccoli and Harry Saltzman, in conjunction with United Artists and Pinewood Studios, throughout the following decade, toned down the Cold War discourse so intrinsic to their sources, turning Soviet-backed villains into megalomaniacal terrorists with outsized ambitions of world dominance. For example, the first Bond film, *Dr. No* (1962), shifted the titular villain's affiliation from SMERSH to SPECTRE (Special Executive for Counter-Intelligence, Terrorism, Revenge, and Extortion), a global criminal organization introduced in Fleming's later novels *Thunderball* (1961) and *On Her Majesty's Secret Service* (1963). In the second Bond film, *From Russia with Love* (1962), the allegiance of Soviet villains—Colonel Rosa Klebb (Lotte Lenya) and Red Grant (Robert Shaw)—was likewise changed from SMERSH to SPECTRE because "Broccoli and Saltzman were concerned that the geopolitics of the Cold War should not be too explicit within the film [series]."[16] This transformation created a deliberate "political unintelligibility" that was missed by many confused film reviewers who still reported that "Bond battled the communists."[17] Writing for the film magazine *Amateur Cine World*, British critic John Sanders called *From Russia with Love* "an interesting example of how the Cold War has cooled since the book was originally written" in 1957. The reviewer cynically added that he was "not sure whether the producers . . . were hoping for a wide distribution of their movie in the Soviet Union, or if this is just their contribution to the easing of international tension."[18] In the third Bond film, *Goldfinger* (1964), Red China—a cinematic surrogate for Fleming's omnipresent Soviet Union—is cast as the sinister sponsor of Auric Goldfinger (Gert Fröbe), a murderous bullion dealer who hatches a plot to knock over Fort Knox with an atomic device provided by communist Chinese agents.

Goldfinger also set a precedent—one that would be followed in *Die Another Day*—in its foregrounding of Korean villain Oddjob (played by Japanese actor Harold Sakata), a boulder-shaped manservant/henchman who menacingly wields a steel-rimmed bowler hat as his unconventional weapon of choice. Celebrated as one of the most memorable villains in the series by "Bondophiles," Oddjob is nevertheless a Cold War–era incarnation of the age-old, archetypal Oriental villain whose muteness and occasional animalistic grunt enhance his race-coded monstrosity. Ten years after the theatrical release of *Goldfinger*, another Korean connection was established in a Bond film when actor Soon-Tek Oh was cast for the role of a Hong Kong secret agent named Hip in *The Man with the Golden Gun* (1974). Unlike Oddjob, Oh's character is an amiable sidekick who assists Roger Moore's Bond in rooting out the notorious Cuban assassin Francisco Scaramanga (Christopher Lee)'s Chinese employer (Hai Fat [Richard Loo]) in Thailand. Once again, the film pulls back the curtain to reveal Red China as the backer of an evil conspiracy. Comparable to post-9/11 Afghanistan, communist China is depicted as a terrorist-harboring threat to international peace and security. Hiding out on a remote island in Chinese territorial waters under the protection of Red patrol guards, the murderous Scaramanga schemes to monopolize world solar power through the stolen "solex agitator."

Although James Bond films of the 1960s and 1970s avoided pigeonholing the Soviet Union as an evil other, the series racialized the Cold War menace by substituting Russia and SMERSH with communist China and conflating the Red Scare with Yellow Peril. In the early to mid-1980s, as the Reagan-Thatcher era's right-wing, anti-communist foreign policies began coloring popular culture, the 007 film series revived the Cold War themes of Fleming's novels, actively recruiting Russian villains in *For Your Eyes Only* (1981), *Octopussy* (1983), *A View to a Kill* (1985), and *The Living Daylights* (1987). As if reflecting the thaw of the Cold War in the late 1980s, *Licence to Kill* (1989) substitutes Russian or Chinese enemies with an international drug syndicate lording over a paramilitary unit on a Latin American island. Although the Cold War officially ended after this film's release with the fall of the Berlin Wall, the collapse of communist regimes in Eastern Europe, and the dissolution of the Soviet Union, the spectral shadows of post–Cold War Russian and Chinese threats lingered on in such Bond films of the 1990s as *GoldenEye* (1995) and *Tomorrow Never Dies* (1997). The latter film, however, recasts the former Chinese enemy as a potential partner in its representation of Mai Lin, a Chinese secret agent played by Hong Kong action star Michelle Yeoh, who joins forces with 007 to uncover a media baron's evil plot to provoke a war between Britain and China. As far as post–Cold War Russia is concerned, Lisa Funnell and Klaus Dodds predict that the country, as an adversary of the West, "will continue to factor into the geopolitical landscape of the Bond films in the foreseeable future," especially in light of their recent military aggressions in Crimea, Ukraine, and Syria.[19]

The Anti-007 Movement and Inter-Korean Nationalism

In his review of *Die Another Day*, the *Village Voice*'s Michael Atkinson, one of the few Western critics to comment on the timeliness of revived Cold War politics, writes "A Cold War artifact that died with Sean Connery's hair follicles but refuses to get buried, James Bond returns, again, using North Korea as a convenient archvillain just as Bush II has."[20] Following the lead of Atkinson, Manohla Dargis of the *Los Angeles Times* states, "Timely—and as demographically savvy as ever—James Bond enters his new adventure off the coast of North Korea with some fast and furious surfing designed to show the 'XXX' generation that the 007 dude still has the stuff."[21] Across the Atlantic, Michael Gove of the *Times* likewise observes, "There had been speculation that in the latest production, as yet teasingly titled only *Bond20*, there were plans to incorporate an Osama bin Laden figure to maintain a contemporary feel. Questions of taste aside, the decision to locate much of the action in Korea . . . may come to seem wiser. As the US turns its attention from Central Asia to the world's other rogue states, the salience of the threat from Pyongyang will move up the news agenda."[22]

For all the critical discourse generated in the West, a vast majority of South Koreans as well as North Korean officials found the film neither timely nor geopolitically savvy but, rather, outright offensive and degrading. The first Korean to criticize *Die Another Day*'s representation of the two Koreas was Ch'a In-p'yo, a television idol-turned-movie star. Ch'a was visiting Los Angeles for the location shooting of his romantic comedy, *Iron Palm* (2002), when he was contacted by MGM casting director Jane Jenkins and asked to audition for the role of *Die Another Day*'s Fu Manchu–like archvillain, Colonel Moon. Three weeks after his screen test, the Korean actor received a congratulatory email from one of the film's producers, Barbara Broccoli, informing him that director Tamahori had cast him for the role. Ch'a, however, demanded reading the entire screenplay before making a decision to appear in a film that heavily featured North Korea. Having read the script sent by MGM, the patriotic actor shocked his agent and MGM personnel by turning down the role, despite the prospect of a $500,000—$1 million contract, plus international stardom. Posting a message on his fan website in January 2002, he explained the reasons behind this decision:

> As expected, Hollywood was once again using another country's current climate for its own entertainment purposes. Especially when 007 arrived at the airport in Korea and went to the DMZ . . . there were no Korean military personnel present, and the US armed forces greeted 007. It seemed that the screenplay kept reminding the audience that North Korea was one of the most likely countries to commit acts of terrorism against the West . . . . I thought of a line of dialogue delivered by General Moon in the screenplay. When facing 007, he says "50 years ago, you people came uninvited and divided the Korean peninsula in two. After all that, what are you trying to teach us at this point?" The producers of 007 are creating the same situation as the dialogue written in their screenplay.[23]

A few days later the actor deleted his message from the website because it had stirred unexpected controversy. However, by that time his writing had been translated into English and sent to a 007 fan site by a Korean netizen, which resulted in the international circulation of a plot spoiler as well as eye-catching web headlines such as "The Man Who Said 'No' to Bond" and "Korean Actor Pulls Out of New 007 Film over 'Anti-Korean' Script."[24] As rumors of his patriotic conduct spread, Ch'a was hailed as a national hero by many South Koreans, from young netizens to veteran politicians including Roh Moo-hyun (who, before taking presidential office in 2003, enthusiastically lauded Ch'a as Korea's "new hope" in a National Assembly speech on February 5, 2002). Ch'a's manifestation of Korean nationalism (traditionally associated with anti-imperial agendas, whether anti-Japanese movements during the colonial period or anti-American student movements of the 1980s) through cultural resistance effectively set the tone of the anti-007 movement to follow.

Even months prior to *Die Another Day*'s theatrical release in South Korea (on December 31, 2002), thousands of netizens had already inundated cyberspace chatrooms and discussion boards with critical invectives against the film. Korean American actor Rick Yune, who had frequently appeared on Korean television commercials and had been popular enough to be invited as one of the 2002 World Cup announcers, suddenly morphed into an object of hatred and contempt for playing a monstrous North Korean villain in *Die Another Day*. The Korean Broadcasting System (KBS) even canceled plans to cast Yune in a morning program due to the public's negative reaction.[25] As the film's arrival in South Korea approached, from mid-December on netizens and civic groups began staging the "Do Not See 007" protest movement. On December 25, the Network for Reunification (T'ongil yŏndae), the main organization behind the nationwide boycott campaign, sent a letter to 20th Century-Fox Korea requesting the cancellation of the film's release in eleven major theaters in Seoul and its vicinity. The civil group reasoned, "This film not only portrays North Korea as cruel and belligerent but also hurts the national pride of South Koreans by depicting the United States and British intelligence as controllers of the war situation." Their request was ignored by the Korean branch of the Hollywood distributor, further fueling the antagonism of protestors.[26]

20th Century-Fox Korea considered delaying the film's December 2002 release until the anti-American feelings stirred by the candlelight protests subsided but decided to push through their original schedule, as the company "concluded that any delay would only embolden the movie's opponents." The distributor tried to decouple their film from its political context by insisting, "It's just a movie. It's meant to be entertaining and fun" and "Viewers must understand that it's fiction."[27] Protestors disagreed. In an interview with the *Los Angeles Times*, Chŏng Hae-gyu, a boycott organizer, complained, "Hollywood takes it for granted that 'good and mighty' America destroys 'evil and savage' Korea."[28] Doug E. Shin, a Los Angeles–based Korean American pastor on a visit to his homeland, opined in his interview with the *New York Times*, "I think there is plenty for Koreans to complain about in this movie. Half the North Koreans were speaking with South Korean accents. That ox looked like it was from the Philippines. That shack at the end looked like it was from Japan.

I guess the director didn't care. But if the movie was about Japan, would they have treated the Japanese that way?" Min Kyŏng-u, a twenty-eight-year-old pacifist picketer in Seoul, mused, "This is Hollywood's strategy toward Northeast Asia. The movie industry is related to politics."[29]

The expression of Korean nationalism through the boycotting of Hollywood blockbusters was not a new thing. When *Titanic* (1997) was released in South Korea in the wake of the IMF Crisis (a 1997 foreign currency crisis that resulted in a $57 billion International Monetary Fund bailout loan), many Korean audiences rejected the film and instead supported the Korean blockbuster *Shiri* (1999), which beat the box office record of not only *Titanic* but of all previous Korean films. Whereas *Titanic* boycotts were staged for the sake of boosting the economy, *Die Another Day* boycotts were motivated by national pride and political agendas. Slogans displayed by hundreds of protesters picketing theaters around the nation read, "Stop showing 007! Stop degrading Korean people!"; "No more war in Korea! No more secret agent in Korea!"; "Gone is 007, which depicts North Korea as an Axis of Evil!" and "Stop showing 007, which distorts the realty of the Korean peninsula!" Apparently, the "Do Not See 007" movement proved to be successful. By the third week of release, the number of theaters screening *Die Another Day* had precipitously dropped from 175 nationwide (40 in Seoul) to 27 (4 in Seoul).[30] The film was taken out of circulation after the first four weeks, and its total Korean box office record stopped short of 640,000 admissions (200,000 in Seoul).[31] This statistic is indeed meager for a Hollywood blockbuster of that size, considering the fact that some popular domestic films, such as the postmodern period piece *Untold Scandal* (*Sŭk'aendŭl*, 2003) and the Korean war epic *Tae Guk Gi: The Brotherhood of War* (*T'aegŭkki hwinallimyŏ*, 2004), reached the one million admission mark over the first weekend of their theatrical releases.

One notable aspect concerning the anti-007 movement is its inter-Korea implications. Such pun-intended newspaper headlines as "The Power of Film: A Bond That Unites Koreans" (*New York Times*, January 2, 2003) and "007 Movie Provides Bond between the Two Koreas" (*Los Angeles Times*, January 11, 2003) playfully describe the phenomenon. Following the lead of Ch'a In-pyo, protesters opposed the film on two grounds: for its portrayal of North Korea as part of the axis of evil, a country terrorizing the world with weapons of mass destruction; and its suggestion that South Korea is little more than a rural, occupied land controlled by U.S. military forces. As James Brooke of the *New York Times* reports, "The correct image of South Korea, people say, is a nation with among the world's highest rates of cellphone ownership, high-speed internet access and college-educated youth. Then there is a scene where an American officer orders a South Korea military mobilization, which prompted someone to write in an Internet chat room that 'Korea in the movie is viewed as America's colony.'"[32]

The implausible storyline of *Die Another Day* can be summarized as follows: Brosnan's James Bond infiltrates North Korea to assassinate Colonel Moon (Will Yun Lee), the son of an influential North Korean general and a graduate of Oxford and Harvard who harbors ambitions of reuniting Korea by force as well as conquering Japan and its Western allies. During the pre-credit fight sequence, Colonel Moon is presumed to die, as he tumbles down a waterfall and disappears into the rapids following his pursuit of Bond. After being captured and tortured by North Koreans, our hero is released fourteen months later, in exchange for Zao (Rick Yune), Moon's right-hand man who had been imprisoned on the sunnier side of the Demilitarized Zone. Eventually, Bond follows Zao to Cuba to uncover the identity of an informer whose betrayal contributed to the failure of his mission in North Korea. On the reclusive isle of Los Oganos, Bond finds Zao undergoing a DNA replacement operation, which will enable him to racially transform himself into a Caucasian. The painstaking procedure is interrupted as Bond infiltrates the clinic and attacks Zao, who—now in the form of a half-yellow, half-white, chrome-domed monster with diamonds engraved on his face—escapes. Zao's trail leads Bond to diamond king Gustav Graves (Toby Stephens), who turns out to be Colonel Moon in disguise. Having survived the deadly fall and changed his racial makeup in the Cuban "beauty parlor," Moon has been developing Icarus, a satellite-operated solar laser weapon, behind the mask of a wealthy entrepreneur/philanthropist knighted by the Queen. Joined by an American agent named Jinx (Halle Berry), Bond eliminates Moon/Graves and his cohorts Zao and Miranda Frost (Rosamund Pike)—the latter being the double spy responsible for Bond's capture—halting the outbreak of a second Korean War in the nick of the time.

The threat posed by North Korea in the film is double: both as a surviving if not thriving communist nation and as a terrorist nation. Red Scare iconography and tropes of the 1950s Korean War POW films are vividly recast during the credit sequence, in which Bond is shown being mercilessly tortured in ice water and being injected with scorpion venom by a North Korean brainwashing team. Although the cruelty of the torture sequence is toned down by its stylistic playfulness (digitized fire pixies and ice sprites careen across the screen to Madonna's propulsive title song), the allusion to POW trauma resulting from the Korean War is too obvious to miss. This striking sequence emphatically evokes the memory of *Prisoner of War* (1954), *The Bamboo Prison* (1954), *The Rack* (1956), *The Manchurian Candidate* (1962), and other films that (as discussed in the previous chapter) explore the theme of POW brainwashing during the Korean War. In *Die Another Day*, James Bond undergoes an experience not unlike that faced by Korean War POWs: upon his release from North Korea through a prisoner exchange, the British spy gets the cold shoulder from his reprimanding boss M (Judi Dench)—who suspects his collaboration in the communist execution of a top American agent—and is deprived of his

FIG. 4.1 The gruesome torture scene of Lee Tamahori's *Die Another Day* (Metro-Goldwyn-Mayer, 2002) evokes images of Korean War POW brainwashing films from the 1950s and 1960s.

triple-digit license to kill. Cruelly telling James Bond "You're no use to anyone now," M orders his transportation to the "reevaluation center." To clear his name through an independent operation, Bond attempts to escape the clinic on a British intelligence ship, where he has been administered treatment for detoxification. A nightmarish memory of North Korean torture returns in a black-and-white montage, as Bond controls his mind to reduce his heartbeat so as to snare the medical team into an emergency alarm and set himself loose during the chaos. This breakout signals the recuperation of a familiar Bond image, that of a debonair, confident super hero—an antithesis to the beaten, discarded, and vulnerable ex-POW.

Seemingly anomalous past images of North Korean atrocities directed toward this cinematically idealized male body—a locus of Anglo-European masculinity for the past six decades—signify the return of repressed anxieties lurking beneath the Western male psyche. In this sense, *Die Another Day* is an uncanny postmodern text in which anachronistic Cold War paranoia is repackaged in state-of-the-art accouterments and ideologically retrofitted for the twenty-first century. In the specific post-9/11 cultural context, the menace of North Korea (as construed by the White House and the Pentagon) exists not simply for its persistent adherence to Stalinist communism and vehement anti-Americanism, but also for its possession of biological, chemical, and nuclear weapons that might be used for blackmailing the Western world or could be sold to terrorist groups such as Al-Qaeda. The production of *Die Another Day* was launched in January 2002, concurrently with Bush's "axis of evil" speech and North Korea's withdrawal from the Nuclear Nonproliferation Treaty, which intensified tensions between the two countries and virtually nullified diplomatic rapprochement achieved by the 1994 U.S.–North Korea Agreed Framework. The timing of the film's release was even more opportune and arrived at the height of the North Korean nuclear crisis, which has since become a regular topic for international news carriers.

While Western critics were busy reading the film's political allegory, Korean audiences were emotionally invested in their own agendas. *Die Another Day* was produced and distributed at a time when Korean nationalism was at an all-time high in the wake of the Kim Dae-jung government's Sunshine policy with Pyongyang, the national euphoria over the miraculous performance of the South Korean soccer team in the 2002 World Cup finals, and the growing civic discontent with the Bush administration's rightist inter-Korea policy. Moreover, this explosion of nationalistic rage occurred after two fourteen-year-old Korean schoolgirls, Sin Hyŏ-sun and Sim Mi-sŏn, had been killed by a U.S. military armored vehicle on June 13, 2002. After being acquitted of all charges (including negligent homicide) in a U.S. military court on November 20, 2002, the two American soldiers responsible, sergeants Mark Walker and Fernando Nino, were hurriedly sent back home. This incident provoked Koreans to release pent-up anger against U.S. military domination, so tainted was it with numerous ignored, unpunished cases of American soldiers' violence against Korean civilians.[33] In a manner reminiscent of the Occupy Wall Street movement initiated by the Canadian anti-consumerist group Adbusters' social media call for camp protests on Wall Street on September 17, 2011, the leaderless, horizontal vigil movement started as an unorganized, spontaneous response to an anonymous netizen's call that went viral: "Let's fill the Kwanghwamun Square [at the heart of downtown Seoul] with candles that symbolize the two dead girls' spirits on November 30, 2001." Nobody expected that tens of thousands of ordinary citizens (from children to the geriatric set) would answer the call and flock to the square with candles, protesting the unjust verdict and demanding Bush's official apology as well as a revision of the unequal U.S.-ROK Status of Forces Agreement (SOFA), which delimits the Korean government's rights to prosecute American soldiers' crimes.[34] As Jiyeon Kang points out, "vigils, which initially simply appeared to be impulsive gatherings of young Koreans, soon escalated into veritable political campaigns, demanding the withdrawal of US troops from South Korea and the election of President Roh Moo-hyun [a human rights lawyer-turned-progressive politician] in December 2002."[35]

Die Another Day thus arrived in South Korea when the anti-American sentiment was at its peak. The anti-007 movement became integrated into the widespread anti-American movement, which included not only the biggest street demonstrations of its kind since the 1980s student movement era but also everyday consumer boycotts of U.S. products such as McDonald's hamburgers and Coca-Cola. In other words, the Korean reception of *Die Another Day* became politicized exactly because of realpolitik tensions surrounding South Korea, North Korea, and the United States. Considering this particular sociopolitical context, it is not difficult to comprehend why Korean audiences directed their anger toward *Die Another Day*, which depicts the containment of a second Korean War through the alliance of British and American super agents, Bond and Jinx. Whereas North Koreans are depicted as belligerent evildoers armed with ultramodern weapons, South Koreans are shown to be disempowered bystanders whose military police forces are like puppets acting under U.S. jurisdiction.

One of the most controversial images are fleeting shots of dumbfounded farmers standing in a rice paddy where two Italian sports cars have dropped headlong from the sky, like lawn darts, during Bond's airborne confrontation with the villain. As a visual gag dependent upon the jarring juxtaposition of a candy-apple-red Lamborghini and an anachronistic ox plow (as opposed to more plausible, less backward agricultural equipment, such as a tractor), this Third World image appeared condescending to a majority of South Korean intellectuals and activists; few of them could regard the film purely as an entertaining spectacle or fantasy when it contained a scene in which an American general barks out the order to "mobilize the South Korean troops" as a North Korean megalomaniac launches an attack across the DMZ. Derisive laughter and bitter feelings pervaded movie theaters when Bond and Jinx, dressed in South Korean civil reservist uniforms (standing in for camouflaged North Korean military uniforms), infiltrate the northern side of the DMZ to save the world.

Although Colonel Moon's ambition to reunite Korea through violence fails due to Western intervention, ironically, the film itself provided a communal ground for the two Koreas to solidify their cultural bonding. Criticizing the film's vilification of North Korea, South Korean boycotters and picketers in fact "spoke for" the North Korean public, who do not have access to American films. Likewise, when North Korean officials announced their own condemnation through the Central News Agency, they resorted to the rhetoric adopted by South Korean protesters: "The U.S. should stop at once the dirty and cursed burlesque . . . a deliberate and premeditated act of mocking at and insulting the Korean nation"; "The film represents the real intention of the U.S., keen on war." North Korea even borrowed Ronald Reagan's Cold War rhetoric, labeling the United States as "an empire of evil" that disseminates "abnormality, degeneration, violence and fin-de-siècle corrupt sex culture."[36] Dubbed "Dr. Evil" by *Newsweek*, notorious cinephile Kim Jong-il no doubt repressed his earlier-publicized attraction to the Bond series for the sake of inter-Korea cultural unity.[37]

It seems that anti-Americanism functioned as a common denominator between North Korean and South Korean criticisms of *Die Another Day*. One might ask, then, if it is accurate to assume that *Die Another Day* represents American ideologies; or, at the risk of sounding more perverse, if it is in fact an American film at all. As mentioned in the opening, although *Die*

FIG. 4.2 A Third World image of poor farmers and an ox plow angered many audiences in South Korea.

Another Day was financed and distributed by Hollywood studios (MGM and 20th Century-Fox), it is officially a U.K./U.S. coproduction involving a multicultural cast and creative personnel of different races, ethnicities, and nationalities (English, Irish British, New Zealanders, African Americans, Korean Americans, Hong Kong Chinese, and Mexicans). One British viewer complained, "What I don't understand is why the South Koreans are angry at the U.S. for the movie. U.S. Yanks had nothing to do with making it . . . a growing anti-U.S. sentiment [in South Korea] should have nothing to do with the movie. They should be upset at the portrayal of Koreans (which they are too)."[38]

Was South Korean resentment simply misdirected, as this homegrown Bond fan points out? Perhaps both Korean protesters and the British public missed the broader transcultural implications of the 007 series in general and of *Die Another Day* in particular. As Tony Bennett and Janet Wollacott argue in *Bond and Beyond: The Political Career of a Popular Hero*, "Bond can be read as a hero of the NATO [North Atlantic Treaty Organization] alliance. Acting in unison with either the American CIA (represented by Felix Leiter) or the French Deuxième Bureau (represented by René Mathis), Bond represents not just Britain . . . but the West in general, as the villain's conspiracy is usually directed against the West as a whole."[39] In *Die Another Day*, this NATO union between Britain and the United States is stressed through the romantic, professional, and multicultural partnership between Bond and Jinx. If the hero is a personification of the West (rather than specifically England), in the dialectical world of James Bond the villain is in turn an embodiment of the non-West or the East (symbolized by classic Oriental villains such as Dr. No and Oddjob or by the abstracted menace of Red China). Considering the transnational tang of the film's ideology and production, its Korean reception should be understood in a larger cultural context, outside of the United States/Korea dichotomy, involving the historical dynamics between global producers of Orientalist films and local audiences of (mis)represented cultures.

Refusing to "Die Another Day": The Asian Question in the Age of Globalization

Let us now consider a perhaps radical proposition: the anti-007 movement in South Korea is, by extension, an expression of Asian nationalism despite its geographical and political particularities. Significantly, the film's title was shortened from *Die Another Day* to *Another Day* for its South Korean release. This change might simply mean that 20th Century-Fox Korea deleted the negative word "die" from the film's Korean title in fear of upsetting audiences. In the film, James Bond kills Colonel Moon, the chief North Korean villain, not once but *twice*: in the pre-credit sequence (as Moon/Will Yun Lee) and the final duel (as Graves/Toby Stephens). After discovering the North Korean's cross-racial masquerade, Bond confidently tells his opponent, aiming a gun at him: "So you lived to die another day."

This line of dialogue provides a self-reflexive moment, since the death of Asian villains and victims has been a recurrent theme of American motion pictures and popular culture for the past century. Famed Chinese American star Anna May Wong once complained about her Hollywood career, "I was killed in virtually every picture in which I appeared. I died so often. Pathetic dying seemed to be the best thing I did."[40] In *Marginal Sights: Staging the Chinese in America*, James S. Moy likewise acknowledges this cultural phenomenon, stating that "both Fu Manchu and dragon-lady characters . . . would live on to die and die again, forever reinscribing the dangers of the Orient and miscegenation while spiraling through seemingly endless cycles of death."[41] As a quintessential white action hero and a guardian of Western imperialism, Bond once again interpellates the death of an Oriental (as opposed to a specifically Korean) villain.

Hence, the critical issue at stake here has a transnational and pan-Asian flavor. When Korean audiences reinterpret "die another day" (predetermined death of screen Asians) as "another day" (a time of cultural resistance), their counter-hegemonic spectatorship engages the concerns of Asian audiences of various ethnic extractions and from diverse cultures whose distinctions have been frequently blurred or ignored in North American films, television series, and stage plays. Thus, *Die Another Day* opens with a Pukch'ŏng coastal scene shot in Maui, Hawaii, while casting Hong Kong performer Kenneth Tsang as a North Korean general. Rick Yune's character Zao likewise bears cross-ethnic characteristics. "Zao" is clearly a Chinese name. In the Korean language, the "z" sound does not exist and the phonetic pronunciation of the name in Korean would be Cho. The mismatch between a Korean character and a Chinese name

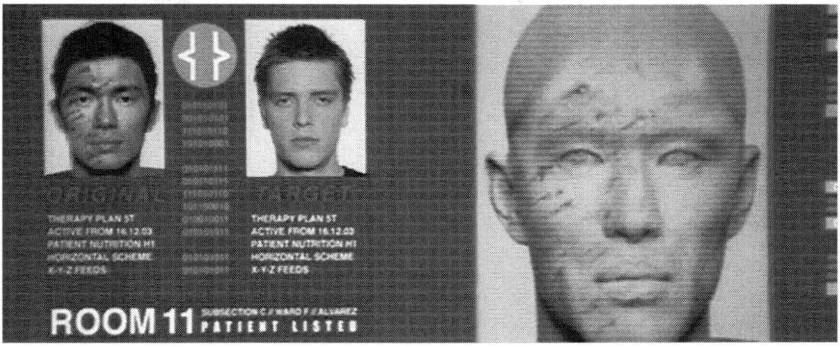

FIG. 4.3 Korean American actor Rick Yune plays a North Korean villain with the Chinese name Zao, whose racial identity is bleached through a DNA replacement operation.

attests to the historical interchangeability of two ethnicities in Hollywood films. The authenticity of Asian names seems to have been of little importance to mainstream producers and audiences alike, so long as they sounded foreign and were easy to remember. Some screen Asians do not even have names fitting their ethnic origin but are rather called by English nicknames (such as Dr. No and Oddjob, the latter parodied in Mike Myers's *Austin Powers* series as Random Task). Like his predecessor Dr. No, a half-Chinese, half-German villain of the first Bond film (played by white actor Joseph Wiseman in yellowface), Zao is a generic Oriental villain whose ethnic identity is bleached. Zao's ethnicity is further amalgamated through a DNA replacement operation, which aims to turn the North Korean into a German. When Bond interrupts the operation, Zao emerges as a bald, blue-eyed monster whose racial/ethnic affiliation is difficult to discern.

Not only are Chinese and Korean actors and appellations mixed, South Korea and Hong Kong constitute mirroring images as subjugated territories in *Die Another Day*. While American military commanders and intelligence agents are shown determining the fate of South Korea at a time of national crisis, Hong Kong appears to be floundering under the heels of British control despite the 1997 handover to mainland China. When Bond, faced with collaboration charges, flees from a British intelligence ship floating near the Hong Kong Harbor, he saunters right into a deluxe hotel filled with affluent Caucasian patrons. In spite of his haggard look and improper dress as an escapee, Bond self-assuredly demands "his usual suite" and all the luxuries (wine, food, clothing, and a masseuse) are instantly prepared and put at his disposal. The hotel manager, Chang (Ho Yi), is later disclosed as a Chinese intelligence agent, and Bond negotiates with him a means of tracking down Zao, who is hiding in Cuba. Although Chang initially resists the British encroachment in his city (declaring, "Hong Kong is our turf now"), he accepts Bond's proposal to retaliate against three Chinese agents' deaths at the hands of Zao, providing our hero faux travel documents. Even after Hong Kong reverted to the People's Republic of China in 1997 and became a Special Administration Region (SAR), where the capitalist system can be retained until 2047 under the "one country, two systems" policy, the Bond series still suggests Great Britain's spectral imperial presence in the former colony. Reminiscent of the *Queen Elizabeth* in *The Man with the Golden Gun*—a half-submerged, completely wrecked ocean liner whose cockeyed compartments contain the British secret service headquarters in Hong Kong—a British intelligence vessel prolongs its presence at the post-1997 Hong Kong port as a reminder of sustained Western influence over the region. *Die Another Day* seems to imply that the SIS (MI6) can reclaim its privileges in Hong Kong at any time despite the PRC's sovereignty.

The intercultural influx of filmic meanings is not exclusively confined to Korea, China, and Hong Kong. One of the remarkable aspects of the resistant forms of spectatorship emerging from *Die Another Day* is the awareness of regional or non-Western alliances. In fact, a number of Korean audiences critically reflected on the unthinking viewing experiences of other "villains" (Arabs, Latin Americans, and Eastern Europeans) in the past and realized the solidarity between "us" and "them." In a personal correspondence, cinephile Cho Mun-sŏn (who, at the time of my interview, was working in New York City) states, "It is an old story that so-called 'Third World' people have been stereotyped, by wholesale, as stupid terrorists in Hollywood films. However, this time I felt particularly disturbed because it was about our country. I am repenting now that I was not critical of other films which cast Latin America, the Middle East or Eastern Europe as villains."[42]

In his review of *Die Another Day* for *Cine 21* (a leading Korean film magazine), Chŏng Han-sŏk offers a similar sentiment, saying, "The pleasure we had for the films which featured Russian enemies and Middle Eastern conspiracies at once disappeared as the current political situations outweigh entertainment."[43] Another viewer, Pak Chŏng-yŏn (who, at the time of my interview, was doing graduate studies in Canada), compares her spectatorial position vis-à-vis *Die Another Day* to that of a Chinese audience watching *Dr. No*. A year prior to the former film's release, Pak had the chance to see *Dr. No* on video with a group of classmates, including a Chinese female student who disliked a scene involving a Chinese "dragon lady" (given the Japanese name Taro) who seduces Bond. Pak's friend complained that the actress (Zena Marshall) was not Chinese, did not speak a word of Chinese, and her costume was not authentic. At that time, Pak thought, "This is just a movie. Why is she so heated up?" When *Die Another Day* was theatrically released, Pak went to see the film with her classmates. This time, Pak could identify with the Chinese student and felt the same way about Korean misrepresentations.[44]

FIG. 4.4 Love, "Oriental" style: James Bond (left: Pierce Brosnan) and Jinx (right: Halle Berry) consummate their passion in a Buddhist temple supposedly located in Southeast Asia.

20th Century-Fox Korea's excuses in the face of mounting criticisms against *Die Another Day* further reinforce the pan-Asian coalition. In his report on the anti-007 movement, Chŏng Min-gyu of *OhMyNews* (a web-based alternative newspaper) quotes 20th Century Fox Korea's responses to two controversial scenes: one featuring the aforementioned farmers and the other the final lovemaking scene taking place in a temple. The distribution company maintained that there was no indication that either scene took place in South Korea, particularly drawing attention to the fact that the temple architecture was in Thai style. At the end of his article, Chŏng identifies *Die Another Day* as "a very peculiar, absurd film in which shabby-looking Asian farmers (whose ethnicity is presumed Korea but is nevertheless unclear) appear and a sex scene takes place in a temple allegedly located somewhere in Southeast Asia."[45] In an attempt to defend the film, the Korean arm of 20th Century-Fox admitted to its Orientalist foregrounding of exotic, Asian backdrops with no geographical and cultural specificity.

What needs to be stressed, however, is that Korean audiences did not protest the film's Orientalism per se rather but its ideological positioning of the West as good and Asia (North Korea in this particular case) as evil. In a sense, the film gestures toward the moral schisms if not mythos of Classical Hollywood Westerns, in which law and order are restored through the elimination or death of corrupt, malevolent forces. The "death" of Asia in *Die Another Day* furthermore has an uncanny link to 1930s melodramas such as *Shanghai Express* (1932), *The Bitter Tea of General Yen* (1933), and *The General Died at Dawn* (1936)—films that culminate with the demise of sinister and cruel Chinese warlords all played by white actors (just as British actor Toby Stephens takes over the role of Colonel Moon on the pretext of racial transformation in *Die Another Day*). As discussed in chapter 1, the Chinese government and people resisted the deaths of their screen surrogates, banning the abovementioned films and influencing Hollywood's representations of China through diplomatic pressure on the U.S. State Department. Despite a seventy-year gap between the Chinese protests of the 1930s and the South Korean anti-007 movement, their intercultural resemblance is indisputable. Their contexts, however, are radically different. The Chinese cultural resistance arose within specific national boundaries, involving both governmental representatives as main negotiators. The South Korean protests, on the other hand, were led by netizens, quickly gaining momentum with the power of the internet and new technology. The latter movement should thus be understood in a broader context of techno-globalization and networked public dissent that would spread around the world, from Tahrir Square to Zuccotti Park, a decade later.

Hollywood studios are no longer the self-sufficient, vertically integrated corporations they were in the 1930s and 1940s. Contemporary Hollywood has become increasingly global and transnational since the era of conglomeration (dating back to the mid-1960s). In 1989, two major Hollywood studios were sold to foreign companies: MGM to Pathé Communications of France and Columbia to Sony of Japan.[46] In 1990, the Japanese corporation Matsushita acquired MCA/Universal, which was subsequently resold to the Canadian company Seagram in 1995, and then to the French media conglomerate Vivendi in 2000, before General Electric bought the American studio back and merged it with NBC in 2003.[47] Global Hollywood maximizes its cost efficiency by outsourcing productions abroad and taking advantage of cheap cultural labor in China, the Czech Republic, India, Mexico, South Africa, Southeast Asia, and elsewhere. Despite Hollywood's domination of most of the movie markets throughout the world (from 40 to 60 percent, with the exception of India, where it accounts for roughly 10 percent of the annual total admissions), the U.S. government continuously strives to lift the protection policies of other film industries through trade pressures. South Korea, the tenth largest market for U.S. films at the time of *Die Another Day*'s release and now the fifth or sixth largest international market, is one of the few countries (along with France, Spain, Brazil, Pakistan, and China) to practice a screen quota system, under which the exhibition of domestic films for a certain number of days a year is guaranteed by law.[48]

In the wake of the pan-Asian financial meltdown of 1997 and the subsequent IMF supervision of the South Korean economy, Washington's pressure to abolish or reduce the Korean screen quota system only increased. In 2006, the South Korean government finally gave in and halved the Korean film screen quota (from 146 to 73 days), in the midst of fierce protests from the film industry and civic groups. During the same period, the Korean film industry has enjoyed an unprecedented boom, with pan-Asian blockbusters such as *Shiri*, *Joint Security Area* (*Kongdong gyŏngbi guyŏk*, 2000), *My Sassy Girl* (*Yŏpgijŏk kŭnyŏ*, 2001), *Friend* (*Ch'ingu*, 2001), *Silmido* (2004), and *Tae Guk Gi: The*

Brotherhood of War. South Korea is one of the few countries in the world where the market share of indigenous films has risen as high as nearly 60 percent (compared to 41 percent in France, 37 percent in Japan, 24 percent in the Czech Republic, 22 percent in Italy, 12 percent in Russia, 4 percent in Canada, and less than 1 percent in Taiwan).[49]

In this context, the anti-007 movement can be interpreted as cultural resistance not only in relation to stereotypical representations of Asia but also in response to Hollywood's global domination. The 1997 Asian currency crisis increased an awareness of the imperative of regional financial cooperation. In May 2000, officials from ten members of the Association of Southeast Asian Nations (ASEN), as well as China, Japan, and South Korea, met at the Asian Development Bank's annual meeting in Chiang Mai, Thailand, and agreed on a plan to prevent a future crisis similar to the one of 1997. Dubbed the Chiang Mai Initiative, the plan laid a blueprint for regional borrowing arrangements, an alternative to the West-dominated IMF system.[50] While Asian economists and politicians were devising plans to solidify regional integration, Asian audiences from China, Japan, and Southeast Asia shared their newfound love of *Hallyu* (Korean Wave) culture. Coined by the Chinese media in 1999, this neologism denotes the contemporary inter-Asia phenomenon in which Korean entertainers are idolized and Korean cultural products are consumed as never before, resulting in not only a wider circulation of South Korean films, television programs, popular songs, and fashion items across national borders but also the popularity of *Hallyu* tourism (the visiting of South Korea to tour location sites of movies or television shows and to catch new theatrical releases featuring *Hallyu* stars).[51]

The emergence of the Korean Wave as a major inter-Asian cultural force in the new millennium is all the more significant precisely because of South Korea's peripheral status throughout the prior century as a nation dominated by Japanese and American imperial influences. Some critics have argued that the popularity of Korean culture in Asia is partly attributed to anti-Japanese, anti-American sentiments shared by many politically minded Asians. As Youna Kim states, the regional popularity of the Korean Wave is "reflective of a region-wide reassertion or imaginary of Asianism, and a key site of decolonization work that may self-reflexively interrogate and unsettle the global hegemony of Euro-America."[52] This assertion may be valid to a degree, but not entirely, as the Korean Wave is primarily propelled by star appeal and consumer desire rather than politics. As Kim explains, "For many Asian audiences, things 'American' are dreams to be yearned for, but things 'Korean' are their 'accessible future,' examples to be emulated and commodities to be acquired."[53] However, one cannot deny that the phenomenon has contributed to enhancing cultural solidarity among peripheral nations without the mediation of hegemonic cultures. What further distinguishes this manifestation of the Korean Wave from the previous pan-Asian craze for Japanese and Hong Kong cultures in the 1980s and the 1990s, at least from the film industry's viewpoint, is South Korea's institutionalization of an organizational network to represent and promote its own as well as other Asian cinemas. Inaugurated in 1996 through public investments, the Busan International Film Festival (BIFF, formerly PIFF) has established a reputation among archivists and critics around the world for being the best venue to sample new Asian films. In 2003, BIFF announced its ambition to become "the heart of the Asian film industry," inviting non-Korean production companies to participate in international sales meetings. It aims to grow into a major marketing arm for Asian films, comparable to the American Film Market in Santa Monica and the Cannes Film Market. Its grand plan for regional cinematic coalition includes the Asian Cinema Fund program, which provides annual cash awards and in-kind services to support script development and postproduction of new projects by promising Asian filmmakers (Kiyoshi Kurosawa of Japan, Aditya Assarat of Thailand, and Murali Nair of India were among past recipients).

In a 2002 interview with *Harvard Asia Quarterly*, Hong Kong filmmaker Peter Chan anticipated a shift in the nexus of the Asian film industry. He states, "Hong Kong was the center of Asian film 15 years ago, when Hong Kong films were made all across Asia. But in the future I don't think this will be the case, because the Koreans are very strong."[54] Chan furthermore emphasizes the importance of a pan-Asian alliance in the film business:

> In terms of film, Asia can really be seen as a single domestic market, and the domestic market is critical for any film industry. In Hong Kong the market is only 6 million, which is too small to support even independent films. But if we add the population of Korea, which has 40 million; Thailand, which has 60 million; Japan, which has 150 million; Taiwan, which has 20 million; and Singapore, which has 3 million—the total population is around 300 million, which is even bigger than the U.S. domestic market. Hollywood films are successful because they have a strong domestic market, and they can produce a large volume of films. If Asian films have a larger domestic market, we can do exactly the same thing.[55]

Based on this calculation, one might even speculate that if the Korean film industry's momentum and leadership in the pan-Asian community continues, Hollywood's dominance in the region could diminish, to an extent, as it did in South Korea over the last two decades.

Foreign sales of Korean films have skyrocketed from $7 million in 2000 to $76 million in 2005. After witnessing a downturn (in the range of $14–$30 million) throughout the period from 2007 to 2015, Korean film exports bounced back at $44 million in 2016 thanks to the global popularity of such horror films as *Train to Busan* (*Pusanhaeng*, 2016) and *The Wailing* (*Koksŏng*, 2016).[56] The influence of Korean cinema is most decidedly felt and visible primarily within the Pacific Rim. In 2005, 87 percent of the export sales were made to Asian countries. In 2016, they were reduced to 63 percent, partly due to the expansion of the North American market to 30 percent (as opposed to 8 percent ten years earlier). With $9 million in sales, the United States topped the list of Korean film importers in 2016 for the first time, thanks to digital distribution deals with such online content providers as Netflix and Hulu.[57] Taking notice of the growing popularity of Korean cinema, Hollywood has also made a move to cash in on that success not only through cross-cultural adaptations (such as *The Lake House* [2007], *Mirrors* [2008], *My Sassy Girl* [2008], *The Uninvited* [2009], and *Oldboy* [2013]) but also through direct investments in local productions. In 2010, 20th Century-Fox opened a local production branch in Seoul (Fox International Productions Korea) and made several commercially successful Korean-language films, including *The Yellow Sea* (*Hwanghae*, 2010), *Running Man* (2013), *Slow Video* (2014), *Intimate Enemies* (*Na ŭi chŏlch'in akdangdŭl*, 2015), and *The Wailing*.[58] Warner Bros. followed suit and opened its production shop in 2016, eventually debuted their first Korean-language project *The Age of Shadows* (*Miljŏng*, 2017), a $57 million smash hit about the Korean resistance movement in the 1920s.[59]

Neoliberalists and internationalists might not welcome the revival of macro-nationalism in Asia. After all, it is not unlike the rhetoric adopted by Japanese colonialists in the first half of the twentieth century to justify the occupation of Taiwan, Korea, Manchuria, the Philippines, and other territories on the pretext of protecting Asia from Western domination. Like other types of nationalisms, macro-nationalism is a precarious concept carrying the potential to be misused as an excuse for such political agendas as colonialism, discrimination, ethnocentrism, xenophobia, and bigotry. The lessons of the anti-007 movement and the Korean Wave at the same time suggest possibilities of resistance to the hegemony of Hollywood. Granting the fact that today's global Hollywood is a composite of capital networks and talents from different nations, races, and cultures (as proven in the case of the 007 series), it anachronistically perpetuates Cold War yellowphobia through an allegorical tale featuring the Asian other/enemy taking over the appearance of the white self/hero. Embracing multiculturalism in its depiction of an interracial romance, this twenty-first century James Bond film—like its predecessors foregrounding Red China—nevertheless divulges abiding anxieties about racial and ideological others threatening to infiltrate the self mentally (via brainwashing) as well as physically (via surgical transformation).[60]

As Snyder rightly points out, the driving force behind pan-Asianism has historically been anti-colonialism since the late nineteenth century.[61] Anti-colonialism in Asia has been double-edged: against external (Western) and internal (Japanese) forces. Despite the official decolonization of Asian nations after the end of World War II, neocolonialism and imperialism still run rampant in the region, masked behind the somewhat friendlier, if abstracted, facades of transnational corporations, global capitalism, the IMF, and the World Trade Organization. As many critics point out, globalization is often a mere disguise for Americanization. Perhaps this equation is particularly true in the case of global Hollywood and its quest to lift local film industries' protection policies through economic and diplomatic pressures of the U.S. government, the single world superpower in the post–Cold War era. South Korea's anti-007 movement is symptomatic of Hollywood's failure to fathom and respond to the complex geopolitics of local markets despite its near monopolistic status as the largest global supplier. In fact, the international market has always been important to Hollywood's survival ever since its ascendancy in the world arena in the wake of World War I, when the heyday of French and Italian silent films was beginning to wane. However, its attempt to incorporate "local flavors," evidenced in the 1930s "China warlord" films or the 1940s Good Neighbor policy films, only aggravated Chinese and Latin American audiences because of their stereotypical ethnic representations. The *Die Another Day* phenomenon demonstrates that situations have not improved much in contemporary Hollywood. What has changed, however, is the emergence of alternative local film industries, which can compete with Hollywood in both domestic and regional markets.

In a metaphoric sense, refusing to "die another day" connotes the ethos of a post–currency crisis Asia facing pressures of restructuring its indigenous economy systems and opening its markets on all fronts. The regional coalition has become a matter not of choice but of necessity for survival in competition against NATO and European Union nations. Perhaps it is this same imperative of the global age that compels one to read the anti-007 movement as a pan-Asian issue beyond the expression of Korean nationalism. For Hollywood executives and filmmakers, the Korean fiasco of *Die Another Day* should serve as a wake-up call. A lesson should be learned that "a Bond-movie tradition of using current events and latent foreign fears"[62] is a relic of the Cold War and needs to be modified to accommodate increasingly important overseas markets. As Toby Miller reminds us, several Bond movies throughout the franchise's history "have rocked the viewers' boats amid charges of racism and cultural insensitivity."[63] Consider, for instance, *You Only Live Twice* (1967), with Sean Connery's appropriation of Japanese language, costumes, and "ninja" martial arts; *Live and Let Die* (1973) with blaxploitation stereotypes and blackface makeup; and *Tomorrow Never Dies* with inauthentic "Vietnamese" settings staged in Thailand. After all, the figure of James Bond was created to represent regressive ideologies of the Cold War era such as "a sop to British imperial decline, a rear-guard response to the rise of feminism [and] a retrogressive colonial fantasy."[64] In the era of Donald Trump and nostalgia for the politically incorrect past, "making Bond great again" at the expense of racial minorities and foreign nationals may not be the safest political vehicle for Hollywood to be in the driver's seat of.

5

The Interview as a Twenty-First-Century *Great Dictator*?

Rethinking Film Regulation and Foreign Relations through the Sony Crisis

The recent scandal surrounding Sony Pictures Entertainment's *The Interview* (2014), Seth Rogen and Evan Goldberg's broad satire depicting the fictional assassination of current North Korean leader Kim Jong-un, highlights the often-overlooked relationship between Hollywood and Washington, as well as the complex correlation between representation and politics. North Korea's filing of official complaints with the United Nations, together with the Obama administration's strengthening of sanctions on the economically strapped country in response to the November 24, 2014, Sony hack,[1] are a testament to the fact that American motion pictures—especially those dealing with contentious, political subjects—continue to present challenges to today's international relations. On December 19, 2014, the Federal Bureau of Investigation (FBI) issued an announcement stating it "has enough information to conclude that the North Korean government was responsible for" the cyberattack on Sony Pictures Entertainment in late November, without releasing specific evidence.[2] Previously, a group called the "Guardians of Peace" claimed responsibility for the hack, which not only stole 100 terabytes of data (movies, emails, company secrets, personal information of employees, 47,000 social security numbers, celebrity data, etc.), but also destroyed the entertainment company's network system. The group also warned of 9/11-style attacks targeting theaters that screened *The Interview*. The North Korean government denied the FBI's allegation and demanded that "if the U.S. is to persistently insist that the hacking attack was made by the [Democratic People's Republic of Korea], the U.S. should produce evidence without fail, though belatedly." North Korea's National Defense Commission further identified Barack Obama as "the chief culprit who forced Sony Pictures Entertainment to 'indiscriminately distribute' *The Interview*" and made a racially offensive analogy between the United States president and "a monkey in a tropical forest" in describing the former's perceived recklessness.[3]

On December 17, 2014, after national theater chains including Carmike Cinemas, Landmark Theaters, and Regal dropped their bookings for security concerns, representatives for Sony Pictures announced the studio's cancellation of the Christmas release of *The Interview* and stated that there were no further plans to release the film in any format. Two days later, in a year-end press conference, President Obama admonished the studio's perceived cowardice, declaring, "We cannot have a society in which some dictator some place can start imposing censorship here in the United States." He added, "I wish they had spoken to me first. I would have told them do not get into a pattern in which you're intimidated by these kinds of criminal attacks."[4] Korean American academic Christine Hong refers to Obama as a "booster-in-chief" for *The Interview*, someone who gave an "invaluable presidential thumbs-up" for a film that can be seen as "government propaganda" against a U.S. enemy. She further points out an ulterior political motive on the part of the commander-in-chief for diverting media attention from the Central Intelligence Agency (CIA) torture reports to North Korea in his final press conference of 2014.[5] Obama's stance on free speech, whether genuine or calculated, was echoed by many commentators and bloggers, including Mark Davis, who stated, "Movie-goers can support Sony by lining up to see *The Interview*. And we should all stand together and resist the temptation of self-censorship out of fear that the cyber-minions of Kim—or Putin, or the Chinese Politburo—will reach into our computers and punish us."[6] Blamed by the president for making a "mistake" by setting a bad precedent, Sony reversed its decision, and, as a result, Rogen and Goldberg's lowbrow action-comedy/bromance lampooning North Korean head of state Kim Jung-un gained a limited theatrical release (300 small and independently owned theaters) and found an audience via digital on-demand platforms (such as Google Play, YouTube, and Xbox Video). Sony is estimated to have spent at least $74 million on *The Interview*'s production and marketing, but lost in excess of $30 million due to the film's limited distribution.[7] As Richard Klein, managing director of film and media advisory practice at McLarty Associates, assesses, the Sony hack became "an international crisis, the cyber-attack that put Americans' vulnerability on display, a free speech cause, an Oval Office gut-check, and a cautionary tale for the future of warfare" in the age of cyberterrorism.[8]

Ever since the United States Supreme Court granted First Amendment protection to motion pictures in 1952 with the *Miracle* decision (reversing its 1915 *Mutual v. Ohio* ruling that denied such protection), freedom of expression in film has been an intensely debated topic.[9] Perhaps it goes without saying that filmmakers in democratic countries *should* exercise their right to express their political and social views without fear of repercussion. However, interpreting the discourses surrounding *The Interview* solely as a threat to American civil liberties and constitutional rights turns a blind eye to the industry's long history of diplomatic negotiations and self-censorship for economic reasons (i.e., protecting Hollywood's prized foreign markets). It was Sony's prerogative, after undertaking a risk assessment, to green-light the Rogen-Goldberg project, which includes a graphic assassination scene in which the current head of the North Korean state is seen disintegrating into flames when his helicopter is hit by a missile launched by the fictional talk show host-turned-CIA henchman Dave Skylar (James Franco). Reportedly, the Department of Homeland Security warned the studio of the risk of retaliation in the summer of 2014, after *The Interview*'s trailer provoked a belligerent response from North Korea's Ministry of Foreign Affairs, which called the film "the most blatant act of terrorism and an act of war."[10]

North Korea is one of the few places in the world where American films are banned, and thus studios have no market concerns there. However, Sony's decision *not* to release *The Interview*—a film loaded with time-honored racial stereotypes, including modern-day variations of Fu Manchu and the Dragon Lady—in the Asia-Pacific region (save for Australia and New Zealand), amounted to the studio's admission of larger problems concerning racial representations.[11] Essentially, the company opted to forfeit four of the six most substantial and lucrative international motion pictures markets: China (first), Japan (second), India (fifth), and the Republic of Korea (sixth).[12] Sony Pictures learned the same lesson that American producers of the studio system era of the 1930s and 1940s had gleaned: that diplomatic crises (resulting from racial, ethnic, and national image–production) equate with loss of profits. From the South Korean anti-007 movement (directed against MGM-UA's *Die Another Day* [2002], which was deemed offensive to the Korean people and detrimental to inter-Korea relations), to North Korea's alleged cyberattack on Sony to stall the release of *The Interview*, recent backlashes and diplomatic crises raise questions about Hollywood's ability to accommodate foreign markets in an era when nearly 70 percent of the industry's box-office revenue comes from overseas markets.[13]

One of the unexpected outcomes of this fiasco is a renewed public interest in Charlie Chaplin's *The Great Dictator* (1940), a political satire about a Jewish barber who is mistaken for the titular autocrat, Adenoid Hynkel (a fictionalized version of Adolf Hitler). The film was released by United Artists, a distributor of independent productions cofounded by Chaplin along with D. W. Griffith, Mary Pickford, and Douglas Fairbanks years earlier (in 1919). In the wake of Sony's announcement of its decision to shelve *The Interview*, the Twitterverse was awash in posts comparing the two films and deploring Sony's failure to uphold the American tradition of free speech. Protest screenings of *The Great Dictator* took place in London, Rome, New York, Los Angeles, and San Francisco, organized by Secret Cinema (a charity-based film group), and were attended by more than 2,000 audiences.[14] Before rushing to the defense of free speech, one should be mindful that *The Great Dictator* was a product of careful negotiations between United Artists and the industry's internal censor, the Production Code Administration (PCA), which ensured that explicit references to the Nazis and their leader were eliminated from Chaplin's script. While reflecting the producer-director-writer's antifascist view, the project had to be reshaped to accommodate the Production Code's respect for foreign governments and nationals (Article Ten, "National Feelings") as well as the U.S. policy of isolation prior to the Pearl Harbor attack of December 7, 1941. Similarly, Sony Pictures' leaked internal documents suggest that the studio was pressured by its Tokyo headquarters to tone down *The Interview*'s representations in fear of potential diplomatic repercussions. Sony's CEO, Kazuo Hirai, personally gave orders to remove the parent company's logo from the film's promotional materials and credits. He also urged American studio executives to remove the gory assassination scene in which Kim Jong-un's face melts away in fire (which ended up being graphically modified to reduce its visceral effect). In addition, Sony pushed the release date of *The Interview* from October to December 2014 and digitally removed thousands of button portraits of Kim Jong-un and his father, Kim Jong-il, in a vain attempt to appease the North Koreans. Both *The Great Dictator* and *The Interview* underwent transformations in consideration of the political ramifications, and neither film was an expression of an unadulterated auteurist vision.

This chapter calls for a shift of the critical discourses surrounding the Sony crisis. Specifically, I wish to reframe this "threat" to American liberties and constitutional rights as a nodal point through which to address crises and complications in representing "others" in contemporary Hollywood productions. It is important to remember that Hollywood's primary goal has always been unrestrained access to global markets, not unrestrained expression on the part of motion picture artists. Sony Pictures preemptively gave up a lucrative market in Asia for *The Interview* even before North Korean threats. That, simply stated, is bad business. One of the lessons of the past, which Chaplin's *The Great*

Dictator so amply demonstrates, is not that filmmakers should be allowed to say anything they want but that Hollywood commercial cinema is a product of compromises between industrial regulatory responsibility and individual artistic freedom.

The Artist and the Dictator: Nazi Germany, the PCA, and Chaplin

In the closing moments of *The Great Dictator*, Charlie Chaplin delivers a message of peace to all of humanity, saying, "I'm sorry, but I don't want to be an emperor. That's not my business. I don't want to rule or conquer anyone. I should like to help everyone if possible; Jew, Gentile, black man, white. We all want to help one another. Human beings are like that. We want to live by each other's happiness, not by each other's misery." Theatrically released at a time when several Asian and European countries were engaged in warfare, this speech could not have been more timely and relevant. As the British-born comedian's first full talkie (*Modern Times* [1936] was his first sound film, but it lacked dialogue), *The Great Dictator* spoke eloquently against Hitler's dictatorship and advocated for the kind of tolerance that the world so desperately needed. In that sense, it was and remains one of the bravest personal statements about tyranny ever committed to celluloid. Chaplin's film generated a great deal of commentary at the time of its release, a period when the United States was still committed to a foreign policy of isolation. Although *The Great Dictator* was lavished with praise by many audiences before garnering four Oscar nominations and cracking the National Board of Review's Ten Best Films list of 1940, it was also criticized for being explicitly opposed to the Nazis' policy on Jews and for being too preachy, as in the above-quoted final speech. For example, Charles S. Aaronson of the *Motion Picture Daily* complained, "In [the concluding] sequence Chaplin plunges headlong into outright propaganda, deserting his medium of satirical expression."[15] Reviewers of the *Hollywood Reporter* also found it "hard to believe Charlie's closing speech [which] was a bit too tough to take as the curtain of a Chaplin picture."[16]

Since the end of World War I, the German government began to impose strict import restrictions on motion pictures, leading up to the 1925 establishment of the quota system, which stipulated that one foreign film could be imported for every German film produced during the previous year. In the revised 1932 quota law, an important provision (Article Fifteen) was added: "The allocation of permits could be refused for films, the producers of which, in spite of warnings issued by the competent German authorities, continue to distribute on the world film market films, the tendency or effect of which could be detrimental to German prestige."[17] Nazi Germany used Article Fifteen to regulate Hollywood's representation of Germany and Germans before the U.S.

entrance into World War II. In 1933, the new German consul Georg Gyssling, a Nazi Party member, arrived in Los Angeles and assumed the task of enforcing Article Fifteen by sending "warnings" to Hollywood studios regarding their film projects. One such warning was sent to Joseph I. Breen, the head of the PCA, in a letter dated October 31, 1938: "I see from a newspaper article under the caption of 'Charlie Chaplin will burlesque Hitler' that Mr. Chaplin will play in this film 'a defenseless little Jew, who is mistaken for a powerful dictator, while in the other role you will see him as the dictator himself.'" Continuing to quote the article, which states that "while naturally Hitler is not mentioned, it doesn't take any Solomon or Sherlock Holmes to see it is the führer, whom Chaplin is burlesquing," Consul Gyssling warned of "serious troubles and complications" should this report turn out to be true.[18]

Breen claimed no knowledge of such a film and forwarded the diplomat's letter to the Charlie Chaplin Film Corporation. On March 2, 1939, Secretary Brooke Wilkinson of the British Board of Film Censors also cabled the PCA chief to express a similar concern, reminding his American counterpart of the "stringent rule that the representation of any living personage without their written consent is disallowed on the screen."[19] Given the "delicacy of the situation," the British censor demanded that they "see [the] scenario before operations are commenced in [the] studio."[20] In his response to Wilkinson, dated March 13, 1939, Breen assured him that "Chaplin has no script and he has no fixed story in his mind. However, he has before him your cablegram and I think clearly understands what the situation is."[21] Pressure against *The Great Dictator* also came from American citizens who were concerned about U.S.-German relations. For example, Senator Robert Reynolds, a member of the Senate Foreign Relations Committee, forwarded to the PCA a letter from Walter McKenna of New Jersey, who wrote, "Regardless of how much we deplore the inhuman persecution of a minority race in foreign lands, [Chaplin as a resident alien] should not be permitted to use the United States as a background and sounding board in the proposed manner with the avowed purpose of stirring up further strife and recrimination between Germany and the United States Government."[22] Joseph Kennedy, then U.S. ambassador to Great Britain and an advocate for appeasement policy, visited Hollywood in 1940 following the release of *The Great Dictator* and reproached a roomful of studio moguls (many of whom were Jewish) for "pushing the United States into war against the Nazis" with their "anti-Hitler [and] anti-German propaganda."[23]

The PCA closely monitored Chaplin's production in accordance with the Production Code's "national feelings" provision and Germany's Article Fifteen, and no direct mention of Hitler, Mussolini, Nazi Germany, or Fascist Italy was allowed to be made therein. As a result, *The Great Dictator* is set in a fictional country, Tomania (standing in for Germany), the titular dictator is named Adenoid Hynkel (a caricature of Adolf Hitler), and his neighboring dictator in Bacteria (standing in for Italy) is named Benzino Napaloni (a caricature of Mussolini). As attested to by actor Jack Oakie, Chaplin took care not to make the film's characters sound too similar to their models: "Charlie originally planned to call me Benzino Gasoline but decided maybe that sounded a little too much like 'Benito Mussolini.' So now I am known as 'Benzino [Napaloni].'"[24] Not surprisingly, Chaplin's film was banned in Germany, Italy, and their allied countries (Japan and Spain) as well as several neutral Latin American territories, including Argentina, Brazil, and Peru.[25] It was also banned in Chicago, a city with a sizable German population.[26] After the United States entered World War II, Chaplin voluntarily withdrew the film from circulation as the situation in both the European and Pacific theaters of war was becoming too tense for Americans to laugh about.

In his 1964 autobiography, Chaplin stated that he regretted making *The Great Dictator*. "Had I known of the actual horrors of the German concentration camps," the actor-director explained, "I could not have made *The Great Dictator*; I could not have made fun of the homicidal insanity of the Nazis."[27] In Kevin Brownlow and Michael Kloft's documentary *The Tramp and the Dictator* (2002), Gitta Senery, a Vienna-born biographer and journalist who, as a young girl, fled to France after the Nazi takeover of Austria in 1938, shares Chaplin's own reservation in hindsight: "When I was young, I thought it was funny... [Chaplin] is a great comic. Later I was politically so opposed to it. When I learned to understand what Hitler was, then I felt it was a terrible thing, to make a comic film about it, because he was a serious man and well, as we all know, a horribly dangerous man. And I think there are two things which are very dangerous: to associate humor with people like that and to diminish them. And both these things were done about Hitler, not just by Chaplin, but Chaplin was an important part of it because everybody saw that film."[28] Another interviewee, Arthur Schlesinger Jr., an American historian, disagrees: "I think there was some dissent, probably from isolationists who regarded this as war propaganda, and probably maybe from people who felt that Hitler was not an object of comedy, an appropriate object of comedy.... I think it is a remarkable film. Historically it was one of the earliest movies to express any kind of repugnance against Hitler and Nazism and it did so, it seems to me, with sublime artistry."[29]

In terms of its artistic and cultural significance, *The Interview*, which, according to Scott Foundas, is "a terror attack against comedy [and] cinematic waterboarding... to any audience with a limited tolerance for anal penetration jokes,"[30] is certainly no match for the legendary silent comedian's much-anticipated first talkie and the boldest political statement of his career. But there is another reason why the comparison between *The Great Dictator* and *The interview* is a questionable one. Simply put, contemporary North Korea, the most isolated country on earth, is no equal to wartime Germany, a military powerhouse in full expansionist mode at the time of the earlier film's theatrical release. As Adam Taylor explains in his article for the *Washington Post*:

> Nazi Germany didn't like Chaplin's film . . . . But ultimately, the Nazis didn't respond . . . . Germany's attention was elsewhere. It was already at war. The film was irrelevant in the broader scheme of things. For North Korea, however, *The Interview* may not be irrelevant. One thoughtful analysis of the current situation with Sony comes from Scott A. Snyder, a senior fellow for Korea studies at the Council on Foreign Relations, who points out that *The Interview* has come out at a time of unprecedented pressure from the international community for North Korea. The battle of perceptions, over Kim Jong Un's leadership and North Korea's human rights record, is North Korea's "war" right now.[31]

No matter how offensive and distasteful the film was for the Nazis (and for Nazi-sympathizers in other countries, including the United States), *The Great Dictator* did not capture Germany's attention in a time of war. In contrast, *The Interview* was of comparatively greater concern for the fragile North Korean government, whose primary goal has long been regime survival.[32] Sony's film provided an opportunity for Kim Jong-un's regime to flaunt its fiery, anti-American rhetoric to rally a disaffected population behind their young leader and the country's political ideology of *Juche* (self-reliance).[33]

"Kill Kim Jong-un": Sony's Crisis Management and the Limits of Responsible Entertainment

With the advent of the Motion Picture Association of America (MPAA)'s rating system, which replaced the PCA's regulatory schema in 1968, matters regarding foreign representations fell outside the purview of Hollywood's self-regulation. While the rating board (the Classification and Ratings Administration [CARA]) continued to regulate sex, profanity, and violence, the Code's respect for national feelings was not among the values inherited by the new system. As Kevin Sandler argues, "The MPAA, through CARA, was able to construct a new model of entertainment, what [can be called] 'responsible entertainment,' an industry standard that functioned much like 'harmless entertainment' during the Production Code. Responsible entertainment required, above all, a collective adherence and commitment by the major distributors and exhibitors to completely abandon the use of X/NC-17 rating product line."[34] This analysis makes it clear that the MPAA/CARA's priority was (and is) suppressing "aberrant sexuality" and sexual explicitness, not encouraging responsible representations of race, ethnicity, and nationality.

More importantly, while PCA regulation was concerned with a variety of compartmentalized constituents, both domestic and international (e.g., churches, women's clubs, civil rights organizations, foreign governments), CARA's focus zeroes in on the interests of a single umbrella group: American parents with children under the age of seventeen. In his memo to the rating board members, dated December 1988, CARA chairman Richard D. Heffner bluntly defines their mission:

> First, last, and always we must recognize the primary purpose of the rating system: to satisfy sufficiently *most* parents' needs in terms of their own youngsters' movie-going in order to avoid widespread pressure for the censorship that itself would be the bane of our free society.... So that the first and most basic question we must ask ourselves *about each film* we see is *not* just whether in it there is or isn't violence, or nudity, or sexuality, or harsh language, or drug content, or what-have-you, but *always*: in its entirety... what will *most* parents of children under 17 likely consider *this film's* most appropriate rating within the framework of our overall classification system ... remembering there's nothing inherently good, or bad, or indifferent about *any* of our ratings. G does *not* mean "Good," any more than R means "Rotten."[35]

In his oral history interviews with *Los Angeles Times* film critic Charles Champlin (conducted between 1995 and 1997), Heffner elaborates, "What does this rating board do when there is something that is offensive to homosexuals or to heterosexuals, or to blacks, or to Jews, or to Catholics, or to people who believe in abortion, to people who don't believe in abortion? We tried very hard not to let... those questions color our ratings beyond G to PG or PG-13. We certainly would never let it get us into the R, X, or NC-17 range."[36] It is notable that Heffner's short list of "special interest" groups (covering diverse categories such as sexual orientation, race, ethnicity, religion, and reproductive rights advocacy) excludes foreign audiences.

To fully understand why CARA's rating operations exclusively privilege domestic concerns of American parents, unlike its more internationally oriented predecessor (the PCA), one should be mindful that the organization was jointly established by the MPAA, the National Association of Theatre Owners (NATO), and the Independent Film Importers and Distributors Association (IFIDA). Since NATO's and IFIDA's concerns pertain only to the domestic film market, it is unsurprising that the content regarding foreign representations dropped off CARA's watch list. According to a survey of NATO members, the three types of movie content posing the biggest problems for exhibition in U.S. theaters are language (39.6 percent), sex (35.4 percent), and violence (30.7 percent).[37] Along with parental pressure, these priorities of American exhibitors understandably helped to shape CARA's regulatory policy.

Neglected by CARA's internal regulation, the MPAA's international constituents remain concerned about national prestige and ethnic/racial images, a matter of significance and sensitivity during the PCA era. For example, Thai censors' banning of both the 1956 Rogers and Hammerstein musical *The King and I* and its 1999 remake *Anna and the King* for their demeaning portrayals of revered nineteenth-century monarch King Mongkut (played by Russian-born Yul Brynner in the former film and Hong Kong star Chow Yun-fat in the latter) highlights the continued relevancy of national feelings in the contemporary period. Both 20th Century-Fox films are based on the memoirs of Anna Leonowens, an Indian-born British widow who worked as a governess for royal children in the Siamese (now Thai) court for five years in the 1860s. According to Leonowens's accounts, King Mongkut and his crown prince Chulaongkorn were greatly influenced by her teaching of Western democratic values and civility. At a press conference, Police Major General Prakat Sataman, the chairman of the nineteen-member National Film Board, explained, "After we viewed the [remake], the majority agreed to ban it because it makes jokes and insults the institution of our monarchy and distorts the facts. It will have a negative impact on the feelings of the people, who love their king."[38] Censorship board member Thepmontri Limpayom complained about an elephant-riding scene in which His Majesty looks and acts like a cowboy and another scene in which the king makes a culturally unacceptable mistake of pushing his crown and portrait down to the floor.[39] Another censor, Patamavadee Charuworn, opined, "Fox wanted to [distribute the film] because it is business. We call this cultural domination."[40] Isorn Pocmontri, a historian and researcher for the Foreign Ministry who served as an advisor to the censorship board, found it difficult to accept that the 1999 remake "portrays the court as rather senseless and subject to the influence of Mrs. Leonowens, and the independence of Siam [now Thailand] and the modernization that King Chulalongkorn subsequently effected derives from Mrs. Leonowens."[41]

It is perhaps too idealistic to expect historical authenticity in Hollywood epics, whether set in the American Wild West or in the Bangkok court. However, one should be mindful that the Thai banning of *Anna and the King* occurred less than twelve months after local environmental groups brought a civil lawsuit against the same studio for damaging the ecosystem of Maya Bay, part of Phi Phi Islands National Park, during the location shooting of *The Beach* (2000). In an attempt to create a fantasy tropical beach setting, 20th Century-Fox's production team bulldozed and relocated the bay's natural dunes in late 1998, which led to the collapse of damaged sand dunes in the region following the next monsoon.[42] Although the studio provided reparation in the form of a donation to the Royal Forestry Department and a joint campaign with the Tourism Authority of Thailand for tie-in promotion for the DiCaprio film and Thai tourism, the internet "was swamped by anti-Hollywood manifestos

(*Boycott The Beach*), both Thai and international, and the film became famous in every corner of the globe for all the wrong reasons."[43] Given this context, it is not difficult to see how the Thai film board's ruling on *Anna and the King* might have represented the general public sentiment against Hollywood's cultural arrogance, beyond the country's cult of the royal family.

Over the past decade and a half, several Hollywood productions concerning North Korean representations likewise drew controversy and negative responses in the regional market. As examined in the previous chapter, the twentieth installment of the James Bond franchise, MGM-UA's *Die Another Day*, generated protests in South Korea for what was perceived to be an insult to national pride and performed dismally at the Korean box office. Only two years after this incident, Paramount's marionette satire *Team America: World Police* (2004) cast North Koreans as arch villains once again. Producer/director/writer Trey Parker performed "yellow voice" in portraying the film's chief antagonist, Kim Jong-il, then head of the North Korean state, and adopted a mock Asian accent ("herro" translates as "hello," "Arec Barrwin" as "Alec Baldwin," and "I am ronery" as "I am lonely").[44] In this hyperbolic satire, the Dear Leader's evil plot to destroy the world with nuclear bombs is thwarted by the titular paramilitary unit. The Korean villain is spiked to death by a Bavarian helmet and is posthumously revealed to be an alien cockroach. As the critic Andy Klein puts it, "To say that Kim is mocked would be putting it mildly: He is portrayed as a half-height, roly-poly lunatic, with the temperament of Ernst Blofeld and an over-the-top 'Asian accent'.... Watching his scenes ... you nervously wonder what the odds are that Kim might actually see *Team America: World Police*. Would he be offended enough to start World War III?"[45] To Kim's credit, no war broke out, but North Koreans were offended enough to request (to no avail) that former Eastern Bloc countries such as the Czech Republic ban the film.[46] North Korea's southern neighbor was more receptive, however. *Team America* was never released in South Korean theaters, and even its DVD release was blocked by the Korea Media Rating Board (KMRB), which indefinitely deferred its rating decision, citing the film's satire of a real-life head of the state and its adverse effect on foreign relations as the reason.[47] This decision contrasts sharply with the nature of the film's trouble with CARA, which initially gave it the dreaded NC-17 rating (for a scene involving puppets' simulated oral sex) before lowering the rating to an R on the studio's tenth resubmission after recuts.[48] It is noteworthy that the KMRB, unlike the MPAA, includes "ideology, religion, customs, race, and nationality" on their list of rating classification standards, along with sexual explicitness, violence, language, horror, drugs, and imitative risks.[49]

Seth Rogen's earlier concept for *The Interview* revolves around the exploits of Kim Jong-il, whom the actor-director considers "the perfect villain, not just because of how unusual he was, but because no rational person would ever try to defend him."[50] Rogen and his production partner Goldberg pitched to Sony Pictures the story of Dave Skylar, a tabloid talk show host who gets an unlikely invitation from North Korea to interview their leader, and his buddy producer Aaron Rapaport (Rogen) who is recruited by the CIA to assassinate Kim Jong-il. When Kim Jong-il died of a heart attack in December 2011 and was succeeded by his Swiss-educated youngest son, Rogen and Goldberg found their new antagonist and renamed the project *Kill Kim Jong-un*. Sony liked the duo's pitch but was hesitant to green-light the use of North Korea and its leader by name. Reflecting this caveat, in earlier scripts, the character was called Kim Il-hwan instead of Kim Jong-un.[51] Rogen and Goldberg, however, felt that "backing down from having the dictator in the film be Kim Jong-il (and ultimately Kim Jong-un) seemed wrong.... That would be like saying, 'Don't make fun of Hitler because it'll piss off Hitler.' Because Hitler's power comes from people being too afraid of Hitler to stop Hitler from being such a Hitler."[52] They ended up persuading Sony Pictures CEO Michael Lynton and co-chairperson Amy Pascal to come on board and allow the naming of the real country and its incumbent ruler.

The problem is that, unlike *The Great Dictator*, which was the first Hollywood feature to openly address Hitler's persecution of Jews, *The Interview* is not a politically conscious film that offers daring social critique in the guise of comedy. As one filmmaker who has worked with Sony puts it, "Why is it necessary to name Kim Jong-un? . . . If you're doing a serious film it's one thing. But it's a fart movie."[53] The same sentiment is shared by Adrian Hong, who wrote in *The Atlantic*: "This film is not an act of courage. It is not a stand against totalitarianism, concentration camps, mass starvation, or state-sponsored terror. It is . . . simply a comedy . . . and intended, like most comedies, to make money and earn laughs. The movie would perhaps have been better off with a fictitious dictator and regime; instead, it appears to serve up the latest in a long line of cheap and sometimes racism-tinged jokes, stretching from *Team America: World Police* to ongoing sketches on *Saturday Night Live*."[54]

When the film's teaser trailer was released online on June 17, 2014, Kazuo Hirai, CEO of the parent Sony Corporation, saw it and became concerned about potential diplomatic repercussions. In one of the leaked Sony emails, Stephen Basil-Jones, executive vice president in Australia, New Zealand, and Northern Asia of Sony Pictures, notified his cohorts in Los Angeles: "Mr. Kaz Hirai, CEO, was very much concerned about this film especially when the Japanese government is negotiating with the North Korean government regarding the returning of the kidnapped Japanese to Japan and has spoken with Mr. Michael Lynton to consider how best Sony Pictures Entertainment LA Home Office could deal with the release especially for international markets."[55] Hirai gave orders to remove the parent company's logo from the film's promotional materials and credits and pressured Sony Pictures executives to remove

FIG. 5.1 Despite the Sony CEO's opposition, star and co-director Seth Rogen insisted that *The Interview* (Sony Pictures Entertainment, 2014) retain the graphic shot of Kim Jong-un (Randall Park)'s head "popping" in fire.

the gory assassination scene in which Kim Jong-un's face melts away in a slow-motion midair explosion. Goaded by his boss in Tokyo, Lynton wrote to Pascal, "We cannot be cute here. What we really want is no melting face and actually not seeing him die. A look of horror as the fire approaches is probably what we need."[56] Rogen, however, put up a fight to preserve what he deemed an "awesome shot" and eventually agreed to "reduce Kim's 'flaming hair by 50%,' cut 'three out of four of the face embers,' and alter 'the color of the head chunks to try to make them less gross."[57] Hirai approved new cuts with the understanding that the scene would be eliminated from overseas prints. On October 31, 2014, Nigel Clark of Sony Pictures Releasing International confirmed to his boss Steven O'Dell, "The U.S. version will have a rather comedic 'head-popping' scene when [Kim Jong-un] is killed . . . . This 'head-pop' will never be shown in an international version."[58]

Sony Pictures preemptively gave up the lucrative Asia market for *The Interview* as early as May 2014 (even before Tokyo headquarters' meddling began), when several internal memos started to circulate confirming that there were no release plans in the region. Preview copies were sent to Sony's Asian offices and negative local responses reaffirmed what had been suspected. Sun Yong Hwang (Hwang Sŏn-yong), managing director of Sony Pictures Releasing in Seoul, wrote to his counterparts in Culver City, recommending the film's suppression in South Korea: "It makes the North Korean head too much a caricature and strange North Korean accent is not acceptable to our audience. Also there would be a big potential to produce the political issue about North Korea as well."[59] Ken Yu, Hwang's counterpart in Taiwan, sent a similar report: "We've just watched *The Interview*, and to be very honest, we are a bit disappointed and don't think the film stands a chance in our market. The concept of *The Dictator* meeting *Argo* may sound fun, but probably due to culture difference, we don't find it entertaining at all. Not to mention our audience doesn't react well to jokes about foreign politics."[60] Robert Crockett, Sony Releasing's managing director in Singapore, Malaysia, and Indonesia, likewise expressed concerns about market sensitivity: "Singapore and Malaysia in particular have very stringent rules and regulations on discriminatory and racial inflammatory content and on those grounds alone without even considering the language or risqué content I believe the film will be banned."[61]

In contrast with the studio system–era filmmakers who consulted and were advised by diplomatic officials of foreign governments (through embassies in Washington, DC, and consulates in New York and Los Angeles), Sony sought independent, private experts to assess the risk of releasing *The Interview* after the so-called rogue nation issued a threat of a "merciless countermeasure" based on the film's trailer. Lynton turned to RAND Corporation, a nonprofit global policy think tank founded in 1948 to provide research and analysis to the United States military, and extensively consulted its North Korean specialist Bruce Bennett. The RAND expert in turn sought the advice of his associate in the State Department—Ambassador Robert King, a U.S. special envoy for North Korean human rights issues—and reported back to Lynton that "their office has apparently decided that this is typical North Korean bullying, likely without follow-up, but you never know with North Korea. Thus, he did not appear worried and clearly wanted to leave any decisions up to Sony."[62] Bennett also shared his own opinion about the film's ending, which depicts U.S.-induced regime change and reform in North Korea:

> I also thought a bunch more about the ending. I have to admit that the only resolution I can see to the North Korean nuclear and other threats is for the North Korean regime to eventually go away. In fact . . . I have been clear that the assassination of Kim Jong-un is the most likely path to a collapse of the North Korean government. Thus while toning down the ending may reduce the North Korean response, I believe that a story that talks about the removal of the Kim family regime and the creation of a new government by the North Korean people (well, at least the elites) will start some real thinking in South Korea and, I believe, in the North once the DVD leaks into the North (which it almost certainly will). So from a personal perspective, I would personally prefer to leave the ending alone. But that is clearly your call.[63]

King's and Bennett's dismissal of North Korean threats makes sense from a political standpoint. According to Van Jackson, "North Korean threats of violence against the United States and its South Korean ally have become so common and colorful that they are rarely taken seriously in the United States, more frequently serving as a source of fodder for late night comedians than a credible national security threat." Jackson goes on to explain, "North Korea's enduring willingness to engage in small-scale violence . . . has led US policy officials to dub this phenomenon a 'cycle of provocation.'" Repeated North Korean threats and militarized violence since the 1960s are not random or irrational; rather, they are "highly rational coercive signals intended to supplement its foreign policy."[64] North Korea's hostile and seemingly suicidal provocations against the United States should be understood in a broader historical context. The United States has long posed a nuclear threat to North Korea. Both General Douglas MacArthur and his successor, Matthew Ridgway, requested the authorization for the use of nuclear bombs against North Korea during the Korean War. In 1958, five years after the ceasefire, the United States deployed ground-based nuclear weapons to South Korea in violation of the armistice agreement. In the yearly "Team Spirit" joint training of U.S. and South Korean troops, nuclear warheads were flown by helicopter to the edge of the Demilitarized Zone (DMZ) as simulated war exercises.[65]

Although the United States withdrew its nuclear weapons from South Korea in 1991 and improved its relationship with Pyongyang during the Clinton years, the post-9/11 Bush doctrine of preemptive strikes against "rogue states" renewed the North Korean fear of U.S. nuclear attacks and forced regime change. As Samuel Kim points out, "Perceiving a clear and present danger based on the regime-change rhetoric and/or strategy of the new Bush administration . . . the DPRK did what most countries under similar circumstances would do: It reactivated its nuclear bargaining chip," which had served Pyongyang as a "potent and fungible instrument for negotiating regime security-cum-survival" throughout the 1990s.[66] Instead of understanding North Korean threats as defensive reactions to hawkish U.S. foreign policy, as pointed out by Roland Bleiker, "the West tends to project a very one-sided image of North Korea—one that sees it solely as an outlaw and thus a source of danger and instability."[67] *The Interview*'s irreverence for the North Korean government and for its incumbent leader, the likes of which is hard to imagine being directed at another sovereign nation even in the silliest Hollywood entertainment, is consonant with the post-9/11 U.S. policy for a handful of targeted "rogue states" (such as Iraq, Iran, North Korea, and Libya), defined by Robert Dujarric as "small or medium nations that have achieved some success in thwarting American policy."[68] As Alex Miles states, "The 'rogue state' label . . . is a distinctly American approach that led to worst-case scenario thinking about the regimes in question and encouraged the perception that they required containing, isolating, and . . . removal from power, rather than diplomatic engagement."[69]

It is unclear how much Bennett's political advice in favor of inducing North Korean regime change had an impact on Sony Pictures' decision to keep the "head-popping" scene in the U.S. version despite mounting pressure from Tokyo. It is more likely that Rogen's star power triumphed over the corporate will to play as safely as possible. As Peter Elkind wrote in *Fortune*, "Sony had final authority over the editing of the movie. But according to interviews and leaked emails, the studio feared that if it imposed its will, Rogen would disassociate himself from the film, creating a box-office and PR debacle."[70] In a desperate and ultimately failed attempt to mitigate North Korea offense, Sony Pictures invested $500,000 to digitally alter thousands of buttons worn by characters, in fear of provoking North Koreans for displaying actual portraits of their deified leaders.[71]

Sony Pictures' publicity machine was set in full motion to spin the crisis. On June 25, 2014, Jean Guerin, senior president of media relations, sent an internal studio memo and shared key talking points for filmmakers and executives in response to the recent news cycle about North Korea's condemnation of *The Interview*:

1 The film is, first and foremost, a comedy.
2 It's as much a skewering of the media and U.S. society as it is of current events or North Korea.
3 This is a different kind of movie for us. It's definitely an all-out comedy, but we wanted to make a movie that was more sophisticated and smarter.
4 Kim Jong-un is such a mysterious figure that he makes an ideal movie character—we could make him anything we wanted.[72]

The memo elaborated on the final talking point: "In the movie it's Kim Jong-un, but . . . *everybody* is also going to realize right away that it's a movie character—it's our hilarious imagination of Kim Jong-un. It had to be that way because *nobody* in the world knows much of anything about the real Kim. He's a 31-year-old guy . . . and he's this mysterious figure that we only see bits and pieces of. Well, that's a great start for a character!"[73] Apparently, Sony's talking points catered to the U.S. press and brushed off the film's potential offense not only to North Koreans but also to Asian audiences at large (as attested by local reports on preview copies). It is presumptuous to expect that "everybody" will accept Randall Park's margarita-loving, Katy Perry–lovestruck Kim Jong-un merely as a harmless movie character when filmmakers and the studio elected to use the real name of North Korea's current head of state. Nor is it accurate to say that "nobody in the world knows much anything about the real Kim" when the brutal executions of his reformist uncle and second most powerful man in North Korea, Jang Song-thaek (Chang Sŏng-t'aek), along with several of his relatives (elder sister, brother-in-law, nephew, and two grandnephews) in January 2014 shocked the world and made international headlines. *The Interview* was also preceded by a series of yellowfaced *Saturday Night Live* skits mocking Kim's despotism, debauchery, and odd friendship with former NBA star Dennis Rodman, who became the first American to visit the new North Korean leader in 2013.

Sony Pictures also prepared a "quick, decisive reactive statement" to counter North Korea's claim that *The Interview* is "an act of war." Two versions of their statement read: "*The Interview* is a fictionalized comedy that is not in any way related to current events" and "*The Interview* is a fictionalized comedy that is solely meant for entertainment purposes." In his email to studio executives, PR chief Charles Sipkins argued, "The North Koreans are using OUR film as bait. My only point in issuing the statement is to remind people that WE are simply making a comedy and are not in any way making a political statement."[74] Sony's disclaimer is reminiscent of a series of appeasement lip-service tactics that Hollywood studios offered to enraged foreign government officials and censors. For example, when Orientalist images of a backward, war-torn China in *The Bitter Tea of General Yen* (1933) provoked members of the National Board of Film Censors in Nanjing to threaten to suppress all future films of Columbia Pictures (incidentally, now Sony Pictures' sister company), the studio agreed to insert a prologue to deflect the situation: "[This] picture represents a mere literary fancy devised by its author, and it does not in any way pretend to depict actual conditions in the real life of China."[75]

Sony's statement contrasts sharply with United Artists' promotional copy in *The Great Dictator* press kit: "Many motion pictures, dealing with controversial subjects, prominently present to the audience the following information: 'The characters and events depicted in this photoplay are fictional. Any similarity to actual persons, living or dead, is purely coincidental.' You may be sure that no such information will be given the people who see Charlie Chaplin's new comedy, *The Great Dictator*. This picture was not made to please the dictators now current in many countries. It is, on the contrary, a devastatingly hilarious lampoon of two of them who have 'an axis to grind.'"[76] Ironically, Chaplin made up fake names for Nazi Germany, Fascist Italy, and their Axis leaders, but United Artists was upfront about their film's political relevancy in press material. Rogen and Goldberg used real names for North Korea and Kim Jong-un, but Sony refused to acknowledge responsibility for a diplomatic affront caused by this decision.

"Putting the Shoe on the Other Foot": Critical Views of *The Interview*

When Sony Pictures announced its decision to pull the controversial title off their release schedule indefinitely in December 2014, several readers of the *Los Angeles Times* sent their letters of opinion. Jennie Fahn of Los Angeles wrote, "I am not a conservative person. I love satire. But let's put the shoe on the other foot for a moment. Imagine if a major North Korean movie studio . . . created a film where there was a really funny plot to kill President Obama. Somehow, I think the CIA might be all over this. And a bunch of politicians would have their hairballs in a wad about the cultural insensitivity [and] the un-funniness of any mention of actually assassinating a real president." Diane Scholfield of Vista, California, pondered the international implications of such a plotline, stating, "It is long past time for the American film industry to realize its products have an immense influence on billions of people around the globe, and what tickles the funny bone of an American junior high student is taken literally in other cultures. The assassination of a world leader caused World War I. The suggestion that a sitting world leader be assassinated—even if it is not meant to be taken seriously—is far too provocative for a movie plot."[77]

A Korean American blogger and New Yorker named Maxine Builder, on the other hand, finds the film's sophomoric satire more forgivable than its racist representations of Asians:

> Most of the celebrity reaction to the movie's cancellation has been outrage and disappointment that the North Koreans "won" because the less than favorable treatment of their Dear Leader was ultimately censored. But many of the jokes in *The Interview* are at the expense of well-worn Asian stereotypes, and the movie's humor relies heavily on one-dimensional depictions of Asians that abound in American media that add little to the satire itself. As a Korean-American woman, I found the movie's orientalism more offensive than any satirical depiction of Kim Jong-un and the North Korean government. . . . Most of the Korean characters speak in clipped sentences with dropped articles like "the," with Rs and Ls reversed, that is typical of the generic Asian accent often heard in American media. What's particularly annoying is when the white male Americans drop in and out of this accent, sometimes to joke with each other, like when Aaron tells Dave, "You no Skylark. You secret agent."[78]

From a slightly different cultural perspective, Builder's offense is shared by Chu Sŏng-ha, a North Korean defector who is currently working as a journalist in South Korea. For his January 2015 review in *Weekly Donga*, Chu saw *The Interview* twice in order to provide a careful analysis from a perspective of both the North Korean government and its people. A few minutes into it, however, he realized that the film was not worth his effort. The former North Korean resident was bewildered and even amused by Hollywood's Pyongyang, where children are clothed in what appears to be Vietnamese traditional dress, Asian American actors speak barely comprehensible Korean dialogue, and ludicrous propaganda slogans (translated as "All Americans should be killed" and "Lift your hands toward Americans") are displayed on helicopters. According to Chu, if Sony's film were to be smuggled into North Korea to encourage rebellions against the Kim regime (for example, a North Korean defector sent 80,000 DVD copies by propaganda balloons across the sky of the DMZ in May 2015), its culturally ignorant caricature of all things North Korea might only

FIG. 5.2 Chu Sŏng-ha, a North Korean defector-turned-journalist in South Korea, was amused by Hollywood's Pyongyang where Asian American actors speak barely comprehensible Korean dialogue and where ludicrous propaganda slogans (translated as "All Americans should be killed" and "Lift your hands toward Americans") are displayed.

intensify the anti-American sentiment of North Korean people. *The Interview* could be used as a perfect tool for anti-American indoctrination as the film gives credence to the government's claim that American imperialists know no boundaries in their slandering and slighting of North Koreans. The defector journalist invites his South Korean readers to put themselves in the shoes of their North Korean brethren: "What if a Japanese film producer mocked the South Korean President to this degree and portrayed his assassination onscreen. Even those who hate the president will explode in anti-Japanese rage. It would be difficult to accept such an insult as 'freedom of expression.'" He goes on to argue, "Only the truth is needed to change North Korea. This type of childish mocking is not helpful at all."[79]

These audiences conjure up the kind of cultural sensitivity and respect for national feelings that is notably missing in Sony's internal correspondences regarding the crisis. But that sentiment was once a core part of American film regulation during the PCA era, even though it would be relegated to the background in CARA's principle of "responsible entertainment" catering to American parental concerns and the policing of X/NC-17 content. For this viewer, it is hard to see anything "responsible" in this satire, which uncritically depicts the longstanding U.S. policy of regime change. According to William Blum, since the end of World War II, the United States has "endeavored to overthrow more than 50 foreign governments, most of which were democratically elected [and] attempted to assassinate more than 50 foreign leaders."[80] Most recently, this very policy was accountable for state collapses in Iraq, Libya, and Syria, destabilizing the entire region of the Middle East, and creating a political vacuum conducive to the rise of extremist terrorist groups such as ISIS.[81] As Sony's aforementioned "talking points" illustrate, humor might lie in the fact that Skylark and Rapaport

FIG. 5.3 As the "least qualified men on earth to pull off regime change," Dave Skylar (left: James Franco), a tabloid talk show host-turned-CIA henchman, and his buddy producer Aaron Rapaport (right: Seth Rogen) nevertheless know what is best for North Koreans.

FIG. 5.4 *The Interview* implicitly justifies U.S. foreign policy and the ethos of American exceptionalism by showcasing the positive effect of regime change, such as television news coverage of liberated North Korea's upcoming democratic elections.

"are maybe the least qualified men on earth to pull off regime change . . . and it turns out, they're perfect for the job, because they don't care about anybody—just their own success."[82] Putting aside its gentle mocking of regime changers, the film implicitly justifies U.S. foreign policy and the ethos of American exceptionalism by showcasing the positive effect of regime change (television news coverage of liberated North Korea's upcoming democratic elections as well as Rapaport's Skype communication with his North Korean sweetheart Sook [Diana Bang] in Pyongyang)—a transformation spearheaded by the "least qualified" Americans who somehow know what is best for North Koreans. *The Interview* forgets history and cheerleads post-9/11 America's arrogant foreign policy, which has pursued reckless, unilateral regime change in "rogue states" rather than a policy of engagement, diplomacy, and international consensus.

On June 12, 2018, a sight that few had ever expected to see captured the world's attention: the United States president Donald Trump and North Korea's "supreme leader" Kim Jong-un shook hands on Singapore's Sentosa island and posed in front of flashing cameras against a backdrop of alternating flags representing their nations, which have been technically at war since 1950. In a stunt dubbed by *Time* as "the riskiest show on earth" and "impulsive diplomacy,"[83] President Trump stunned foreign policy experts by offering the North Korean leader something that none of his predecessors had: respect and legitimacy on the world stage. Many political commentators are skeptical that this historic summit will lead to the "complete, verifiable, irreversible denuclearization" of the Korean peninsula, Washington's professed aim, in the foreseeable future. However, as evaluated by Victor Cha, former National Security Council director for Asia, "Mr. Trump's diplomacy, however unconventional, has pierced the isolation bubble of the North Korean leadership, which no previous president could do" and set the stage for future talks and negotiations on a lower level.[84] While watching the first U.S.–North Korean summit on television, I could not help but think about that closeup shot of Kim's face exploding in fire near the end of *The Interview*. To borrow the PCA's phrase cited in the opening of this book's Introduction, Sony's film is in hindsight a "serious embarrassment to our State Department" (now headed by Mike Pompeo, who, as the outgoing CIA chief, was sent as Trump's envoy to Pyongyang twice before the summit) as it makes efforts to engage in diplomatic dialogue with North Korea and work toward a peaceful resolution to the nuclear crisis. The film already seems anachronistic and irrelevant a mere four years after its release, especially in light of Trump and Pompeo's new policy toward North Korea.

This case study of *The Interview* demonstrates that Hollywood's "cautious and reductive approach, essentially designed to minimize international offense rather than maximize international appeal,"[85] has remained unchanged since the classical period. But it also reminds us that a single film can lead to damaging consequences. For its stateside defenders, *The Interview* is a light comedy whose expression should be protected under the United States Constitution; for the North Korean government, it is a grave foreign relations faux pas that warrants retaliatory reactions on the part of a much weaker power as a means of resisting a greater power's cultural domination. The case demonstrates that international crises could affect the interests of NATO members as well, since theaters could be as vulnerable to terrorist attacks as studio networks to cyber vandalism. More crises like *The Interview* could trigger the mass migration of "risky" studio films from multiplexes to video on demand (VOD) platforms.[86] Of course, the biggest casualty of such crises would be foreign markets. Few studio executives and industry insiders would deny that Hollywood's future is more dependent on foreign markets than it has ever been. For the sake of the industry's own financial well-being, not to mention its international prestige, serious consideration should be given to formulating a long-term, twenty-first-century policy that makes fundamental, *positive* changes in terms of curtailing racial and ethnic stereotypes and respecting the national feelings of overseas audiences.

Conclusion

Chinese Censors Return to Hollywood

The proverbial phrase "history repeats itself" comes to mind when thinking about the current state of Chinese censorship and Hollywood. There is an uncanny similarity between what went on in the early 1930s (as discussed in depth in chapter 1) and what is happening today. On November 7, 2016, the Chinese National People's Congress passed the Film Industry Promotion Law, the first national law coming out of the People's Republic of China to regulate its film industry (the 1930 Motion Picture Censorship Law was promogulated by the Republic of China, now Taiwan, before the founding of the PRC). The law, which took more than a decade to draft, went into effect on March 1, 2017. In China, unlike in most countries, there is no rating system, and film regulation is overseen by the State Administration of Press, Publication, Radio, Film, and Television (SAPPRFT), which issues release licenses for films that pass censorship.[1] Since the provisions of the Regulations on the Administration of Movies were issued by the State Council in 2001, film content has been regulated (cuts of objectionable scenes are ordered or, in severe cases, entire films are banned) in accordance with the following guidelines of prohibited subjects:

1. that which defies the basic principles determined by the Constitution;
2. that which endangers the unity of the nation, sovereignty or territorial integrity;
3. that which divulges secrets of the State, endangers national security or damages the honor or benefits of the State;

4 that which incites national hatred or discrimination, undermines the solidarity of nations, or infringes upon national customs and habits;
5 that which propagates evil cults or superstition;
6 that which disturbs the public order or destroys the public stability;
7 that which propagates obscenity, gambling, violence or instigates crimes;
8 that which insults or slanders others, or infringes upon the lawful rights and interests of others;
9 that which endangers public ethics or the fine folk cultural traditions;
10 other contents prohibited by laws, regulations or provisions of the State.[2]

As its title suggests, the new law aims to protect the Chinese film industry and liberalizes domestic regulation policy to a certain degree. For example, filmmakers no longer are required to submit complete scripts for preproduction review unless they deal with "sensitive topics, including China's national security, foreign relations, ethnic groups, religion, and military affairs."[3] Likewise abolished is a preproduction licensing system that had previously restricted independent filmmakers and small companies from entering the field. In terms of content regulation, the new rulebook reinforces and expands the above-cited taboo subject list. Article Sixteen stipulates that motion pictures must not contain:

1 violations of the basic principles of the Constitution, incitement of resistance to or undermining of implementation of the Constitution, laws, or administrative regulations;
2 endangerment of national unity, sovereignty or territorial integrity; leaking state secrets; endangering national security; harming national dignity, honor, or interests; advocating terrorism or extremism;
3 belittling exceptional ethnic cultural traditions, incitement of ethnic hatred or ethnic discrimination, violations of ethnic customs, distortion of ethnic history or ethnic historical figures, injuring ethnic sentiments or undermining ethnic unity;
4 [undermining] of national religious policy, advocating cults or superstitions;
5 endangerment of social morality, disturbing social order, undermining social stability; promoting pornography, gambling, drug use, violence, or terror; instigation of crimes or imparting criminal methods;
6 violations of the lawful rights and interests of minors or harming the physical and psychological health of minors;
7 insults [or] defamation of others or spreading others' private information and infringement of others' lawful rights and interests.[4]

Moreover, Articles Fourteen and Twenty-Two prohibit Chinese nationals and organizations from cooperating with foreign film companies in creating film content that is harmful to China's "dignity, honor, or interests" or might hurt its "[ethnic/national] feelings." Remarkably, the new law uses almost the exact same phrases chosen by Hollywood's Production Code (Article Ten) and the 1930 Chinese Motion Picture Law (Article Two) in suppressing similar content, as elaborated in chapter 1.[5]

Like its 1930 predecessor, China's new film industry law triggered a censorship scare across the Pacific, in Tinseltown. Under the telling headline "China Advances Film Industry Law, Cracks Down on 'Western' Values," the trade paper *Hollywood Reporter* essentially labeled the law "anti-Western": "much of the language surrounding the draft law concerns the 'moral integrity' of those engaged in the film industry and what the Chinese Communist Party calls 'core socialist values.' Throughout his four-year tenure, Chinese President Xi Jinping has pushed an unprecedented campaign to limit the influence of 'Western lifestyles' in China and to censor media that do not reflect the official Communist Party line. The discussion surrounding the new film law reflects these imperatives."[6] Leading up to the promulgation of this long-awaited law, American politicians and policy analysists joined the "freedom defense" bandwagon, collectively warning Hollywood about the price of appeasing Chinese censors for increased access to the world's largest movie market outside the United States. In the Motion Picture Association of America (MPAA)'s 2017 market analysis report, four out of the top five international markets were Asian: China tops the list with $7.9 billion ticket sales, followed by Japan with $2 billion, and India and South Korea with $1.6 billion each.[7] Not only is China the most important foreign market for the American entertainment industry for its size, but its protection quota on the number of annual foreign imports (increased from twenty to thirty-four in 2012, after a trade deal with the United States) incentivizes Hollywood studios to please the SAPPRFT in order to gain coveted spots.

In their October 2015 research report for the U.S.-China Security Review Commission, Sean O'Connor and Nicholas Armstrong list several examples of China's "chilling effects" on Hollywood:

> Ultimately, due to the limit on foreign films and the size of the market, U.S. filmmakers have significant motivation to work with Chinese regulators, even if they have to remove important scenes or themes from their movies to do so. For example, Chinese screenings of *Mission Impossible 3* omitted a scene showing clothes drying on a clothesline in Shanghai because it was not a positive portrayal of Shanghai, despite the fact that the film was partially shot in Shanghai, where many people do not own dryers. *Skyfall* had to remove a scene in which James Bond kills a Chinese security guard because Chinese

> regulators were unwilling to tolerate a Chinese citizen being killed by a foreigner. . . . The internal debates within film studios over how and when to alter a movie or script extend beyond the direct dictates of Chinese censors, however. U.S. filmmakers self-censor scenes, dialogue, images, and themes they fear will jeopardize their film's chance of receiving Chinese approval for import. During the production of the movie *Pixels*, content was eliminated prior to viewings by Chinese censors to forestall any objections, including a scene where the Great Wall is destroyed, references to an e-mail hack attributed to a "Communist" source, and a connection between the movie's antagonists and the Chinese government. That this content was edited out of both the film's international and U.S. releases, partially as a result of concern over media backlash if two versions of the film—one for China and another for the rest of the world—were released, highlights China's encroaching influence in Hollywood.[8]

Other recent examples of direct and indirect Chinese censorship include postproduction digital alterations of invaders' military uniforms and flags from those of the PRC to the People's Democratic Republic of Korea (North Korea) in *Red Dawn* (2012); the cutting of thirteen minutes from *Men in Black 3* (2012) to eliminate scenes of aliens disguised as Chinese restaurant workers and Agent J (Will Smith)'s erasing Chinese bystanders' memories; a Chinese market-only inserted scene showing Chinese movie stars playing doctors who discuss surgery on the titular superhero in *Iron Man 3* (2013); the change of the zombie pandemic's origin from China to Russia in *World War Z* (2013); and the transformation of the Ancient One (Tilda Swinton)'s ethnicity from Tibetan to Celtic to avoid any reference to Tibet in *Doctor Strange* (2016).

This latter example in particular—suppression of the Tibetan theme—has been singled out as a kind of "bad censorship" that advocates of political freedom on American screens abhor. In his opinion piece for the *Washington Post* dated September 15, 2016, former Virginia congressman Frank Wolf states,

> By controlling the financing and distribution of American movies, and subjecting them to censorship to gain access to the Chinese market, Beijing could effectively dictate what is and isn't made—providing powerful control over America's greatest cultural exports . . . . One Chinese company, Dalian Wanda, has purchased the Hollywood movie studio Legendary Entertainment for $3.5 billion and is now seeking a 49 percent stake in Paramount Pictures, as well as purchases of America's two largest movie theater chains: AMC and Carmike Cinemas . . . . What will be the impact of state-controlled Chinese companies owning more of the Western media? Would movies like *Seven Years in Tibet* be put on ice for fear of offending major studio owners?[9]

The ex-lawmaker calls for a congressional intervention to investigate "authoritarian foreign ownership of U.S. media" in order to "keep the United States a place where people aren't afraid to challenge human rights and religious freedom abuses—in Tibet and beyond."[10]

In another opinion piece for the *Los Angeles Times*, published on October 7, 2016, Robert Daly, director of the Kissinger Institute on China and the United States at the Wilson Center, shares similar concerns:

> We no longer see movies like *Red Corner, Seven Years in Tibet* and *Kundun*, all of which were released in 1997, before China's box office became the force it is today. It's not that we need anti-Chinese or Yellow Peril fare. But Americans have always used movies to help them make sense of major challenges . . . . China is something new for filmmakers and the U.S. government—a nation of grave concern to us that we also want to sell to and cooperate with. If a free culture is essential to our national well-being, it matters that the U.S. is surrendering its ability to respond to this historic challenge through film. Congress is right to worry that Hollywood's global business model has implications for national security. The film industry needs to prove it is protecting creative freedom in the face of Chinese pressures and temptations, before the invitations arrive from Capitol Hill.[11]

To be clear, I agree that the Chinese government's mistreatment of dissident journalists, filmmakers, and bloggers and its brutal suppression of the Tibetan independence movement are reprehensible. However, the above opinion pieces simplistically characterize China's ownership of U.S. media corporations and censorship of Hollywood films for exhibition within its own territory as imposing authoritarian censorship on American culture and betraying the latter's democratic principles. This is akin to accusing local production companies owned or joint-ventured by American studios (Warner China Film HG Corp., Fox International Productions, etc.) of conspiring to sully their own motion pictures with U.S. government or corporate propaganda. Ironically, Daly acknowledges that Hollywood does not need "anti-Chinese or Yellow Peril fare," while neglecting to consider that collaborating with Chinese media professionals and regulators might be an opportunity for Hollywood to fix its century-old problems with Asian representations and better serve its biggest regional market (the Asia-Pacific region accounted for nearly 40 percent, or $16 billion, of the total global box office of $40.6 billion in 2017).[12] I have yet to see an argument that successfully invalidates the common-sense demand of Chinese censors: not to harm China's "dignity, honor, or interests" or hurt its "ethnic/national feelings" in films intended for commercial exhibition in China.

If individual studios want to say no to censors and forgo the Chinese market (or possibly, the entire Asian market, as Sony Pictures planned for *The Interview* [2014] months before the cyberattack), they are free to do so. But it does not make sense from a business angle, given what the above market statistics indicate. If free-speech advocates scold studios for making adjustments to their products in order to please international customers, they go against the core American principle of free enterprise on the premise of protecting another. To insist that foreign audiences should just relent in the face of Hollywood stereotypes—that they should just accept those images uncritically—because changing them would be an infringement on the freedom of American film producers is like telling potential car buyers that they should consent to whatever design or model available at their local dealership and not demand any customizations or improvements from auto manufacturers. Neither makes sense from the vantage of commerce and public relations.

Explaining the aforementioned controversial decision to change the ethnic identity of the Marvel sorcerer, *Doctor Strange*'s co-screenwriter C. Robert Cargill reasons in his interview with the *New York Times*, "The Ancient One was a racist stereotype who comes from a region of the world that is in a very weird political place. He originates from Tibet, so if you acknowledge that Tibet is a place and that he's Tibetan, you risk alienating one billion people." Beyond admitting the intention of appeasing the Chinese government and people, however, the writer puts a positive spin on British actress Swinton's casting as an originally Tibetan character, stating that "because the original character of the Ancient One was a racist stereotype, the role would be hard to pull off with modern sensibilities. . . . if a Tibetan had been cast, it would result in the stereotypical narrative of a white hero, Dr. Stephen Strange . . . being indoctrinated into Eastern mysticism."[13] Of course, one can counter this excuse and argue that Marvel Studios could have changed the character into a non-Tibetan Asian (Chinese, Japanese, Korean, Nepalese, or Vietnamese) without casting a white actress and sparking the "whitewashing" controversy.

Another key character transformation that has received far less attention is supporting Chinese character Wong, who was a manservant and sidekick to the neurosurgeon-turned-mystic-arts-master Strange in the original comics created by Stan Lee and Steve Ditko. The big screen version of this character, portrayed by Benedict Wong, is upgraded to a librarian-turned-master in Kamar-Taj, a secret Nepalese compound where Strange (Benedict Cumberbatch) is trained by the Ancient One, and joins forces with the hero in protecting the Hong Kong Sanctum from the attacks of Kaecilius (Mads Mikkelsen), a former disciple gone rogue. In his interview with the *Hollywood Reporter*, another screenwriter, Jon Spaihts, explains, "Wong—as rendered in the original comics—is so problematic that we weren't sure he was going to

FIG. C.1 Marvel Studios, a subsidiary of Disney, changed the ethnicity of the mythical sorcerer Ancient One (left: Tilda Swinton) from Tibetan to Celtic in order to avoid political trouble in the Chinese market for Scott Derrickson's *Doctor Strange* (2016).

make the cut. He needed to be more than a Man Friday to our hero. He needed to be a complex human being with power and agency and a presence of his own."[14] A lifelong Marvel comic fan and collector, the British actor Wong had always asked himself while watching Marvel films, "Where are super Asians? People are looking to be represented by their heroes," without realizing that he would be given a chance to depict the first Asian Marvel superhero on screen.[15] If one is to blame Chinese censorship for suppressing the Ancient One's Tibetan identity, by the same token its contribution (even if it was indirect) to pressuring studios to improve Asian characters like Wong should be acknowledged.

As we have seen through the various case studies mobilized throughout this book, film censorship is never an exercise of absolute repressive power by one party over another. It is a complex, discursive process of negotiations and compromises through which Hollywood studios modify, transform, and fine-tune their commodities to respond to various market demands and restrictions. This regulatory feedback structure is essential for the industry's long-term fiscal well-being, enabling it to achieve the primary goal of maximizing the market potential of their multimillion-dollar investments. Local production insiders based in China would be the first to inform us that there is ample room for flexibility in creating complex Chinese characters in negotiation with government regulators. In his interview with the *Daily Telegraph*, Robert Cain, a partner in Pacific Bridge Pictures specializing in Chinese productions, acknowledges that Chinese regulators want to see "a flattering image of Chinese people" but that "there is room for negotiation with the censors, particularly if a film is more nuanced and if there is a balance between good and bad Chinese characters." Dan Mintz, the head of DMG Entertainment, a Beijing production company, echoes this view, elaborating that "Chinese censors were sympathetic if characters were more nuanced" and that SAPPRFT regulation is not a problem when "you get to the level of making a thought-provoking film."[16]

As cited in chapter 1, Willys R. Peck, the American consul general in Nanjing who mediated many diplomatic crises between the Chinese government and studios throughout the 1930s, wrote to Frederick L. Herron, the foreign manager of the Motion Picture Producers and Distributors of America (MPPDA, now MPAA), in an advisory capacity on January 5, 1934. His letter states, "There is no advantage to be gained . . . in irritating Chinese public opinion. It is, of course, essential that scenario writers should retain their literary independence and not be compelled invariably to depict China as the one perfect country and all Chinese as free from fault, but a little attention to Chinese susceptibilities will probably bring worthwhile returns in avoiding annoyance."[17] The consular opinion was expressed when the Chinese market was miniscule compared with its European counterparts, and foreign markets as a whole accounted for only one-third of Hollywood's revenues (rather than two-thirds, as it is today). This lesson from the past cannot be more relevant at a time when China is about to surpass the United States as the world's largest movie market.[18]

Instead of adjusting to new challenges and demands of global markets in the twenty-first century, a substantial section of American society seems to be addled by the idea of a "foreign invasion" in a manner reminiscent of the mid-twentieth-century Joseph McCarthy–led Red Scare. On September 15, 2016, Representative Robert Pettinger of North Carolina and fifteen other lawmakers wrote a joint letter to the U.S. Government Accountability Office, informing Comptroller General Gene L. Dodaro that concerns "have been raised about Dalian Wanda's acquisition of major movie studios, including Legendary Entertainment and Paramount Studios, and the AMC and Carmike theatre chains due to growing concerns about China's efforts to censor topics and exert propaganda controls on American media." The concerned members of Congress further questioned, "Should the definition of national security be broadened to address concerns about propaganda and control of the media and 'soft power' institutions?"[19] In his interview with *Variety*, Representative Chris Smith of New Jersey, one of the letter authors, elaborates his position, stating, "We should worry that movies about Tibet will never again get made. Hollywood fought against the 'blacklist,' but will it accept without question the red-lining of scripts and content to show authoritarian China in the best possible light? It better not."[20] While I find Congressman Smith's concern for Tibet touching (and his reference to the blacklist ironic, as congressional HUAC hearings on Hollywood in 1947–1952 were responsible for the rise of the practice), I wonder why he and his colleagues do not raise the same question over Hollywood's silence about recent U.S. atrocities and war crimes (civilian killings, rapes, kidnappings, extrajudicial detention, torture, random "signature" drone strikes, targeted assassinations of "terrorists" including U.S. citizens and children, etc.) in Afghanistan, Iraq, Pakistan, Somalia, Yemen, and elsewhere. The expectation that Hollywood should tackle either topic—China's oppression of Tibetans or America's dirty wars in the Middle East (which are risky both commercially and politically)—seems to misconstrue the purpose and function of the entertainment industry in the United States.

Under increased public scrutiny of Hollywood's practice of making "China concessions," the MPAA's spokesperson Howard Gantman defended the industry, explaining, "The adjustment of some of our films for different world markets is a commercial reality, and we recognize China's right to determine what content enters their country. Overall, our members make films for global audiences and audience's tastes and demands evolve and our members respond to those changes. But we also stand for maximum creative rights for artists."[21] Although this cautious statement might sound like an obligatory public relations gesture to appease all parties, it succinctly encapsulates the regulatory dilemmas that have persisted in Hollywood over the past century. Balancing market pressures and creative freedom is indeed no easy feat. If history is a wellspring of inspiration, it is worth remembering that Hollywood reached its golden age in the 1930s and 1940s, not in spite of or against the Production Code Administration's self-regulation and external censorship, but by collaborating with various regulatory bodies in developing a sophisticated textual system that served audiences of all ages while capturing the hearts and minds of moviegoers around the world.

In *Movie-Made America: A Cultural History of American Movies*, Robert Sklar acknowledges the Production Code's positive contributions to American film history. He writes, "What is interesting to speculate about is not what the code prevented Hollywood from doing, but what it enabled it to do. If there was a golden age of Hollywood film production in the 1930s—the creation of a glamorous, appealing, mythical world of satisfying values in life and on the screen—it is important to know what role the Production Code played in its creation."[22] Similarly, in his study of video game regulation, Zach Saltz contends that the industry's guidelines protect artist creativity and prosperity through the maintenance of positive public relations and social respectability. The author goes on to state, "It may be ironic that defenders of sexual content, in their attempts to eliminate the ratings board mandate and forge an unregulated market of video game content, may actually be doing themselves more harm than good by eradicating the industry's credibility . . . . [T]he existing mechanism of video game ratings attempts to protect more than just underage users . . . in a roundabout way, it protects the very sexual content it ostensibly seeks to censor."[23] Saltz comes to this conclusion by comparing film and video game industries' regulation histories. Although the above-quoted passage focuses on sexual content, its insight can be applied to other areas of regulation including matters of race and nationality (for instance, Chinese/East Asian representations in twenty-first-century Hollywood). Perhaps "true freedom" is not, in the final analysis, an entitlement to offend one's biggest customers, but the privilege and opportunity to build new, better relationships with partners around the world while working together toward realizing the U.S. motion picture industry's dream of "correctly [portraying] the habits and customs of every country to the citizens of every other country"—a sentiment expressed nearly a full century ago (in 1927) by Hollywood's first public spokesman, MPPDA president Will H. Hays.[24]

Appendix

Thirteen Regulations on Film Censorship, the Republic of China's Ministry of the Interior, September 3, 1928

In recent years movie making has experienced a boom; film's impact on society is great and has influence and repercussions over social order and mores. Thus, film censorship is necessary in order to prevent negative social impact. This ministry has drafted the following regulations which should be enforced uniformly.

I. All films, whether domestically made or foreign imports, are prohibited from public screening without being reviewed and approved by this ministry. Documentaries are exempted, needing only approval from the head of the local public security bureau.

II. Upon applying for review, the applicant must provide an application form and three explanatory pamphlets of the film in question to the censorship institution. The application should have the following information: (1) the name and address of the applicant; (2) the title of the movie (if it is a foreign film, both the original and translated titles must be given); (3) the name of the producer and the number of cans of film.

III. If the applicant has met the above requirements and the contents of the film submitted for review are deemed not detrimental to the Nationalist Party's political doctrines, government apparatus, public order and social mores, a stamp of approval will be issued to such films. The approval should also be indicated on the three pamphlets submitted. A record of each case will be kept by the censoring committee and a duplicate of such record will be given to the applicant.

IV. Approval given from the interior ministry will be valid for three years; approval given by the local public security bureau will be valid for three months within this bureau's jurisdiction.

V. The censorship institution is authorized to limit the time and locations of the exhibition of films approved by the local security bureau when the situation requires it.

VI. Even if a film has been approved, the approval can still be revoked if it is found violating Article III of these regulations. In such case, the proprietor of such a film must turn in the film and pamphlets for removal of the approval stamps.

VII. If an approved film changes its title, the censorship institution should be informed. If the approved film changes its contents, it will have to re-apply for approval.

VIII. Censors and police must go to the movie houses for inspection. When doing so, they should have their ID cards with them and require the exhibitors to display the approved copy and pamphlets.

IX. In the event that the stamped film copy or pamphlets are worn out or lost, the proprietor must explain to the censorship institution and apply for re-issuing the approval stamp.

X. A penalty of thirty days in jail or a maximum 100 yuan fine will be imposed on anyone who (1) violates Article I of this regulation; (2) goes beyond the time limit justified by Articles IV and V, and does not meet the requirement of Article VI of this regulation; (3) fails to re-apply when the contents of the film are changed; (4) falsifies documentation.

XI. A maximum 50 yuan fine will be imposed on those who (1) fail to turn in the films and pamphlets whose exhibition permits have been revoked; (2) fail to inform the censorship institution of name-changing of approved films; (3) fail to co-operate with the inspecting officials.

XII. In the event that the violator of this regulation has not reached adulthood or does not have property, the penalty will be imposed on the person's legal guardian.

XIII. This regulation will be effective by January 1, 1929.

(Source: Zhiwei Xiao, "Film Censorship in China, 1927–1937," PhD diss., University of California, San Diego, 1994)

Sixteen Regulations on Film Exhibitions, the Republic of China's Ministries of Education and the Interior, April 17, 1929

I. All films, whether domestically made or foreign imports, have to be reviewed and approved based on the principles set forth in these regulations.

II. The following standards will apply to films: (1) no harm to the party's doctrine and the government apparatus; (2) no negative impact on social mores and order; (3) no advocacy of superstition and feudalistic ideology.

III. Film censorship should be conducted jointly by the civil bureau and education department of the provincial governments, or through the university officials in a college district. In special cities and counties film censorship should be conducted jointly by the local police department, social bureau and education department. The local party branch should be informed and send its representative to supervise such activities.

IV. For domestic films, the producers must submit a proposal to the local censorship committee for approval before production begins. The finished film, along with four explanatory pamphlets, is then subject to a formal review before release.

V. For foreign films, the distributor or proprietor must submit four application forms and explanatory pamphlets, a copy of the film and the comments made by the censors from its country of origin.

VI. The application should provide the following information: (1) the title of the film (if it is a foreign film, including both the original and translated title); (2) the number of cans and scenes of film; (3) the market value of the film; (4) the date and place of the production; (5) the names and addresses of the producer and actors; (6) the name and address of the applicant.

VII. If a film is deemed to have violated none of the standards set forth in Article II of this regulation, the censorship committee will issue a temporary permit for the film and a stamp on the film indicating the completion of the review. In addition, film censorship institutions in special cities should send the file of the film being reviewed to the Ministries of Education and the Interior for recording keeping. In other cities and counties, the local censorship institutions should send their decisions on each film, along with the original application and pamphlets to the Ministries of Education and the Interior via their local civil and education bureau; when such decisions are approved by the two ministries, the local censorship institutions can then issue an exhibition permit.

VIII. Each exhibition permit is valid for three years. When it expires, the proprietor should re-apply for approval.

IX. Upon approval, it is the exhibitor's responsibility to show the exhibition permit to the local censors; the local censorship institutions must send its people to the movie house to inspect the movie at least once.

X. If the approved film is found violating any of the provisions in Article II of this regulation, a ban will be imposed and a request will be sent to the two ministries to revoke the exhibition permit.

XI. When a proprietor changes the title of an approved film, he must inform the two ministries through local censorship institutions; if he changes the contents of the film, a new application must be submitted for re-review.

XII. Censorship institutions should send their members to movie theaters regularly; these certified inspectors are authorized to request the exhibitor to submit the copy of the film as well as the exhibition permit.

XIII. In the event the exhibition permit is worn out or lost, the proprietor should go to the censorship institution to apply for a new permit, with reasons clearly stated.

XIV. A maximum 50 yuan penalty will be imposed on producers and exhibitors if the above regulations are violated, or if their applications are found to have false statements.

XV. From the date of the implementation of these regulations, the previous thirteen regulations published by the Ministry of the Interior on September 3, 1928, will be null and void.

XVI. This regulation will become effective by July 1, 1929.

(Source: Zhiwei Xiao, "Film Censorship in China, 1927–1937," PhD diss., University of California, San Diego, 1994)

The Republic of China's Motion Picture Censorship Law, November 3, 1930

I. All motion picture films, either of domestic or foreign production, are not allowed to be shown unless they have passed censorship in accordance with this Law.

II. Motion Picture films will not be approved if they are:

1. Injurious to the dignity of Chinese people.
2. Contrary to the Three Principles of the People.
3. Detrimental to good morality or public order.
4. Promoting superstition or heterodoxy.

III. The censorship of films shall be done by a Motion Picture Censorship committee consisting of four members appointed by the Ministry of Education and three members appointed by the Ministry of the Interior. When films are censored by the Committee, the Propaganda Department of the Central Party Headquarters shall be requested to send representatives to participate in and to conduct the censoring.

IV. Holders of motion picture films, either of domestic or foreign production, shall, before such films are sold or shown, submit an application and a detailed explanation of the film, each in duplicate, together with the films to the Motion Picture Censorship Committee for examination.

V. The application shall contain the following information:

1. Title and synopsis of the film. If the film is foreign made, both the original title and its translation must be mentioned.
2. Numbers of reels and parts, and length.
3. Value of the film.
4. Month, year, and place made.
5. Names, addresses and brief biographical sketches of the maker and important actors.
6. Name, address and brief biographical sketch of the applicant.

VI. When the Motion Picture Censorship Committee, in censoring a film, considers that it does not contain any of the features mentioned in Article II above, a permit to show shall be issued.

VII. The permit to show motion picture shall be valid for a period of three years. Applicant for re-examination should be submitted at the time of expiration (of the permit). If a permit to show is destroyed or lost during the period of its validity, an application may be submitted for the issuance of a new permit.

VIII. Before a motion picture covered by a permit is shown, the party showing the film shall present the permit to the competent local educational organ for examination. No fee shall be collected. If a motion picture, when it is shown, is found to have gone beyond the limit with which approval was originally given, the competent local educational organ may, besides forbidding the showing, submit a petition to the Motion Picture Censorship Committee requesting cancellation of the permit.

IX. In case of change of title or synopsis of a motion picture covered by a permit, an application shall be submitted for reexamination in accordance with this Law.

X. The Motion Picture Censorship Committee may send officers, bringing with them certificates of censorship, to the places where pictures are shown for the purpose of investigation. The above mentioned officers may request the party showing the film to produce for examination the original film and permit.

XI. The applicant, or the party showing the film, who violates the provisions of this Law, shall be punished with a fine not more than 300 yuan.

XII. The Motion Picture Censorship Committee, in censoring films, shall charge as censorship fee 10 yuan for each 500 meters. Films less than 500 meters in length should be accounted for as 500 meters. Domestic made films may be exempt.

XIII. The Detailed Rules for Enforcement of the Motion Picture Censorship Law shall be enacted by the Executive Yuan.

XIV. This Law shall take effect from the date of promulgation.

(Source: Record Group 59, State Department files on China, box 7220, 893.4061 Motion Pictures, National Archives and Records Administration at College Park, MD)

Acknowledgments

The author wishes to thank several individuals and institutions whose many contributions to this project helped to bring it to fruition. The research at the heart of this book benefitted tremendously from travel grants provided by Colorado State University's Department of Communication Studies, which enabled me to visit several archives and libraries in Los Angeles, Washington, DC, and New York City. Special thanks go to Department Chair Dr. Greg Dickinson for his ongoing support of my archival research. I would also like to thank my graduate research assistants at CSU—Brad Kaye, Clarence Sanon, and Jordin Clark, who helped me to compile and organize historical and archival materials at various stages. I am grateful for the assistance provided by the reference librarians at the Margaret Herrick Library, the National Archives and Records Administration, Georgetown University Special Collections Research Center, and the Columbia University Oral History Archive. Particularly, I would like to acknowledge Jenny Romero and Marisa Duron, research archivists at Margaret Herrick Library, Scott S. Taylor, manuscript archivist of Georgetown University, and David A. Olson, oral history archivist of Columbia University Rare Book & Manuscript Library. Their assistance was vital in my gaining access to the Academy of Motion Picture Arts and Sciences' Special Collections, the Department of Defense Film Collection, and the Richard Heffner papers, respectively.

No one contributed more to this project than David Scott Diffrient, my partner and colleague, who watched all of this book's case study films with me, shared his thoughts and ideas, and significantly improved the entire manuscript with his editorial insights. My intellectual life and personal well-being depend greatly on him. My parents (Sang Ho Chung and Eunok Shim) and sister (Hyeuk Jung) in Seoul have supported me every step of the way through this and earlier book projects, and without their love I could not have come this far as a scholar. The final two years of writing this book were transformed by an addition to our family: Pepper Diffrient, a precocious baby girl whose joyous embrace of life (in all of its wonderful messiness) motivated my final sprint toward the finish line. I am deeply indebted to Pepper's dad, grandparents (Harry and Donna), and daycare teachers, who helped me focus by sharing childcare responsibilities.

Early, shorter versions of chapter 2 and chapter 4 were previously published as "From *Die Another Day* to 'Another Day': The South Korean Anti-007 Movement and Regional Nationalism in Post–Cold War Asia," *Spectator* 27, no. 2 (Fall 2007), 64–78; and "Hollywood Diplomacy and *The Purple Heart* (1944): Preserving Wartime Alliances through Film Regulation," *Historical Journal of Film, Radio and Television* 38, no. 3 (2018). The author wishes to thank *Spectator* guest editor Dr. Hyungsook Lee and *Historical Journal of Film, Radio and Television* editor Dr. James Chapman for their support. Last, but not least, I would like to acknowledge my editor, Lisa Banning of Rutgers University Press, for her faith in the project and effective editorial interventions throughout the long process of completing this manuscript.

Note: The Romanization of Korean names in chapters 4 and 5 follows the McCune-Reischauer system, which is the academic standard endorsed by the Library of Congress. Exceptions to this rule are city names and political figures whose spellings are known to English-speaking readers, such as Seoul, Busan, Pyongyang, Kim Il Sung, and Kim Dae-jung. Korean and other East Asian names appear in their native standard, with surname first (except for names printed otherwise in English-language publications). Finally, all quotations from Korean-language sources have been translated by the author.

Notes

Introduction

1 PCA chief Joseph I. Breen to Robert L. Lippert, October 16, 1950, *The Steel Helmet*, Production Code Administration (PCA) files, Margaret Herrick Library (MHL), Academy of Motion Picture Arts and Sciences (AMPAS). Before the founding of the Republic of Korea in 1948, "Auld Lang Syne" was indeed used as the melody for the national anthem of the exiled government (during the Japanese colonial period). The use of the Scottish song as the Korean anthem in *The Steel Helmet* is not historically accurate as the film is set in 1950.
2 "Memo for the Films Re: *The Steel Helmet*," October 17, 1950, ibid.
3 "Memo for the Films Re: *The Steel Helmet*," October 19, 1950, ibid.
4 Michel Foucault, *The History of Sexuality*, vol. 1, *An Introduction* (New York: Vintage Books, 1990), 92, 95.
5 Thomas Doherty, *Hollywood's Censor: Joseph I. Breen and the Production Code Administration* (New York: Columbia University Press, 2007), 109. Emphasis in original.
6 Ibid., 98.
7 Foucault, *The History of Sexuality*, 45.
8 Daniel Biltereyst and Roel Vande Winkel, eds., *Silencing Cinema: Film Censorship around the World* (New York: Palgrave MacMillan, 2013), 2.
9 Matthew Bernstein, ed., *Controlling Hollywood: Censorship and Regulation in the Studio Era* (New Brunswick, NJ: Rutgers University Press, 1999), 1–2.
10 Doherty, *Hollywood's Censor*, 8.
11 Clayton R. Koppes and Gregory D. Black, "Blacks, Loyalty, and Motion-Picture Propaganda in World War II," *Journal of American History* 73, no. 2 (September 1986): 400.
12 Ibid., 404.
13 Ellen C. Scott, "Black 'Censor,' White Liberties: Civil Rights and Illinois's 1917 Film Law," *American Quarterly* 64, no. 2 (June 2012): 219.
14 It took $100 million and a full year to repair Sony Pictures' computer network. "Despite Ongoing Attack, Trump Didn't Discuss North Korean Hacking at Summit with Kim," *Japan Times*, June 16, 2018, https://www.japantimes.co.jp

/news/2018/06/16/asia-pacific/despite-ongoing-threat-trump-didnt-discuss-north-korean-hacking-summit-kim/#.WzRaVExFw2w.

15 "Address Delivered by Will H. Hays, President of Motion Picture Producers & Distributors of America, Inc. before the Harvard School of Business at Harvard University," March 15, 1927, MPPDA Digital Archive, reel 3, record #330, 20, 22, https://mppda.flinders.edu.au/records/330.

Chapter 1 Censorship as Cultural Resistance

1 The other six were in Pennsylvania, Ohio, Maryland, New York, Florida, and Virginia.

2 Some English-language scholarship uses different English names for the National Board of Film Censors and the Central Motion Picture Censorship Committee—respectively, the National Film Censorship Committee and the Central Film Censorship Committee. I honor the English names used in the diplomatic correspondences between the Chinese authorities and the State Department.

3 I am referring to the lack of federal censorship for the mainstream film industry's commercial feature films. An exception to this rule can be found in the Sims Act, which sanctioned the federal ban on the importation and theatrical exhibition of "fight films" (photographic recordings of prize boxing matches) between 1912 and 1940. For information on this rare instance of federal-level motion picture censorship, see Dan Streible, *Fight Pictures: A History of Boxing and Early Cinema* (Berkeley: University of California Press, 2008).

4 "Mutual Film Corp. v. Industrial Commission of Ohio, 236 U.S. 230 (1915)," United States Supreme Court, https://supreme.justia.com/cases/federal/us/236/230/.

5 After Hays's appointment, out of the thirty pending state-level film censorship bills at the end of 1921, only Virginia's became law. Robert Sklar, *Movie-Made America: A Cultural History of American Movies*, rev. ed. (New York: Vintage Books, 1994), 132.

6 "Report of the Sub-Committee on Eliminations," May 24, 1927, MPPDA Digital Archive, reel 3, record 341, https://mppda.flinders.edu.au/records/341.

7 Richard Maltby, "The Production Code and the Hays Office," in *Grand Design: Hollywood as a Modern Business Enterprise, 1930–1939*, ed. Tino Balio (New York: Charles Scribner's Sons, 1993), 38.

8 David A. Cook, *A History of Narrative Film* (New York: W. W. Norton, 1981), 267.

9 Thomas Doherty, *Pre-Code Hollywood: Sex, Immorality, and Insurrection in American Cinema, 1930–1934* (New York: Columbia University Press, 1999), 6.

10 Thomas Doherty, *Hollywood's Censor: Joseph I. Breen and the Production Code Administration* (New York: Columbia University Press, 2007), 46.

11 Maltby, "The Production Code and the Hays Office," 42.

12 Doherty, *Pre-Code Hollywood*, 2. Emphasis in original.

13 Richard Maltby, "More Sinned against than Sinning: The Fabrications of 'Pre-Code Cinema,'" *Senses of Cinema* 29 (December 2003), http://sensesofcinema.com/2003/feature-articles/pre_code_cinema/.

14 Ibid.

15 Ruth Vasey, *The World According to Hollywood, 1918–1939* (Madison: University of Wisconsin Press, 1997), 55.

16 Jason S. Joy to Harold Hurley, Paramount Publicity Corp., July 21, 1932; Joy to Hurley, October 8, 1932, in *Trouble in Paradise*, Production Code Administration (PCA) files, Margaret Herrick Library (MHL), Academy of Motion Picture Arts and Sciences (AMPAS).

17 Vasey, *The World According to Hollywood*, 143.

18 See Yat-sen Sun, *The Three Principles of the People* (Taipei: China Publishing Co., 1981).

19 Zhiwei Xiao, "Anti-imperialism and Film Censorship during the Nanjing Decade, 1927–1937," in *Transnational Chinese Cinemas: Identity, Nationhood, Gender*, ed. Sheldon Hsiao-peng Lu (Honolulu: University of Hawai'i Press, 1997), 35–36.

20 Jubin Hu, *Projecting a Nation: Chinese National Cinema Before 1949* (Hong Kong: Hong Kong University Press, 2003), 16.

21 For detailed information on early Chinese film censorship and its historical context, see Zhiwei Xiao, "Film Censorship in China, 1927–1937" (PhD diss., University of California, San Diego, 1994).

22 Zhiwei Xiao, "Prohibition, Politics, and Nation-Building: A History of Film Censorship in China," in *Silencing Cinema: Film Censorship around the World*, ed. Daniel Biltereyst and Roel Vande Winkel (New York: Palgrave MacMillan, 2013), 114.

23 Ibid., 115.

24 Ibid. For the full text of the "Thirteen Regulations" and "Sixteen Regulations," see Appendix.

25 A translated copy of the Motion Picture Censorship Law (promulgated on November 3, 1930, and effective on June 15, 1931), attached to American Minister in Beijing Nelson Trusler Johnson's report to the Secretary of State, Washington, DC, August 11, 1931, Record Group 59, State Department files on China, box 7220, 893.4061 Motion Pictures, National Archives and Records Administration (NARA) at College Park, MD. See Appendix for the full text of this law.

26 Xiao, "Prohibition, Politics, and Nation-Building," 116.

27 Ibid. Although the law was not usually applied to American motion pictures, the Chinese government later defined the second clause of Article Two as films "advocating ideologies other than Three Principles of the People," such as imperialism, capitalism, feudalism, or socialism. See Xiao, "Film Censorship in China," 300–301.

28 Johnson's report to the Secretary of State, September 23, 1931, State Department files, box 7221, NARA.

29 Xiao, "Film Censorship in China," 114–115.

30 Peck's report to Johnson, "Subject: The Chinese Government and the Motion Picture Industry," June 21, 1933, State Department files, box 7221, NARA.

31 Ibid.

32 National Educational Cinematographic Society of China, "An Open Letter to European and American Film Producers," July 1933, attached to Peck's report to the Secretary of State, "Subject: The Chinese Government and the Motion Picture Industry," September 21, 1933, State Department files, box 7221, NARA.

33 Peck to Herron, November 4, 1933, letter attached to Peck's report to the Secretary of State, "Subject: The Chinese Government and the Motion Picture Industry," November 4, 1933, ibid.

34 "Mutual Film Corp. v. Industrial Commission of Ohio, 236 U.S. 230 (1915)," United States Supreme Court.

35 Hu, *Projecting a Nation*, 16.
36 Xiao, "Film Censorship in China," 123.
37 Ibid., 125.
38 Peck's report to the Secretary of State, "Subject: Changes in the Organization Controlling the Motion Picture Industry in China," April 23, 1934, State Department files, box 7221, NARA.
39 Counselor of the United States legation in Beijing Mahlon F. Perkins's report to the Secretary of State, February 23, 1932, ibid.
40 Xiao, "Anti-imperialism and Film Censorship During the Nanjing Decade," 42.
41 Ibid., 47.
42 Ibid., 37.
43 Consul General in Shanghai Edwin S. Cunningham's report "Regarding: Protest by Kuomintang against *Welcome Danger*, a sound picture by Harold Lloyd," March 13, 1930, State Department files, box 7220, NARA.
44 Ibid.
45 Xiao, "Anti-imperialism and Film Censorship during the Nanjing Decade," 39.
46 Cunningham's report "Re: Protest by Kuomintang against *Welcome Danger*."
47 Golden to Smith, April 1, 1930, Record Group 151, Records of the Bureau of Foreign and Domestic Commerce, 281 Motion Pictures, Canada 1929–Cuba 1939, box 1306, NARA.
48 Shu-mei Shih identifies the Republic of China of the 1920s and 1930s as a "semi-colonized" era. See "Introduction to Part I," in *Embodied Modernities: Corporeality, Representation, and Chinese Culture*, ed. Fran Martin and Larissa Heinrich (Honolulu: University of Hawai'i Press, 2006), 10.
49 Huston's memorandum of conversation, April 17, 1930, attached to Cunningham's report to Johnson, "Subject: Prohibition against the Exhibition of Harold Lloyd Films," April 25, 1930, State Department files, box 7220, NARA.
50 Lloyd to Chang, May 29, 1930, letter attached to Cunningham's report to Johnson, "Subject: Prohibition against the Exhibition of Harold Lloyd Films," August 9, 1930, ibid.
51 Consul General in Shanghai Clarence E. Gause's report to Johnson, "Subject: Confiscation of Motion Picture Films by Central Film Censorship Committee," June 19, 1936, attached to Johnson's report to the Secretary of State, July 9, 1936, State Department files, box 7222, NARA.
52 Xiao, "Anti-imperialism and Film Censorship during the Nanjing Decade," 41.
53 Will H. Hays to Under Secretary of State William R. Castle Jr., May 25, 1932, State Department files, box 7221, NARA.
54 Merrell's report to the Secretary of State, "Subject: Objections of the Italian Government to the Screening of *Give Us This Night*," July 2, 1936, ibid.
55 Phillips to Johnson, August 8, 1933, State Department files, box 7222, NARA.
56 Peck to Herron, November 4, 1933, State Department files, box 7221, NARA.
57 Vasey, *The World According to Hollywood*, 154–155.
58 Eric Smoodin, *Regarding Frank Capra: Audience, Celebrity, and American Film Studies, 1930–1960* (Durham, NC: Duke University Press, 2004), 66.
59 Cunningham's report to the Secretary of State, "Subject: Prohibition of Exhibition of Film *East Is West*," June 18, 1931, State Department files, box 7220, NARA.
60 Paramount Pictures press sheet, clippings file on *Shanghai Express*, MHL, AMPAS.
61 Carole Zucker, "Some Observations on Sternberg and Dietrich," *Cinema Journal* 19, no. 2 (Spring 1980): 17–18.

62 Gina Marchetti, *Romance and "Yellow Peril": Race, Sex, and Discursive Strategies in Hollywood Fiction* (Berkeley: University of California Press, 1993), 58.
63 Joseph von Sternberg, *Fun in a Chinese Laundry* (London: Columbus Books, 1987), 262.
64 Ibid., 263. According to Sternberg, "The film featured, loosely based on a single page by Harry Hervey, a hold-up by bandits. This caused the Chinese to resent the slur on their national law and order, and they banned the film wherever they could, and I was told that if I ever appeared in China I would be arrested and punished."
65 Ibid., 263–264.
66 Edward W. Said, *Orientalism* (New York: Vintage Books, 1979), 5, 12.
67 Paramount Pictures press sheet, clippings file on *Shanghai Express*, MHL, AMPAS.
68 Yiman Wang, "Screening Asia: Passing, Performative Translation, and Reconfiguration," *positions: east asia cultures critique* 15, no. 2 (Fall 2007): 324–325.
69 Said, *Orientalism*, 5.
70 Lamar Trotti's memorandum to Joy, September 18, 1931, *Shanghai Express* (1932), PCA files, MHL, AMPAS.
71 Joy to Schulberg, September 28, 1931, ibid.
72 Joy to Schulberg, October 8, 1931, ibid.
73 Lasky to Joy, January 14, 1932, ibid.
74 Joy to Hays, January 20, 1932, ibid.
75 Joy to Schulberg, January 21, 1932, ibid.
76 Xiao, "Anti-imperialism and Film Censorship during the Nanjing Decade," 42.
77 Johnson's report to the Secretary of State, December 7, 1936, "Subject: The Chinese Government and the Motion Picture Industry," State Department files, box 7222, NARA.
78 For more information about the Chinese reception of Charlie Chan, see Yunte Huang, *Charlie Chan: The Untold Story of the Honorable Detective and His Rendezvous with American History* (New York: W. W. Norton, 2010), 251. According to Dorothy B. Jones, head of the Office of War Information (OWI) film reviewers during World War II, "The Charlie Chan series has been extremely successful in the Far East. Audiences in the Far East appreciate this American tribute to Chinese wisdom .... I was told of a back region in Java [where], according to the report of this American GI, the Charlie Chan films were the favorite among all American films, and even had a larger turnout than did most Hollywood class-A features." *The Portrayal of China and India on the American Screen, 1896–1955* (Cambridge: Massachusetts Institute of Technology Center for International Studies, 1955), 35.
79 Enjoying the popularity over two decades and generating forty-four entries during the sound era, the Charlie Chan series officially retired in 1949 with Monogram's *The Sky Dragon*. There were several attempts to revive the series, such as NBC's pilot of a television series starring Ross Martin produced in 1970 but never broadcast. An active Asian American lobby kept not only remakes but also the originals off air. The Chan controversy escalated in 1980 when the producer/writer Jerry Sherlock cranked in a big-budget big screen remake entitled *Charlie Chan and the Curse of Dragon Queen*, starring Peter Ustinov and Angie Dickinson in Chinese roles. Many civil rights groups (including the Coalition of Asians to Nix Charlie Chan, the Chinese for Affirmative Action, the Japanese American

Citizens League, and the League of Black Cinema Artists) protested the casting of white actors and anachronistic Asian stereotypes in Sherlock's remake. In his interview with *Variety*, Sherlock defended his casting decision, arguing that "There are no bankable Asian-American stars" (Richard Goldstein, "The Chan Syndrome," *Village Voice*, May 5, 1980). In 1997, Miramax announced its plan to remake the film with Steven Soderbergh as director and Russell Wong as the new, hip, sexy Chan, a project that never materialized. In the summer of 2003, Fox Movie Channel's programming of the twenty-three-film Chan fest came under fire. Pressured by complaints and protests from various civil rights groups and Asian American constituents, Fox canceled the fest, instead showing only four Chan films with follow-up discussions with prominent Asian American commentators, such as the actor George Takei and the scholar Peter Feng (Steve Brennan, "Complaints Doom Chan Fest," *Hollywood Reporter*, July 1, 2003, 1, 79; Andrew Wallenstein, "Discussions Added to Chan Fest," *Hollywood Reporter*, September 2, 2003, 75).

80 Fred W. Beetson, executive vice president of the Association of Motion Picture Producers, to Schulberg, October 8, 1931, *Shanghai Express*, PCA files, MHL, AMPAS.

81 Joy to Schulberg, September 28, 1931, ibid.

82 Jules Furthman's first script of *Shanghai Express*, September 14, 1931, file S-540, C-3, Paramount Scripts Collection, MHL, AMPAS.

83 Ibid., B-2.

84 Marchetti, *Romance and "Yellow Peril,"* 64.

85 Robert G. Lee, *Orientals: Asian Americans in Popular Culture* (Philadelphia, PA: Temple University Press, 1999), 116.

86 See Ella Shohat, "Gender and Culture of Empire: Toward a Feminist Ethnography of the Cinema," in *Visions of the East: Orientalism in Film*, ed. Matthew Bernstein and Gaylyn Studlar (New Brunswick, NJ: Rutgers University Press, 1997), 45.

87 Peck's report to the Secretary of State, August 9, 1932, "Subject: Unusual Demand by the Chinese National Motion Picture Censorship Committee," State Department files, box 7221, NARA.

88 Peck's report to Johnson, June 21, 1932, "Subject: Motion Picture Film *Shanghai Express*," ibid.

89 Peck's report to the Secretary of State, August 9, 1932, ibid.

90 Ibid.

91 Peck's report to Johnson, June 21, 1932, State Department files, box 7221, NARA.

92 Peck's report to the Secretary of State, August 9, 1932, ibid.

93 North to Herron, December 13, 1932, Records of the Bureau of Foreign and Domestic Commerce, box 1306, NARA.

94 Ibid.

95 C. L. Hsia, first secretary of Chinese legation, to Kiang, June 26, 1933, attached to Peck's report to the Secretary of State, September 21, 1933, "Subject: The Chinese Government and the Motion Picture Industry," State Department files, box 7221, NARA.

96 Heron to Peck, May 31, 1933, attached to Peck's report to the Secretary of State, July 3, 1933, ibid.

97 Peck's report to the Secretary of State, September 21, 1933, ibid.

98 Herron to Peck, January 26, 1934, attached to Peck's report to the Secretary of State, March 3, 1934, ibid.

99 Peck to Herron, January 5, 1934, attached to Peck's report to the Secretary of State, January 5, 1934, "Subject: The Chinese Government and the Motion Picture Industry," ibid.

100 Johnson's report to the Secretary of State, December 7, 1936, State Department files, box 7222, NARA.

101 Central Motion Picture Censorship Committee's Notification no. 71, November 23, 1936, attached to Peck's report to Johnson, November 28, 1936, ibid.

102 Johnson's report to the Secretary of State, December 7, 1936; Peck to Herron, June 16, 1937, attached to Peck's report to the Secretary of State, June 16, 1937, ibid.

103 Chang to Liu Chieh, Counselor of the Chinese Embassy in Washington, DC, September 29, 1942, *The General Died at Dawn* file, General Records of the Chief, Lowell Mellett, Records of the Bureau of Motion Pictures, Record Group 208, Office of War Information (OWI) files, box 1433B, NARA.

104 Ku to Paramount Pictures, September 29, 1943, ibid.

105 J. Z. Huang, secretary to Dr. T. V. Soong, Foreign Minister, Chinese Embassy, to Chief Lowell Mellett, OWI Bureau of Motion Pictures, November 6, 1942, ibid.

106 Minderman's memorandum to Mellett, November 6, 1942, "Subject: *The General Died at Dawn*," ibid.

107 Herron to Breen, April 16, 1937, *Shanghai Express*, PCA files, MHL, AMPAS.

108 Ibid.

109 The memorandum is referenced in Breen's letter to Paramount vice president Henry Hezbrun, May 14, 1937, *Shanghai Express*, PCA files, MHL, AMPAS.

110 Hezbrun to Breen, May 6, 1937, ibid.

111 For more information about MGM's negotiations and contract with the Chinese government in the production of *The Good Earth*, see chapter 4 of Hye Seung Chung, *Hollywood Asian: Philip Ahn and the Cross-Ethnic Performance* (Philadelphia, PA: Temple University Press, 2006).

112 Ibid., 89–103.

113 The PCA's inaugural staff included Islin Auster (a college graduate), Karl Lischka (a former professor of history at Georgetown University), Douglas Mackinnon (a former employee of educational companies), John McHugh Stuart (a former newspaperman), Geoffrey Shurlock (a former literary secretary and Breen's successor-to-be), and Dr. James Wingate (a former board of regents member of the Department of Education of the New York State). Doherty, *Hollywood's Censor*, 82–83.

114 Vice Minister of Foreign Affairs Hsu Mo's opinion quoted in Peck's report to Johnson, November 28, 1936, State Department files, box 7222, NARA.

115 John M. Begg, assistant chief, State Department's Division of Cultural Relations, to Robert Rubin, Metro-Goldwyn-Mayer, February 22, 1943, State Department files, box 5865, NARA.

116 Peck to A. J. Healy, chief of Press and Pictorial Section, Office of Censorship, February 4, 1943, ibid.

117 Begg to Rubin, February 22, 1943, ibid.; C. R. Moffatt, director of advertising, United Steel Corporation, to Begg, February 15, 1943, ibid.

118 Begg to Charles Goldsmith, chief of distribution, Motion Picture Bureau, OWI Overseas Branch, July 19, 1943, ibid.

119 Report from Guass, Embassy of the United States in Chungking, to the Secretary of State, January 29, 1943, "Subject: Cultural Relations, Motion Pictures," ibid.

120 Begg to Goldsmith, July 19, 1943, ibid.

121 Mansfield to Roosevelt, January 3, 1945, *Foreign Relations of the United States: Diplomatic Papers, 1945, The Far East, China,* vol. 7 (Washington, DC: United States Government Printing Office, 1969), 18.

122 Joy to Laemmle Jr., October 24, 1929, *The Shanghai Gesture* (1942), PCA files, MHL, AMPAS.

123 Hays's interoffice memorandum to Joy, December 20, 1929, ibid.

124 Breen to Pressburger, April 26, 1941, ibid.

125 Another potential Code violation that was avoided by this change is the anti-miscegenation provision. In his letter to the MPPDA dated July 14, 1939, Jay Sanford Fush of International Film Exchange defended his treatment of *The Shanghai Gesture*, arguing, "The point of Poppy's consorting with an oriental, we think, does not violate the code—Poppy is not a white girl—as is found at the end—she is Eurasian. Another moral point is brought out—it is not right to intermingle races." Fush also pointed out the original Code's anti-miscegenation clause was subsequently narrowed to be the specific prohibition on "relations between Blacks and Whites." Fush to F. S. Harmon, MPPDA, July 14, 1939, ibid.

126 The PCA to Pressburger, June 21, 1941, ibid.

127 Chang to Pressburger, August 21, 1941, ibid.

128 Ibid.

129 Pressburger to Chang, August 22, 1941, ibid.

130 Chang to Pressburger, August 25, 1941, ibid.

131 Chang to Geoffrey Shurlock, PCA, September 23, 1941, ibid.

132 Shurlock's memorandum, "Re: *The Shanghai Gesture*," September 26, 1941, ibid.

133 Ibid.

134 Karen Kuo, "*The Shanghai Gesture*: Melodrama and Modern Women in the East/West Romance," *Quarterly Review of Film and Video* 29, no. 2 (2012): 108–109.

135 Ibid., 108.

136 Pressburger to Vice Consul S. C. Hsu, September 25, 1941, *The Shanghai Gesture*, PCA files, MHL, AMPAS.

137 For example, on April 21, 1943, OWI staff member Warren Pierce wrote to MGM producer Maurice Revnes to give the studio a warning about the Chinese consulate objection to their treatment of a proposed film entitled *Army Brat* with a queue-wearing Chinese servant character (who is later revealed to be a mandarin). Citing Consul T. K. Chang's opposition that "traditionally the Chinese have so often been represented as house boys and servants and such a picturization contributes nothing to an understanding of modern China," the OWI urged MGM to "work as closely as possible with the Chinese Consulate" in Los Angeles to ensure that there should be "no harm to American-Chinese relations." Whether it is due to the Chinese problem or not, the project got scraped. Warren Pierce, OWI's Bureau of Motion Pictures, to Maurice Revnes, April 21, 1943, General Records of the Chief, Lowell Mellett, OWI files, box 1445, NARA. Pierce had also advised the same producer on another project, *Right about Face* (later retitled *Swing Fever* [1944]), "There is a Chinese comedy character who appears briefly during the story as [a] valet. In view of the natural distaste for the Chinese government to have their people usually portrayed as menials and comics in motion pictures, it would be a good thing for Chinese-American relations either to eliminate this part or to change the nationality of the character." MGM complied, changing the valet's ethnicity to African American and casting Mantan Mooreland for the role. Pierce to Revnes, January 13, 1943, ibid.

Chapter 2 Justified Patricide and (Im)Properly Directed Hatred

1 See Thomas Doherty, *Projections of War: Hollywood, American Culture, and World War II* (New York: Columbia University Press, 1993), and Clayton R. Koppes, "Regulating the Screen: The Office of War Information and the Production Code Administration," in *Boom and Bust: American Cinema in the 1940s*, ed. Thomas Schatz (Berkeley: University of California Press, 1999).

2 For more information about the NAACP's protests against *The Birth of a Nation*, see Arthur Lenning, "Myth and Fact: The Reception of *The Birth of a Nation*," *Film History* 16, no. 2 (2004): 117–141.

3 Gerald R. Butters Jr., *Banned in Kansas: Motion Picture Censorship, 1915–1966* (Columbia: University of Missouri Press, 2007), 85–86.

4 Sumiko Higashi, *Cecil B. DeMille and American Culture: The Silent Era* (Berkeley: University of California Press, 1994), 101.

5 Daisuke Miyao, *Sessue Hayakawa: Silent Cinema and Transnational Stardom* (Durham, NC: Duke University Press, 2007), 26–28.

6 Ibid., 28.

7 Ibid., 128.

8 H.D.R., "The Secret Game," *Dramatic Mirror*, December 8, 1917, *The Secret Game*, clippings files, Margaret Herrick Library (MHL), Academy Motion Picture Arts and Sciences (AMPAS), Beverly Hills, CA.

9 Miyao, *Sessue Hayakawa*, 129.

10 Kerry Segrave, *American Films Abroad: Hollywood's Domination of the World's Movie Screens* (Jefferson, NC: McFarland, 1997), 5.

11 Robert Sklar, *Movie-Made America: A Cultural History of American Movies*, rev. ed. (New York: Vintage Books, 1994), 47.

12 Ruth Vasey, *The World According to Hollywood, 1918–1939* (Madison: University of Wisconsin Press, 1997), 19–20.

13 Segrave, *American Films Abroad*, 21–22.

14 Kia Afra, *The Hollywood Trust: Trade Organizations and the Rise of the Studio System* (Lanham: Rowman & Littlefield, 2016), 227.

15 Vasey, *The World According to Hollywood*, 38.

16 "Resume of Dinner-Meeting of the Studio Relations Committee," December 14, 1927, MPPDA Digital Archive, reel 3, record #337, https://mppda.flinders.edu.au/records/337.

17 Ibid.

18 Leonard J. Leff and Jerold L. Simmons, "Appendix: The Motion Picture Production Code," *Dame in Kimono: Hollywood, Censorship, and the Production Code* (Lexington: University of Kentucky Press, 2001), 289, 300.

19 Vasey, *The World According to Hollywood*, 159.

20 Ibid.

21 Quoted in John Trumpbour, *Selling Hollywood to the World: U.S. and European Struggles for Mastery of the Global Film Industry, 1920–1950* (Cambridge: Cambridge University Press, 2002), 70.

22 De Martino to Herron, June 3, 1932, *Scarface*, Production Code Administration (PCA) files, MHL, AMPAS.

23 Ibid.

24 Jason S. Joy, director of the Studio Relations Committee (SRC), to E. B. Derr, Caddo Company, June 4, 1931, *Scarface*, PCA files, MHL, AMPAS.

25 Joy's interoffice memorandum to Hays, November 3, 1931, ibid.

26 "Memorandum in Re: *Scarface*: A Brief of the Record," March 4, 1932, ibid. Along with scenes with an incest theme, a new ending with Camonte's hanging was added. After getting a green light for this version from the SRC, Hughes showed the unaltered, original version for a press screening at the Grauman's Chinese Theater in Hollywood on March 2, 1932. Hughes got into trouble with the MPPDA by insisting that he would release the original version in all states without censorship boards. However, Joseph Schenck, president of United Artists, gave his word to Hays that he would not release the film unless it was "entirely satisfactory under the Code." United Artists and MPPDA compromised, and the revised version without Camonte's execution was released in most of states except for New York and Pennsylvania. "Memorandum for Mr. Hays," March 5, 1932; "Re: *Scarface*," March 1932, ibid.

27 "Memorandum in Re: *Scarface*," March 4, 1932, ibid.

28 "Report and criticism of scenario of talking picture *Scarface*," June 1, 1931, ibid.

29 History of *Scarface* (1932), American Film Institute Catalog, http://www.afi.com/members/catalog/DetailView.aspx?s=&Movie=1134.

30 Herron to Joy, June 17, 1932, *Scarface*, PCA Files, MHL, AMPAS.

31 History of *Scarface*.

32 Herron to Joy, June 7, 1932, *Scarface*, PCA files, MHL, AMPAS.

33 Eric Smoodin, *Regarding Frank Capra* (Durham, NC: Duke University Press, 2004), 75.

34 Thomas Doherty, *Hollywood's Censor: Joseph I. Breen and the Production Code Administration* (New York: Columbia University Press, 2007), 115. Seven states with motion picture censorship boards were Pennsylvania, Ohio, Kansas, Maryland, New York, Florida, and Virginia. The number of state censorship boards is sometimes counted as six because Florida did not have an autonomous board and followed the decisions made by the New York State.

35 See Thomas Doherty, *Pre-Code Hollywood: Sex, Immorality, and Insurrection in American Cinema: 1930–1934* (New York: Columbia University Press, 1999); Doherty, *Hollywood's Censor*; Lea Jacobs, *The Wages of Sin: Censorship and the Fallen Woman Films, 1928–1942* (Berkeley: University of California Press, 1997); Stephen Prince, *Classical Film Violence: Designing and Regulating Brutality in Hollywood Cinema, 1930–1968* (New Brunswick, NJ: Rutgers University Press, 2003); Vasey, *The World According to Hollywood*.

36 Breen to Heron, June 11, 1937, quoted in Vasey, *The World According to Hollywood*, 179.

37 Doherty, *Hollywood's Censor*, 224.

38 Ibid., 236.

39 Nelson Poynter's reply to *Hollywood Reporter*, General Records of the Chief, Lowell Mellett, Records of the Bureau of Motion Pictures, Record Group 208, Office of War Information (OWI) files, box 1443, National Archives and Records Administration (NARA) at College Park, MD.

40 "Activities of Hollywood Office, Bureau of Motion Pictures, OWI (May 1942 to April 1943)," General Records of the Chief, Lowell Mellett, OWI files, box 1442, NARA.

41 Mellett's letter of December 9, 1942, to the heads of studios, requesting that they submit treatments, synopses, scripts, and preview prints of *all* films, generated alarmist headlines from the trade press and resistance on the part of studio

executives, who feared government censorship. In a statement for Appropriation Committee hearings dated May 21, 1943, the OWI insisted that the controversial letter was "in line with the voluntary cooperation between the motion picture industry and the government" as the producers "are completely free to disregard any of [OWI] views or suggestions" made by its Hollywood office in response to submitted scripts. "Statement for Appropriation Committee Hearings," May 21, 1943, General Records of the Chief, Lowell Mellett, OWI files, box 1447, NARA.

42 Koppes, "Regulating the Screen," 269.

43 Clayton R. Koppes and Gregory D. Black, *Hollywood Goes to War: How Politics, Profits and Propaganda Shaped World War II Movies* (Berkeley: University of California Press, 1990), 141.

44 Ellen C. Scott, *Cinema Civil Rights: Regulation, Repression, and Race in the Classical Hollywood Era* (New Brunswick, NJ: Rutgers University Press, 2015), 42.

45 *Government Information Manual*, condensed and updated version, April 29, 1943, 10, General Records of the Chief, Lowell Mellett, OWI files, box 1438, NARA. The original *Government Information Manual* was circulated in the summer of 1942.

46 Randolph Seiler to William S. Cunningham, acting chief, Los Angeles Overseas Branch, March 21, 1944, *Keys of the Kingdom*, Motion Picture Reviews and Analyses files, OWI files, box 3518, NARA.

47 Poynter to Sandrich, October 26, 1942, General Records of the Chief, Lowell Mellett, OWI files, box 1438, NARA.

48 *Government Information Manual*, 8–9, 18.

49 After the airmen's capture, their fates were debated for weeks in Tokyo. General Hajime Sugiyama, chief of the Imperial General Staff, pressured for death sentences, while Prime Minister Tojo was in favor of life imprisonment. After a brief, untranslated military tribunal in which the predetermined death sentence was handed to the eight (who were neither informed of their charges nor offered defense counsel, unlike in *The Purple Heart*), Emperor Hirohito commuted the sentence for five of them but not for two pilots and the engineer-gunner who were found guilty of killing schoolchildren. For more information, see Duane Schultz, *The Doolittle Raid* (New York: St. Martin's Press, 1988), 260–270.

50 Eleanor Berneis, feature review, July 7, 1943, *Behind the Rising Sun*, Motion Picture Reviews and Analyses files, OWI files, box 3512, NARA.

51 Alton Cook, "War Film *Purple Heart* Depicts Prison Atrocities of Bestial Japs," *New York World-Telegram*, February 18, 1944, *The Purple Heart*, clippings files, MHL, AMPAS.

52 Doherty, *Projections of War*, 136.

53 Erskine Johnson, "Zanuck's Second Guess," *Los Angeles Daily News*, February 9, 1944, *The Purple Heart*, clippings files, MHL, AMPAS.

54 Prince, *Classical Film Violence*, 67.

55 Eleanor Berneis, feature review, February 23, 1944, *The Purple Heart*, Motion Picture Reviews and Analyses files, OWI files, box 3524, NARA.

56 Prince, *Classical Film Violence*, 67–68.

57 Ibid., 208.

58 Ibid., 220.

59 The "souvenir" photo was taken by a Japanese private at the request of Chikao, and a copy was found on a dead Japanese major's body near Hollandia, New Guinea by American troops in April 1944.

60 Associated Press, "Story of Atrocities by Japs on Hapless Prisoners Is Released by the U.S.: Deliberate Starvation, Torture, Death," January 28, 1944, http://www.angelfire.com/nm/bcmfofnm/atrocities/atrocities01.html. Emphasis added.
61 Prince, *Classical Film Violence*, 208.
62 Ibid., 207.
63 Breen to Joy, October 14, 1943, *The Purple Heart*, PCA files, MHL, AMPAS.
64 Pierce to Joy, October 21, 1943, *The Purple Heart*, OWI files, NARA.
65 Ibid.
66 Ibid.
67 While the Doolittle Raid targeted military and industrial installations such as factories, warehouses, oil tanks, and shipyards, some incendiary bombs hit residential areas of Tokyo, causing collateral damage (albeit minuscular compared to an estimated 100,000 civilian casualties suffered by the firebombing of Tokyo on May 9, 1945). As a wartime propaganda film, *The Purple Heart* discredits the Japanese court's claim of civilian killings as outright falsification. However, Japanese records and eyewitness reports suggest otherwise. For example, "At the Waseda Middle School in Tokyo, students poured onto the playground after lunch. An airplane roared overhead, sounding to them like a freight train. Kikujiro Suzuki assumed the plane was theirs until he saw an object fall from the sky. It was an incendiary. It hit one of Suzuki's schoolmates. The boy fell down and did not move." Schultz, *The Doolittle Raid*, 160. A postwar analysis of civilian casualties of the Doolittle Raid counts 87 dead and 151 injured. James M. Scott, *Target Tokyo: Jimmy Doolittle and the Raid That Avenged Pearl Harbor* (New York: W. W. Norton, 2015), 309.
68 Berneis, feature review, February 23, 1944.
69 Ibid.
70 Ibid.
71 Eleanor Berneis, script review, November 11, 1943, *Thirty Seconds Over Tokyo*, Motion Picture Reviews and Analyses files, OWI files, box 3527, NARA.
72 William S. Cunningham, feature review, September 15, 1944, ibid. While the OWI's recommendations focused on Chinese images, the PCA requested that MGM delete a reference to the "fall of the Alamo" as "a gesture to our Mexican friends." Breen to Louis B. Mayer, September 9, 1943, *Thirty Seconds Over Tokyo*, PCA files, MHL, AMPAS.
73 Koppes, "Regulating the Screen," 269.
74 Dr. Chung is a fictional version of Dr. Chen in Ted Lawson's memoir. Unlike his screen surrogate, Captain Lawson never had a chance to say goodbye to the Chinese doctor and thank him.
75 *The Purple Heart* script, 2nd revised final, October 14, 1943, 21, Lewis Milestone Papers, File 89, MHL, AMPAS.
76 In the film's narrative, a Swiss Red Cross representative ironically reminds Loo's character that over 100,000 Japanese nationals are interned in the United States.
77 John Stanley, "Master Kan of *Kung Fu*—Wisdom in a Shaolin Temple," *San Francisco Examiner and Chronicle*, undated clipping (presumed to have been printed in 1973), Philip Ahn clippings file, Ahn Family Collection, Korean Heritage Library, University of Southern California, Los Angeles.
78 Eddie Wong, "H. T. Tsiang, A Free Spirit Imprisoned on Ellis Island," *Immigrant Voices,* Angel Island Immigration Station Foundation, https://www.immigrant-voices.aiisf.org/stories-by-author/h-t-tsiang-a-free-spirit-imprisoned-on-ellis-island/.

79 After studying political economy at the University of Nanking and working as an aid to the secretary of Sun Yun-sen, the founder of the Republic of China, H. T. Tsiang (Hsi Tseng Tsiang) fled to the United States in 1926 in fear of the political purge against leftist sympathizers. While taking classes in law, economics, and history at Columbia University, he became involved in the proletariat art movement of Greenwich Village during the 1920s and 1930s. In addition to self-publishing experimental novels about unemployed laborers and alienated immigrants such as *The Hanging on Union Square* (1935) and *And China Has Hands* (1937), he contributed revolutionary poems about workers' struggle in the *Daily Worker* and *New Masses*. After being rejected by the literary establishment in New York and nearly deported to China when his student visa expired (left-wing writers' appeals helped him stay), Tsiang relocated to Los Angeles in 1943 and started a new career in wartime Hollywood, where Asian actors were in high demand. For more information about Tsiang's life and career, see Huo Hsu, "The Remarkable Forgotten Life of H. T. Tsiang," *New Yorker*, July 16, 2016, https://www.newyorker.com/books/page-turner/the-remarkable-forgotten-life-of-h-t-tsiang.

80 Warren I. Cohen, "American Perceptions of China," in *Dragon and Eagle: United States–China Relations: Past and Future*, ed. Michel Oksenberg and Robert B. Oxnam (New York: Basic Books, 1978), 55, 62.

81 Chang to Arnold Pressburger, August 21, 1941, *The Shanghai Gesture*, PCA files, MHL, AMPAS.

82 Luca Gabbiani, "Insanity and Patricide in Late Imperial China," *International Journal of Asian Studies* 10, no. 2 (July 2013): 115–141.

83 Kate Cameron, "*The Purple Heart*, A Powerful Picture," *New York Daily News*, March 8, 1944, *The Purple Heart*, clippings files, MHL, AMPAS.

84 Ted W. Lawson, *Thirty Seconds Over Tokyo* (New York: Random House, 1943), 168.

85 Owen Lattimore to Harry B. Price, November 10, 1943, *The Purple Heart*, OWI files, NARA. A scholar of Chinese and Mongolian history (who taught at Johns Hopkins University from 1938 and returned to instruction and research after a brief political career during World War II), Lattimore became an unlikely primary target for Senator Joseph R. McCarthy's anti-communist scapegoating and was blamed for the "loss of China" due in part to his vocal criticism of Chiang Kai-shek's corrupt regime. The academic was thrown into a public spotlight when McCarthy falsely accused him of being "the top Soviet espionage agent" in the United States in March 1950.

86 *The Purple Heart* script, 52.

87 Doherty, *Projections of War*, 122.

88 *Government Information Manual*, 7.

89 Ibid., 7–8.

90 Doherty, *Projections of War*, 123.

91 Pierce to Joy, October 21, 1943, *The Purple Heart*, OWI files, NARA.

92 *Government Information Manual*, 8.

93 *The Purple Heart*, clippings files, MHL, AMPAS.

94 Louella O. Parsons, "*Purple Heart* Strong Indictment of Tokyo," *Los Angeles Examiner*, March 10, 1944, 12.

95 Lee Mortimer, "*Purple Heart* Has Timely Wallop," *New York Mirror*, March 9, 1944, *The Purple Heart*, clippings files, MHL, AMPAS.

96 James Lindsley, "Zanuck Completes Picture of Doolittle's Tokyo Raid," *Hollywood Citizen-News*, February 3, 1944, ibid.
97 Evaluations Division, OWI Overseas Branch, "Motion Picture Reactions—Turkey: Turkish Responses to *The Purple Heart*," April 27, 1945, OWI files, NARA.
98 Ibid.
99 Lillian R. Bergquist, feature script review, October 15, 1943, *The Purple Heart*, OWI files, NARA.
100 Ibid.
101 Koppes and Black, *Hollywood Goes to War*, 271.
102 Ibid., 267.
103 Thomas Schatz, *The Genius of the System: Hollywood Filmmaking in the Studio Era* (New York: An Owl Book, 1988), 6.
104 Doherty, *Hollywood's Censor*, 6.
105 Dalton Trumbo, *Thirty Seconds Over Tokyo* script, October 20, 1943, MGM Legal Department Records, folder 162, MHL, AMPAS.
106 Koppes and Black, *Hollywood Goes to War*, 277.
107 Ibid., 276.
108 Cunningham to Joy, February 29, 1944, *The Purple Heart*, OWI files, NARA.
109 Sailer to Cunningham, March 21, 1944, *Keys of the Kingdom*, Motion Picture Reviews and Analyses files, OWI files, box 3520, NARA.
110 Quoted in Scott, *Target Tokyo*, 389.
111 Quoted in Carroll V. Glines, *The Doolittle Raid: America's Daring First Strike against Japan* (New York: Orion Books, 1988), 152.
112 Lawson, *Thirty Seconds Over Tokyo*, 171–172.
113 Schatz, *Boom and Dust*, 141.
114 Scott, *Cinema Civil Rights*, 12–41.
115 J. E. Johnston, feature script review, August 29, 1945, *Charlie Chan in Mexico*, Motion Picture Reviews and Analyses files, OWI files, box 3513, NARA.
116 Gene Kern, OWI Los Angeles Overseas Bureau, Motion Picture Division, to Marie Quigley, Monogram Pictures Corporation, September 7, 1945, ibid.

Chapter 3 Beyond the Propaganda Model

1 Carl Boggs and Tom Pollard, *The Hollywood War Machine: U.S. Militarism and Popular Culture*, 2nd ed. (New York: Routledge, 2016), 1, 10.
2 Edward S. Herman and Noam Chomsky, *Manufacturing Consent: The Political Economy of Mass Media*, 2nd ed. (New York: Pantheon Books, 2002), 1–2.
3 Boggs and Pollard, *The Hollywood War Machine*, 38.
4 David L. Robb, *Operation Hollywood: How the Pentagon Shapes and Censors the Movies* (New York: Prometheus Books, 2004), 26.
5 Lawrence H. Suid, *Guts and Glory: The Making of the American Military Image in Film* (Lexington: University Press of Kentucky, 2002), 136.
6 Ibid., 137.
7 RKO Radio Studio handbook of publicity data, *One Minute to Zero*, December 7, 1961, Lincoln Quarberg Collection, folder 50, Margaret Herrick Library (MHL), Academy of Motion Picture Arts and Sciences (AMPAS), Beverly Hills, CA.
8 Ibid.; History of *One Minute to Zero* (1952), American Film Institute Catalog, http://www.afi.com/members/catalog/DetailView.aspx?s=&Movie=50606.

9 "Army Nixes Cooperation for RKO's *Zero* Over 'Objectionable Scene,'" *Variety*, July 30, 1952.

10 Breen to Harold Melniker, RKO Radio Pictures, July 11, 1951, *One Minute to Zero*, The Production Code Administration (PCA) files, MHL, AMPAS.

11 Lt. Col. Clair E. Towne to Anthony Muto, 20th Century Fox, March 27, 1953, *Hell and High Water*, Department of Defense (DoD) Film Collection, box 5, folder 18, Georgetown University Special Collections Research Center (GUSCRC), Washington, DC.

12 Ibid.

13 Robb, *Operation Hollywood*, 16–17.

14 "Industry Gift to Army: $38,500,000," *Motion Picture Herald*, September 15, 1952, 46.

15 These files include the Korean War feature films *Frogmen in Korea* (1953 story, unproduced), *Prisoner of War*, *The Bamboo Prison*, *The Bridges at Toko-Ri* (1954), *The Rack* (1956), *Battle Hymn* (1957), *Men in War* (1957); Cold War thrillers or crime dramas *Hell and High Water* (1954) and *House of Bamboo* (1955); and short subjects *Korean Orphan Story* (1954), *Korean Folk Story* (1955), and *Boy from Korea* (1956).

16 The American Legion, American Business Consultants, and editors of the public blacklists *Counterattack* and *Red Channels* were among "a host of self-appointed Grand Inquisitors and 'clearance' agencies in the private section" empowered to handle "a process of self-abasement" of those who were pressured to "come clean [by] denouncing one's friends . . . [and] confessing one's own guilt by association." David A. Cook, *A History of Narrative Film*, 3rd ed. (New York: W. W. Norton, 1996), 456.

17 Ibid., 458.

18 After retirement from the armed services, some veterans became professional military advisors for the film and television industry, operating independently from the Pentagon's official technical advising. Well-known private military advisors include R. Lee Ermey, a former marine corps drill instructor who played Sergeant Hartman in Stanley Kubrick's *Full Metal Jacket* (1987), and Dale Dye, a former marine captain who founded Warriors, Inc., a technical advisory company that provides training and consultation for realistic portrayals of military action in Hollywood films and television. Dye's technical advising credits include *Platoon* (1986), *Casualties of War* (1989), *Saving Private Ryan* (1998), and the HBO miniseries *Band of Brothers* (2001).

19 Paul Edwards, *A Guide to Films on the Korean War* (Westport, CT: Greenwood Press, 1997), 45.

20 In a January 1954 press conference sponsored by the Chinese, the leader of the twenty-one American defectors, Richard G. Gorden, called for "real democracy and racial equality" rather than "witch-hunts and McCarthyism." Except for James Veneris (whose parents had been communists in Greece before immigrating to the U.S.), defecting POWs returned to the United States by 1966. Racism in the United States was a determining factor for the defection of three African Americans in the group (Clarence Adams, William White, and Larance Sullivan). For more information, see Lewis H. Carlson, *Remembered Prisoners of a Forgotten War: An Oral History of Korean War POWs* (New York: St. Martin's Griffin, 2002), 202–212.

21 Other sources estimate the actual POW death rate was considerably higher than 38 percent of the official figures. Ibid., 2–3.

22 For statistics of alleged misconduct, investigation, and prosecution, see Albert D. Biderman, *March to Calumny: The Story of American POWs in the Korean War* (New York: Macmillan, 1963), 27–37. For the testimonies of Korean War POWs on post-repatriation experience, see Carlson, *Remembered Prisoners of a Forgotten War*, 213–224.

23 Carlson, *Remembered Prisoners of a Forgotten War*, 9.

24 Eugene Kinkead, *In Every War But One* (New York: W. W. Norton, 1959), 16, 34. In his revisionist study of Korean War POWs, sociologist Albert D. Biderman criticized Kinkead's erroneous equation of collaboration and misconduct and emphasized that "by strictly *legal criteria*, only 10 of 4,000 have been proved guilty of 'collaboration.'" Biderman, *March to Calumny*, 37. Emphasis in original.

25 "Momism" is a neologism that was sprung on the American public in Philip Wylie's *Generation of Vipers* (1942), which blames overprotective American mothers for producing weak, inadequate men. The idea strongly influenced Richard Condon's 1959 novel *The Manchurian Candidate* and its 1962 film adaptation by John Frankenheimer.

26 Carlson, *Remembered Prisoners of a Forgotten War*, 157.

27 Charles S. Young, "Missing Action: POW Films, Brainwashing, and the Korean War, 1954–1968," *Historical Journal of Film, Radio, and Television* 18, no. 1 (March 1988): 49.

28 Susan L. Carruthers, "Redeeming the Captives: Hollywood and the Brainwashing of America's Prisoners of War in Korea," *Film History* 10, no. 3 (1998): 279.

29 Ibid.

30 Orville Crouch, MGM, to Towne, DoD, August 21, 1953, *Prisoner of War*, DoD Film Collection, box 9, folder 2, GUSCRC.

31 Memorandum from Towne for the chief of information, DA, November 3, 1953, ibid.

32 Memorandum from Howard Horton, MGM, to the Studio Executive Committee, November 13, 1953, attached to the DoD memorandum, Pictorial Branch, Office of Public Information, "Subject: MGM *The POW Story*," date of action: November 13–17, 1953, ibid.

33 DoD memorandum, date of action: November 13–17, 1953, ibid.

34 Memorandum from Patrick Welch, chief of DA Public Information Division, attached in Towne's letter to Crouch, MGM, November 20, 1953, ibid.

35 DoD Memorandum, Pictorial Branch, Office of Public Information, "Subject: MGM *POW Story*," date of action: February 11, 1954, ibid.

36 Memorandum, February 18, 1954, DA, Staff Communication Office, ibid.

37 "*Prisoner of War* Had, But Lost, Defense Okay," *Variety*, March 24, 1953.

38 "Rivkin Says Army Praised His Film," *New York Times*, March 19, 1954, 11.

39 Joe Hyams, "Defense Dept. Won't Back Film on Germ Fare Issue," *Motion Herald Tribune*, March 19, 1954.

40 Ibid.

41 MGM's interoffice memorandum from R. Monta to Henry Berman, "Subject: *The POW Story*," November 24, 1953, Andrew Marton Papers, *Prisoner of War* Production, file 137, MHL, AMPAS.

42 Ibid.

43 Ibid.

44 DoD memorandum, date of action: February 11, 1954, *Prisoner of War*, DoD Film Collection, GUSCRC.

45 Allen Rivkin, temporary complete screenplay, October 30, 1953, Turner/MGM Scripts, *Prisoner of War* (1954), file P-980, 82, MHL, AMPAS.
46 Rivkin, "The P.O.W. Story," August 23, 1953, ibid., file P-978, 37.
47 Rivkin, temporary complete screenplay, November 17, 1953, ibid., file P-986, 80.
48 MGM's interoffice memorandum from Monta to Berman.
49 "*Prisoner of War* Audience Research," Andrew Marton Papers, file 135, MHL, AMPAS.
50 Arthur Knight, review of *Prisoner of War*, *Saturday Review*, April 17, 1954, *Prisoner of War*, clippings files, MHL, AMPAS.
51 Memorandum from Welch, November 20, 1953.
52 Kathryn Weathersby, "Soviet Aims in Korea and the Origins of the Korean War, 1945–1950: New Evidence from Russian Archives," working paper no. 8., Cold War International History Project, Woodrow Wilson International Center for Scholars, November 1993, 36, https://www.wilsoncenter.org/sites/default/files/Working_Paper_8.pdf.
53 Ibid.
54 Lester H. Brune, "The Soviet Union and the Korean War," in *The Korean War: Handbook of the Literature and Research*, ed. Brune (Westport, CT: Greenwood Press, 1996), 214–215.
55 Ibid., 215.
56 Ruth Vasey, *The World According to Hollywood, 1918–1939* (Madison: University of Wisconsin Press, 1997), 54, 59.
57 Tony Shaw, *Hollywood's Cold War* (Amherst: University of Massachusetts Press, 2007), 15.
58 Ibid., 17.
59 Breen to Warner, December 23, 1942, *Mission to Moscow*, PCA files, MHL, AMPAS.
60 John Dewey and Suzanne La Follette, "Several Faults Are Found in *Mission to Moscow* Film," *New York Times*, May 9, 1943, clippings, ibid. The Dewey Commission investigated Stalin's treason charges against the exiled leader Leon Trotsky and his followers in the Moscow trials (most Trotskyists in the Soviet Union were executed during the Great Purge of 1936–1938, and Trotsky was assassinated by a Spanish communist in Mexico City in 1940) and published its findings in the book-length report *Not Guilty* (1937).
61 Script review, November 30, 1942, *Mission to Moscow*, Motion Picture Reviews and Analyses files, Record Group 208, Office of War Information (OWI) files, box 3521, National Archives and Records Administration (NARA) at College Park, MD; Carol A. Salig to Mellett, April 20, 1943, OWI files, box 1455.
62 Mellott to Salig, April 26, 1943, OWI files, box 1445, NARA.
63 Harlow Robinson, *Russians in Hollywood, Hollywood's Russians: Biography of an Image* (Lebanon, NH: University Press of New England, 2007), 158.
64 Vasey, *The World According to Hollywood*, 122. Examples include Paramount's *Desire* (1936), in which Marlene Dietrich plays a jewel thief whose ethnicity is unclear, and MGM's *Idiot's Delight* (1937), set in an Italian mountain resort at the beginning of a new world war and featuring a group of stranded Europeans whose country origins are made nondescript.
65 Cyndy Hendershot, "The Bear and the Dragon: Representations of Communism in Early Sixties American Culture," *Journal of American and Comparative Culture* 23, no. 4 (2000): 67.

66 Rivkin, complete file copy screenplay, December 10, 1953, Turner/MGM Scripts, *Prisoner of War* (1954), file P-994, 13, MHL, AMPAS.
67 "*Prisoner of War*," *Variety*, March 24, 1954.
68 Edward Hunter, *Brainwashing: The Story of the Men Who Defied It* (New York: Farrar, Straus, and Cudahy, 1956), 259–260.
69 Edward Hunter, *Brain-Washing in Red China* (New York: Vanguard, 1951), 10.
70 Ibid. As Susan L. Carruthers points out, "the brainwashing methods depicted in *The Manchurian Candidate* are more akin to CIA-sponsored research into 'mind control' techniques [MKUltra experiments] than to anything experienced by western POWs in Korea." Carruthers, "*The Manchurian Candidate* (1962) and the Cold War Brainwashing Scare," *Historical Journal of Film, Radio, and Television* 18, no. 1 (March 1988): 87.
71 Hendershot, "The Bear and the Dragon": 71.
72 Ibid.
73 Rivkin, "The P.O.W. Story," 18.
74 Ibid, 41.
75 William Stueck, *The Korean War: An International History* (Princeton, NJ: Princeton University Press, 1995), 6–7.
76 Robert J. Lentz, *Korean War Filmography* (Jefferson, NC: McFarland, 2000), 34, 36.
77 Bell to Baruch, February 18, 1954, *Bamboo Prison*, DoD Film Collection, box 2, folder 19, GUSCRC.
78 Welch's memorandum to the chief of Pictorial Branch, DoD, OPI, "Subject: Columbia Pictures Corp. Film, *Those Reported Missing*," March 2, 1954, ibid.
79 Baruch to Bell, March 3, 1954, ibid.
80 *Citizen-News*, January 17, 1951.
81 Samuel Fuller, *A Third Face: My Tale of Writing, Fighting, and Filmmaking* (New York: Alfred A. Knopf, 2002), 262.
82 Breen to Robert L. Lippert, October 16, 1950, *The Steel Helmet*, PCA files, MHL, AMPAS; "Memorandum for the Files Re: *The Steel Helmet*," October 17, 1950, ibid.
83 "Memorandum for the Files Re: *The Steel Helmet*," October 19, 1950, ibid.
84 Ibid.
85 Fuller, *A Third Face*, 264.
86 Towne to Manning Clagett, MPAA, February 1, 1951, *The Steel Helmet*, PCA files, MHL, AMPAS.
87 Breen to Joyce O'Hara, MPAA, January 17, 1951, ibid. Emphasis in original.
88 Towne to Clagett, February 1, 1951.
89 Welch's memorandum, "Subject: Columbia Pictures Corp. Film, *Those Reported Missing*," March 2, 1954, *Bamboo Prison*, DoD Film Collection, GUSCRC.
90 Ibid.
91 Baruch to Bell, March 3, 1954.
92 Breen to Harry Cohn, Columbia Pictures, February 15, 1954, *The Bamboo Prison*, PCA files, MHL, AMPAS.
93 E. A. Wheat to Senator Carl Hayden, December 12, 1954, attached in Hayden's letter to the Secretary of Defense, DoD, December 17, 1954, *Bamboo Prison*, DoD Film Collection, GUSCRC.
94 C. Herschel Schooley, DoD public information director, to Hayden, December 20, 1954, ibid.

95 "L.A. Catholic Tidings Hits Attack on Col Pic by Rival Catholic Paper," *Daily Variety*, December 22, 1954, *The Bamboo Prison*, clippings files, MHL, AMPAS.

96 Among the most notorious cases of "Binfordization" was *Curley* (1947), Hal Roach's *Little Rascals*–like innocent comedy featuring one scene with white and black children in the same classroom. It was banned in Memphis because, according to the film censorship board, "the South does not permit Negroes in white schools nor recognize social equality between the races, even among children." The film's distributor, United Artists, took the case to the Tennessee Supreme Court, which upheld Binford's decision on the jurisdictional grounds that UA was not licensed to do business in the state. For more information about Lloyd Binford and the Memphis Board of Film Censors, see Michael Finger, "Banned in Memphis," *Memphis Flyer*, May 18, 2008, https://www.memphisflyer.com/memphis/banned-in-memphis/Content?oid=1144204; Whitney Strub, "Black and White and Banned All Over: Race, Censorship and Obscenity in Postwar Memphis," *Journal of Social History* 40, no. 3 (Spring 2007): 685–715.

97 "Memphis Censors Fail to Understand Plot, Ban *Bamboo Prison*," *Variety*, February 1, 1955.

98 Ibid.

99 Binford to Schooley, March 23, 1955, *Bamboo Prison*, DoD Film Collection, GUSCRC.

100 Schooley to Binford, March 30, 1955, ibid.

101 Bell to Baruch, March 25, 1955, ibid.

102 Peter Lev, *Twentieth Century-Fox: The Zanuck-Skouras Years, 1935–1965* (Austin: University of Texas Press, 2013), 236.

103 Suid, *Guts and Glory*, 193.

104 Although I was not able to access the DoD's 1964 directive itself, these criteria and principles are included in the DoD instruction "Delineation of DoD Audio Visual Public Affairs Responsibilities and Policies," November 3, 1966, reprinted in Daniel Dancis, "With the Pentagon's Blessing: Hollywood, the Military, and Don Baruch," National Archives Text Message Blogs, March 18, 2018, https://text-message.blogs.archives.gov/2018/03/01/with-the-pentagons-blessing-hollywood-the-military-and-don-baruch/.

105 Ibid.

106 Suid, *Guts and Glory*, 197.

107 Lawrence H. Suid, "Arthur Sylvester Oral History Interview," August 16, 1973, John F. Kennedy Presidential Library Archives, 7, https://www.jfklibrary.org/sites/default/files/archives/JFKOH/Sylvester%2C%20Arthur/JFKOH-AUS-01/JFKOH-AUS-01-TR.pdf.

108 Ibid.

109 Ibid., 6.

110 Aly Weisman, "One Man in the Department of Defense Controls All of Hollywood's Access to the Military," *Business Insider*, March 5, 2014, http://www.businessinsider.com/phil-strub-controls-hollywoods-military-access-2014-3.

111 Ibid.

112 Strub to Hendrix, June 8, 1993, quoted in Robb, *Operation Hollywood*, 50–51.

113 Ibid., 19.

114 Phil Strub, "Pentagon's Entertainment Office Brings Military Science to Hollywood," *Armed with Science*, May 20, 2010, http://science.dodlive.mil/2010/05/20/pentagons-entertainment-office-brings-military-science-to-hollywood/.

Chapter 4 From *Die Another Day* to "Another Day"

1 Toby Miller, Nitin Govil, John McMurria, Richard Maxwell, and Ting Wang, *Global Hollywood*, no. 2 (London: BFI Publishing, 2005), 139.
2 *Die Another Day* poster, *Hollywood Reporter*, March 11, 2003.
3 For an elaborate definition of macro-nationalism, see Louis L. Snyder, *Encyclopedia of Nationalism* (New York: Paragon House, 1990), 200–203.
4 Ibid., 279–281.
5 Charles Lyons, "The Paradox of Protest: American Film, 1980–1992," in *Movie Censorship and American Culture*, ed. Francis G. Couvares (Washington, DC: Smithsonian Institute Press, 1996), 277–278. Emphasis in original.
6 It was reported that the film was pulled out of circulation early, within ten days of its release, in a number of theaters in Seoul, Chuncheon, and Wonju. Other theaters alternated films on the screens showing *Die Another Day* and minimized the number of daily screenings of the controversial film. A theater representative in Seoul explained, "We reduced the number of showings because of the social atmosphere created by the [anti-007] campaign and the problem of film content which contributed to low audience turnout. Other theaters are probably doing the same thing. We respect civil groups' expression of opinion but theaters also have to think about our relationship with distributors." Song Chŏng-mi, "Nationwide Campaigning of 'Do Not See 007'" [Chŏnguk aesŏ "007 yŏnghwa anbogi undong" chinhaeng], *Tongil News*, January 11, 2003, http://www.tongilnews.com/news/articleView.html?idxno=27160.
7 Heather Hendershot, *Saturday Morning Censors: Television Regulation before the V-Chip* (Durham, NC: Duke University Press, 1998), 94.
8 Ellen C. Scott, *Cinema Civil Rights: Regulation, Repression, and Race in the Classical Hollywood Era* (New Brunswick, NJ: Rutgers University Press, 2015), 186.
9 Jiyeon Kang, "Internet Activism Transforming Street Politics: South Korea's 2008 'Mad Cow' Protests and New Democratic Sensibilities," *Media, Culture & Society* 39, no. 5 (2017): 751.
10 Zeynep Tufekci, *Twitter and Tear Gas: The Power and Fragility of Networked Protest* (New Haven, CT: Yale University Press, 2017), 26.
11 Kang, "Internet Activism Transforming Street Politics," 753.
12 Lyons, "The Paradox of Protest," 277.
13 Although it is arguable whether the Cold War really ended in Asia in the light of the North Korean nuclear crisis, in this chapter I use the term "post-Cold War" in a conventional sense to refer to the new world order that emerged in the wake of the fall of the Berlin Wall, the collapse of the Eastern Bloc, and the market liberalization of mainland China.
14 James Chapman, *License To Thrill: A Cultural History of the James Bond Films* (London: I. B. Tauris, 1999), 30.
15 Klaus Dodds, "Screening Geopolitics: James Bond and the Early Cold War Films (1962–1967)," *Geopolitics* 10, no. 2 (2005): 272.
16 Klaus Dodds, "Licensed to Stereotype: Popular Geopolitics, James Bond, and the Spectre of Balkanism," *Geopolitics* 8, no. 2 (Summer 2003): 134.
17 Thomas M. Barrett, "Desiring the Soviet Woman: Tatiana Romanova and *From Russia, with Love*," in *For His Eyes Only: The Women of James Bond*, ed. Lisa Funnell (London: Wallflower, 2015), 47.

18 Quoted in Dodds, "Licensed to Stereotype," 143.

19 Lisa Funnell and Klaus Dodds, *Geographies, Genders, and Geopolitics of James Bond* (London: Palgrave Macmillan, 2017), 105.

20 Michael Atkinson, "Realpolitik for the People: *A View to a Kill*," *Village Voice*, November 20, 2002.

21 Manohla Dargis, "Bond's 40 but Refuses to Behave," *Los Angeles Times*, November 22, 2002, http://articles.latimes.com/2002/nov/22/entertainment/et-dargis22.

22 Michael Gove, "We Meet Again, Mr. Bond. Only This Time in Korea," *The Times*, January 12, 2002.

23 This translated message appeared at such websites as Bond 20: The Unofficial Site and CommanderBond.net, which are no longer available.

24 These headlines were circulated at the Bond 20: The Unofficial Site and Ananova websites, which are no longer available.

25 Im Kyŏng-gyu and Kim Ha-yŏng, "Popular Stars Go to the 'Square of Anger'" [Taejung sŭt'adŭl, "Punno ŭi kangjang" ae nasŏda], *Pressian*, December 2, 2002, http://www.pressian.com/news/article.html?no=23565.

26 Yi T'ae-ho, "Will 007 *Die Another Day* Succeed in Korea?" ["007 Dai ŭnadŏ dei," kuknae sangyŏng sŏnggonghalgga?], *OhMyNews*, December 27, 2002, http://www.ohmynews.com/NWS_Web/View/at_pg.aspx?CNTN_CD=A0000100410.

27 Mark Magnier, "007 Movie Provides Bond between the Two Koreas," *Los Angeles Times*, January 11, 2003, http://articles.latimes.com/2003/jan/11/world/fg-bond11; James Brooke, "Seoul Journal; The Power of Film: A Bond That Unites Koreans," *New York Times*, January 2, 2003, https://www.nytimes.com/2003/01/02/world/seoul-journal-the-power-of-film-a-bond-that-unites-koreans.html.

28 Magnier, "007 Movie Provides Bond between the Two Koreas."

29 Brooke, "Seoul Journal; The Power of Film."

30 Editorial in the *Chosun Daily* [*Chosŏn Ilbo*], January 23, 2003.

31 Box office statistics were provided by 20th Century-Fox Korea.

32 Brooke, "Seoul Journal; The Power of Film."

33 According to official records, between 1967 and 1998, 56,904 American soldiers committed 50,082 crimes in South Korea. Based on this statistics, scholars and activists infer that over 100,000 crimes had been committed by U.S. soldiers stationed in Korea between 1945 and 1999. See Anti-U.S. Military Crime Movement Headquarters, ed., *A History of Unfinished Pain: U.S. Military Crimes* [*Kkŭtnaji anjŭn ap'ŭm ŭi yŏksa migun pŏmjoe*] (Seoul: Kaemasŏwŏn, 1999).

34 The candlelight demonstration reached its peak during the week of December 7–14, 2002, when nearly 100,000 citizens gathered in the Kwanghwamun Square.

35 Jiyeon Kang, "The Corporeal Memory and the Making of a Post-Ideological Social Movement: Remembering the 2002 South Korean Candlelight Vigils," *Journal of Korean Studies* 17, no. 2 (Fall 2012): 330.

36 "North Korea Denounces James Bond Film," *New York Times*, December 15, 2002; Magnier, "007 Movie Provides Bond between the Two Koreas."

37 Cover story, *Newsweek*, January 13, 2003.

38 Message Board, Universal Exports 007, http://www.universalexports.net.

39 Tony Bennett and Janet Wollacott, *Bond and Beyond: The Political Career of a Popular Hero* (London: MacMillan Education, 1987), 99.

40 Neil Okrent, "Right Place, Wong Time," *Los Angeles Magazine*, May 1990.

41 James S. Moy, *Marginal Sights: Staging the Chinese in America* (Iowa City: University of Iowa Press, 1993), 91.

42 Personal correspondence. November 25, 2002.

43 Chŏng Han-sŏk, "Using the Korean Politics as Film Subject in *Die Another Day*" [Hanbando ŭi chŏngsega yŏnghwa ŭi sojero, *007 Another Day*], *Cine 21*, no. 383, December 24–31, 2002, http://www.cine21.com/news/view/?mag_id=16017.

44 Personal correspondence. December 7, 2002.

45 Chŏng Min-gyu, "Netizens'. Do Not See 007 Movement" [Net'ijŭn 007 yŏnghwa anbogi undong], *OhMyNews*, November 29, 2002, http://star.ohmynews.com /NWS_Web/OhmyStar/at_pg.aspx?CNTN_CD=A0000096403.

46 Thomas Shatz, "The Return of the Hollywood Studio System," in *Conglomerates and the Media*, ed. Erik Barnouw et al. (New York: New Press, 1997), 84–85.

47 Gill Branston, *Cinema and Cultural Modernity* (Buckingham: Open University Press, 2000), 53.

48 South Korea ranked the sixth largest international market in 2013, 2014, and 2016 in the Motion Picture Association of America's annual theatrical market statistics reports. In 2015 and 2017, the country's rank was raised to fifth. For full reports and statistics, see https://www.mpaa.org/research-policy/. South Korea's screen quota system originated in 1962, when the government mandated that theaters show at least six Korean films a year over the period of at least ninety days. In 1983, the protection quota for domestic films increased to 40 percent of their operation days (up to 146 days per year). For more information about the screen quota in South Korea and its controversy, see Cho Hee-moon, "Is the 'Screen Quota' System Really Relevant?" June 14, 2003, *Dong-A Daily* [*Dong-A Ilbo*], translated and reprinted in *Korea Focus*, http://www.koreafocus.or.kr/design1 /layout/content_print.asp?group_id=428.

49 Market share statistics are based on 2004 data. The Korean film industry's domestic market share has consistently been over 50 percent between 2004 and 2016 (reaching its peak at 64 percent in 2006). See Park Shin-young, *Status and Insight: Korean Film Industry 2016* (Seoul: Korean Film Council, 2016), downloadable at the Korean Film Council website, http://www.kofic.or.kr.

50 Tae-Jun Kim, Jai-Won Ryou, Yunjong Wang, *Regional Arrangements to Borrow: A Scheme for Preventing Future Asian Liquidity Crises* (Seoul: Korean Institute for International Economic Policy, 2000), 3.

51 According to a 2003 survey of 2,000 mainland Chinese, Hong Kong, and Taiwanese tourists conducted by the Korea National Tourism Organization (Han'guk kwangwang kongsa), 44.9 percent of respondents visited Korea to see film and television location sites, 20.7 percent to attend pop concerts, and 17.4 percent to participate in tour packages guided by popular stars. When one of the most popular *Hallyu* stars, Bae Yong-joon (Pae Yong-jun), made his much-anticipated cinematic debut in *Untold Scandal*, an estimated 20,000 Japanese tourists crossed the Sea of Japan to see the film upon its release. See the related reports in *Chosun Daily* [*Chosŏn Ilbo*], November 24, 2003, and *Cine 21*, October 3, 2003.

52 Youna Kim, "Hallyu: Korean Wave Media Culture in a Digital Age," in *Communication, Digital Media, and Popular Culture in Korea*, ed. Dal Yong Jin and Nojin Kwak (Lanham, MD: Lexington Books, 2018), 430.

53 Ibid., 429.

54 Jin Long Pao, "The Pan-Asian Co-production Sphere: Interview with Director Peter Chan," *Harvard Asia Quarterly* 6, no. 3 (Summer 2002): 47.

55 Ibid., 45.

56 The slump in exports from the mid-2000s can be attributed to the diminished appeal of Korean films in Japan, the biggest importer until 2014, when China overtook the role. For example, exports to Japan plummeted from $60 million in 2005 to $3 million in 2007 (it is at $4–$5 million as of 2015–2016). By contrast, the Chinese market for Korean films increased from $500,000 in 2005 to $8 million in 2014.

57 For year-by-year Korean film export statistics, see the Korean Film Council's *Korean Cinema* and *Korean Film Industry* reports at http://www.koreanfilm.or.kr/jsp/publications/books.jsp.

58 Sonia Kil, "Fox International Productions Seeks Increase in Korean Movie Making," *Variety*, May 3, 2016, https://variety.com/2016/film/asia/fox-international-productions-seeks-increase-in-korean-movie-making-1201765241/.

59 Lee Hyo-won, "Studio Head Jay Choi on Warner Bros.," *Hollywood Reporter*, March 14, 2017, https://www.hollywoodreporter.com/news/jay-choi-warner-bros-immediate-success-south-korea-importance-localization-985944.

60 In a sense, *Die Another Day* racially retools the 1950s Red Scare allegory on view in such films as *Invasion of the Body Snatchers* (1956), a sci-fi classic in which alien pod creatures infiltrate and take over the bodies of sleeping townspeople.

61 Snyder, *Encyclopedia of Nationalism*, 200, 279–281.

62 Quoted in Magnier, "007 Movie Provides Bond between the Two Koreas."

63 Ibid.

64 Dodds, "Screening Geopolitics," 271–272.

Chapter 5 *The Interview* as a Twenty-First-Century *Great Dictator*?

1 In January 2015, the White House announced a new executive order that targets North Korean officials, preventing them from accessing property, operating agencies, and entering the United States as a part of the "proportional response" that President Obama promised after the Sony hack. Jim Acosta, "U.S. Slaps New Sanctions on North Korea after Sony Hack," CNN Politics, January 3, 2015, http://www.cnn.com/2015/01/02/politics/new-sanctions-for-north-korea-after-sony-hack/index.html.

2 "Update on Sony Investigation," National Press Release, FBI, December 19, 2014, https://www.fbi.gov/news/pressrel/press-releases/update-on-sony-investigation. Several high-profile security experts (including Marc Rogers, a hacker–turned–security manager, and Jack Goldsmith, a Harvard law professor) expressed skepticism about the FBI's conclusion based on sketchy evidence. See Sam Biddle, "A Lot of Smart People Think North Korea Didn't Hack Sony," *Gawker*, December 22, 2014, http://gawker.com/a-lot-of-smart-people-think-north-korea-didnt-hack-sony-1672899940.

3 Holly Yan and Ben Brumfield, "North Korea Lambasts U.S. over *The Interview*, Says Obama Is the 'Culprit,'" CNN World, December 29, 2014, http://www.cnn.com/2014/12/27/world/asia/north-korea-the-interview-reaction/.

4 Hunter Walker, "Obama Might Have Forced Sony to Release *The Interview*," *Business Insider*, December 20, 2014, http://www.businessinsider.com/obama-may-have-just-forced-sony-to-release-the-interview-2014-12.

5 Christine Hong, "Stranger than Fiction: *The Interview* and U.S. Regime-Change Policy Toward North Korea," *Asia-Pacific Journal* 12, no. 52 (2014), http://www.globalresearch.ca/the-hollywood-demonization-script-the-interview-and-u-s-regime-change-policy-toward-north-korea/5421932.

6 Mark W. Davis, "Stand by Sony," U.S. News, December 16, 2014, http://www.usnews.com/opinion/blogs/mark-davis/2014/12/16/see-the-interview-to-stand-by-sony-and-stick-it-to-north-korea.
7 Pamela McClintock, "*The Interview* Lost Sony $30 Million, Says Theater Group," *Hollywood Reporter*, January 16, 2015, https://www.hollywoodreporter.com/news/interview-lost-sony-30-million-764366.
8 Mark Seal, "An Exclusive Look at Sony's Hacking Saga," *Vanity Fair*, February 4, 2015, http://www.vanityfair.com/hollywood/2015/02/sony-hacking-seth-rogen-evan-goldberg.
9 In 1952, the Supreme Court reversed its 1915 ruling (*Mutual v. Ohio*) in the *Miracle* case (*Joseph Burstyn, Inc. v. Wilson*) regarding the New York State's banning of the Italian short film *Il Miracolo* on the ground of sacrilege.
10 Paul Fischer, "North Korea's Fear of Hollywood," *New York Times*, July 3, 2014, http://www.nytimes.com/2014/07/04/opinion/sunday/north-koreas-fear-of-hollywood.html?_r=1; Meg James, Daniel Miller, and Josh Rottenberg, "Sony Pictures Execs Debated Risk of *The Interview* before Cyberattack," *Los Angeles Times*, December 9, 2014, http://www.latimes.com/entertainment/envelope/cotown/la-et-ct-sony-hack-north-korea-the-interview-20141210-story.html.
11 Mark Schilling, "*The Interview* to Have Only Limited Release in Asia," *Variety*, December 10, 2014, http://variety.com/2014/film/news/the-interview-to-have-only-limited-release-in-asia-1201376806/.
12 Motion Picture Association of America, "Theatrical Market Statistics 2014," 5, http://www.mpaa.org/wp-content/uploads/2015/03/MPAA-Theatrical-Market-Statistics-2014.pdf. In 2017, India's and Korea's rankings raised to fourth and fifth, respectively.
13 Tom Brock, "How the Global Box Office Is Changing Hollywood," *BBC News*, June 20, 2013, http://www.bbc.com/culture/story/20130620-is-china-hollywoods-future.
14 Josh Constine, "*The Interview* Censorship Protestors Screen Chaplin's Hitler Parody *The Great Dictator*," *Techcrunch*, December 21, 2014, http://techcrunch.com/2014/12/21/no-appeasement/.
15 Charles S. Aaronson, "*The Great Dictator*," *Motion Picture Daily*, October 16, 1940, 6.
16 "*Dictator* Disappointing; Lacks the Chaplin Wallops," *Hollywood Reporter*, October 15, 1940.
17 Ben Urwand, *Collaboration: Hitler's Pact with Hollywood* (Cambridge, MA: Harvard University Press, 2013), 48.
18 Gyssling to Breen, October 31, 1938, *The Great Dictator*, Production Code Administration (PCA) files, Margaret Herrick Library (MHL), Academy of Motion Picture Arts and Sciences (AMPAS), Beverly Hills, CA.
19 Wilkinson's cable to Breen, March 2, 1939, ibid.
20 Ibid.
21 Breen to Wilkinson, March 13, 1939, ibid.
22 McKenna to Reynolds, February 27, 1939, ibid.
23 "Joseph Kennedy, 'Patriarch' of an American Dynasty," Author Interviews, *NPR Books*, http://www.npr.org/2012/12/12/166488040/joseph-kennedy-patriarch-of-an-american-dynasty.
24 Frederick C. Othan, "Chaplin Seeks Berlin Premiere of 'Dictator,'" *Motion Picture Herald*, March 27, 1940.

25 Confidential reports from local censor boards, *The Great Dictator*, PCA files, MHL, AMPAS.
26 Dan Kamin, "Who Is This Man? (Who Looks Like Charlie Chaplin)," in *Chaplin: The Dictator and the Tramp*, ed. Dan Kamin (London: British Film Institute, 2004), 9.
27 Charlie Chaplin, *My Autobiography* (Harmondsworth: Penguin Books, 1966), 387–388.
28 "*The Great Dictator* in Historical Context: As Reflected in *The Tramp and the Dictator* Interviews," *Chaplin: The Dictator and the Tramp*, 97.
29 Ibid., 99.
30 Scott Foundas, "Film Review: *The Interview*," *Variety*, December 12, 2014, http://variety.com/2014/film/reviews/film-review-the-interview-1201376293/.
31 Adam Taylor, "Why *The Interview* Is Not *The Great Dictator* of Our Times," *Washington Post*, December 18, 2014, https://www.washingtonpost.com/news/worldviews/wp/2014/12/18/why-the-interview-is-not-the-great-dictator-of-our-times/.
32 For more information about North Korea's policy of regime survival, see Young Whan Kihl and Hong Nack Kim, *North Korea: The Politics of Regime Survival* (London: Routledge, 2005).
33 As historian Bruce Cumings elaborates, *Juche* "means self-reliance and independence in politics, economics, defense, and ideology; it first emerged in 1955 as [Pyongyang] drew away from Moscow, and then appeared full-blown in the mid-sixties as [Kim Il Sung] sought a stance independent of both Moscow and Beijing. . . . [*Juche*] is the opaque core of North Korean national solipsism." Cumings, *Korea's Place in the Sun: A Modern History*, rev. ed. (New York: W. W. Norton, 2005), 413–414.
34 Kevin S. Sandler, *The Naked Truth: Why Hollywood Doesn't Make X-Rated Movies* (New Brunswick, NJ, Rutgers University Press, 2007), 43–44.
35 Heffner's memorandum ("How to Do What We Do") to Rating Board members, December 1988, Pre-Oral History Memoranda Year 1990, Richard Heffner Papers, vol. 13, Columbia University Oral History Archive, New York City. Emphasis in original.
36 Richard Heffner Papers, vol. 1, session 6, 56, ibid.
37 Pre-Oral History Memoranda Year 1978, Richard Heffner Papers, vol. 4, 13, ibid.
38 "Thai Censors Ban *Anna* Movie as an Insult to King," *Chicago Tribune*, December 28, 1999, http://articles.chicagotribune.com/1999-12-28/news/9912290154_1_king-mongkut-gen-prakard-satamarn-censorship-board.
39 Emily Farache, "*Anna and the King* Banned in Thailand," *E! News*, December 28, 1999, http://www.eonline.com/news/39189/anna-and-the-king-banned-in-thailand.
40 Justin Pritchard, "Even Updated *King* Banned in Thailand," *Christian Science Monitor*, December 27, 1999, https://www.csmonitor.com/1999/1227/p1s4.html.
41 Keith B. Richburg, "Not Playing: *Anna and the King*," *Washington Post*, January 17, 2000, http://www.washingtonpost.com/wp-srv/WPcap/2000-01/17/021r-011700-idx.html.
42 Toby Miller, Nitin Covil, John McMurria, Richard Maxwell, and Ting Wang, *Global Hollywood 2* (London: British Film Institute, 2005), 167.
43 Rodanthi Tzanelli, *The Cinematic Tourist: Explorations in Globalization, Culture and Resistance* (New York: Routledge, 2007), 49.

44 For a detailed discussion of yellow voice in *Team America*, see Hye Seung Chung, "From 'Me So Horny' to 'I'm So Ronery': Asian Images and Yellow Voices in American Cinema," in *Film Dialogue*, ed. Jeff Jaeckle (New York: Columbia University Press, 2013), 172–191.

45 Andy Klein, "Puppet Dictator: The South Park Gang Goes Marionette Mad in *Team America: World Police*," *Citybeat*, October 14–20, 2004, 21.

46 Will Tizard, "Czechs Take One for *Team*," *Variety*, March 13, 2005, http://variety.com/2005/film/news/czechs-take-one-for-team-1117917821/.

47 It appears that the lucrative Korean theatrical market was voluntarily given up in the case of *Team America*. In his interview with the *Hollywood Reporter*, United International Pictures Korean manager Douglas Lee said, "There are no plans to release *Team America* at this time." Although Lee elaborated that *Team America* was just one of the many American films, particularly comedies, that missed theatrical releases in South Korea, it is hard to imagine that the political factor was not behind this suppression. Mark Russell, "S. Korea Likely to Shun 'Team,'" *Hollywood Reporter*, October 19, 2004. The KMRB's decision to defer the rating for the film's DVD release came at a bad time, after Paramount Pictures had already run a big advertising campaign in major film magazines for its anticipatory June 2005 launch. Sŏl Wŏn-t'ae, "American Popular Culture, 'Demonization of Kim Jong-il'" [Mi taejung munhwa "Kim Chŏng-il Atdanghwa"], *Kyunghyang Daily* [*Kyŏnghyang sinmun*], June 2, 2005, http://news.khan.co.kr/kh_news/khan_art_view.html?artid=200506020833491&code=960100.

48 Gary Susman, "*Team America* Finally Earns an R Rating," *Entertainment Weekly*, October 6, 2004, http://ew.com/article/2004/10/06/team-america-finally-earns-r-rating/.

49 Korea Media Rating Board, *Film Rating Classification Standards Workbook* [*Yŏnghwa tŭnggŭp kijun*] (Seoul: Korea Media Rating Board, 2012), 11.

50 Seal, "An Exclusive Look at Sony's Hacking Saga."

51 Peter Elkind, "Sony Pictures: Inside the Hack of the Century," *Fortune*, July 1, 2015, http://fortune.com/sony-hack-part-1/.

52 Seal, "An Exclusive Look at Sony's Hacking Saga."

53 Elkind, "Sony Pictures: Inside the Hack of the Century."

54 Adrian Hong, "North Korea: Not Funny," *The Atlantic*, December 18, 2014, http://www.theatlantic.com/international/archive/2014/12/north-korea-is-not-funny-the-interview-sony/383885/.

55 Basil-Jones's email, June 23, 2014, "Re: Interview," email ID: 191563, WikiLeaks, https://wikileaks.org/sony/emails/.

56 Lynton's email, July 14, 2014, "Re: Seth/Evan," email ID: 27823, WikiLeaks.

57 Ibid.

58 O'Dell's email, October 30, 2014, "Re: *The Interview*—new edits," email ID: 186797, WikiLeaks.

59 Hwang's email, June 3, 2014, "Re: *The Interview*—DCP Screenings," email ID: 193874, WikiLeaks.

60 Yu's email, June 2, 2014, "Re: *The Interview* DCP Screening—Taiwan Reaction," email ID: 191840, WikiLeaks.

61 Crockett's email, June 16, 2014, "Re: *The Interview*—DCP Screenings," email ID: 195749, WikiLeaks.

62 Bennett's email, June 26, 2014, "Re: Kim Myong-chol details KJI's 'plans for thermo-nuclear war,'" email ID: 139029, WikiLeaks.

63 Ibid.

64 Van Jackson, *Rival Reputations: Coercion and Credibility in US–North Korean Relations* (Cambridge: Cambridge University Press, 2016), 2.

65 Roland Bleiker, "A Rogue Is a Rogue Is a Rogue: US Foreign Policy and the Korean Nuclear Crisis," *International Affairs* 79, no. 4 (2003): 725–726.

66 Samuel S. Kim, "North Korea's Nuclear Strategy and the Interface between International and Domestic Politics," *Asia Perspective* 34, no. 1 (2010): 61, 69.

67 Bleiker, "A Rogue Is a Rogue Is a Rogue," 720.

68 Robert Dujarric, "North Korea: Risks and Rewards of Engagement," *Journal of International Affairs* 54, no. 2 (Spring 2001): 467.

69 Alex Miles, *US Foreign Policy and the Rogue State Doctrine* (New York: Routledge, 2013), 1.

70 Elkind, "Sony Pictures: Inside the Hack of the Century."

71 Ibid; Tatiana Siegel, "Sony Altering Kim Jong Un Assassination Film *The Interview*," *Hollywood Reporter*, August 13, 2014, http://www.hollywoodreporter.com/news/sony-altering-kim-jong-assassination-725092.

72 Guerin's email, June 25, 2014, "Re: *The Interview* Talking Points," email ID: 99976, WikiLeaks.

73 Ibid. Emphasis added.

74 Sipkins's email, June 25, 2014, "Re: Korea/*The Interview*," email ID: 29353, WikiLeaks. Emphasis in original.

75 Willys Peck to Nelson Johnson, November 21, 1933, Record Group 59, State Department files on China, 893.4061 Motion Pictures, National Archives and Records Administration (NARA) at College Park, MD.

76 "Charlie Chaplin in *The Great Dictator*," United Artists Press Kit, *The Great Dictator*, Clippings files, PCA files, MHL, AMPAS.

77 Paul Thornton, "Sony Pulls *The Interview*: Some Sympathy for North Korea," *Los Angeles Times*, December 17, 2014, http://www.latimes.com/opinion/opinion-la/la-ol-north-korea-sony-the-interview-pulled-readers-react-20141217-story.html.

78 Maxine Builder, "The Real Problem with *The Interview* Is Its Racism, Not Its Satire," *Medium*, December 18, 2014, https://medium.com/@maxine_builder/the-real-problem-with-the-interview-is-its-racism-not-its-satire-4d0cd30d5f0d#.3svhh1s3m.

79 Chu Sŏng-ha, "The Reason Why the Movie *Interview* Is Absurd" [*Yŏnghwa Int'ŏbyu ka ŏi ŏpnŭn iyu*], *Weekly Dong-a* [*Chugan Tong-a*], no. 970, January 7–13, 2015, 22–23.

80 William Blum, *America's Deadliest Export: Democracy*, 2nd ed. (London: Zed Books, 2013), 1.

81 For a detailed account of failed U.S. policy of regime change in Iraq, see Toby Dodge, "Iraq in Transitions: From Regime Change to State Collapse," *Third World Quarterly* 26, no. 4/5 (2005): 705–721.

82 Guerin's email, "Re: *The Interview* Talking Points."

83 Brian Bennett, cover story, *Time*, June 28, 2018, 20–28.

84 Victor Cha, "Trump and Kim Have Just Walked Us Away from the Brink of War," *New York Times*, June 12, 2018, https://www.nytimes.com/2018/06/12/opinion/trump-kim-north-korea-summit.html.

85 Ruth Vasey, *The World According to Hollywood, 1918–1939* (Madison: University of Wisconsin Press, 1997), 159.

86 *The Interview* was touted by some observers for initiating a "paradigm shift toward day-and-date theatrical and VOD releases." While most insiders still see this dual

strategy (which Sony was forced to adopt as last-minute crisis management) as economically unviable due to its negative effect on box office performance, the fact that the NATO vice president Patrick Corcoran publicly disputed the claim that Sony's unorthodox release strategy was "a game changer" attests to the threat of this new business model to traditional exhibitors. Pamela McClintock, "Sony Hack: *Interview*'s VOD Strategy Probably Won't Change Anything," *Hollywood Reporter*, January 8, 2015, https://www.hollywoodreporter.com/news/sony-hack-interviews-vod-strategy-761463; Dave McNary, "*The Interview* Will Lose $30 Million, 'Not a Game-Changer,' Says NATO," *Variety*, January 16, 2015, http://variety.com/2015/film/news/the-interview-will-lose-30-million-not-a-game-changer-says-nato-1201407514/.

Conclusion

1 The SAPPRFT was formed in 2013 by merging two regulatory bodies, the State Administration of Radio, Film, and Television (SARFT) and the General Administration of Press and Publication. In March 2018, the Chinese government submitted a proposal for legislative deliberation to replace the SAPPRFT with a new regulatory body directly under the State Council, a move that is expected to tighten the government's control of media and entertainment industries. Patrick Frater, "China to Put Media under Cabinet-Level Control, Abolish SAPPRFT," *Variety*, March 13, 2018, https://variety.com/2018/film/asia/china-media-under-cabinet-level-control-abolish-sapprft-1202725104/.

2 "Regulations on the Administration of Movies" [*Dianying Guanli Tiaoli*], (issued December 12, 2001, effective February 1, 2002), World International Property Organization (WIPO), http://www.wipo.int/wipolex/en/text.jsp?file_id=182159.

3 Laney Zhang, "China: First Law on Film Industry Effective in March," Library of Congress Global Legal Monitor, February 28, 2017, http://www.loc.gov/law/foreign-news/article/china-first-law-on-film-industry-effective-in-march/.

4 For an unofficial English translation of the law, see "Film Industry Promotion Law 2016" [Zhonghua Renmin Gongheguo Dianying Chanye Cuijin Fa], China Law Translate, November 7, 2016, https://www.chinalawtranslate.com.

5 Ibid.

6 Patrick Brzeski, "China Advances Film Industry Law, Cracks Down on 'Western' Values," *Hollywood Reporter*, August 30, 2016, https://www.hollywoodreporter.com/news/china-advances-film-industry-law-924201.

7 Motion Picture Association of America, "2017 THEME Report: A Comprehensive Analysis of and Survey of the Theatrical and Home Entertainment Market Environment," 8, https://pmcdeadline2.files.wordpress.com/2018/04/mpaa-theme-report-2017.pdf.

8 Sean O'Connor and Nicholas Armstrong, "Directed by Hollywood, Edited by China: How China's Censorship and Influence Affect Films Worldwide," U.S.-China Security Review Commission Staff Research Report, October 28, 2015, 11–12, https://www.uscc.gov/Research/directed-hollywood-edited-china-how-china%E2%80%99s-censorship-and-influence-affect-films-worldwide.

9 Frank Wolf, "Will China Soon Control American Movies?" *Washington Post*, September 15, 2016, https://www.washingtonpost.com/opinions/global-opinions

/will-china-soon-control-american-movies/2016/09/15/968539b6-79e2-11e6-bd86-b7bbd53d2b5d_story.html?utm_term=.feb20fb48178.

10 Ibid.

11 Robert Daly, "Hollywood's Dangerous Obsession with China," *Los Angeles Times*, October 7, 2016, http://www.latimes.com/opinion/op-ed/la-oe-daly-hollywood-20161007-snap-story.html.

12 MPAA, "2017 THEME Report," 8.

13 Edward Wong, "*Doctor Strange* Writer Explains the Casting of Tilda Swinton as Tibetan," *New York Times*, April 26, 2016, https://www.nytimes.com/2016/04/27/world/asia/china-doctor-strange-tibet.html.

14 Aaron Couch, "*Doctor Strange*: Wong's Journey from Stereotype to Unlikely Symbol of Progress," *Hollywood Reporter*, November 3, 2016, https://www.hollywoodreporter.com/heat-vision/doctor-strange-wongs-journey-stereotype-symbol-progress-943871.

15 Brian Truitt, "Benedict Wong Gives *Doctor Strange* a Needed Asian Superhero," *USA Today*, November 7, 2016, https://www.usatoday.com/story/life/movies/2016/11/07/benedict-wong-doctor-strange/93236974/.

16 Malcolm Moore, "Chinese Villains Censored from *Men in Black 3*," *Daily Telegraph*, May 30, 2012, https://www.telegraph.co.uk/news/worldnews/asia/china/9300092/Chinese-villains-censored-from-Men-in-Black-3.html.

17 Peck to Herron, January 5, 1934, letter attached to Peck's report to the Secretary of State, January 5, 1934, "Subject: The Chinese Government and the Motion Picture Industry," State Department files, box 7221, National Archives and Records Administration (NARA) at College Park, MD.

18 For the past few years, it has been widely predicted that China will become the largest movie market by 2020. This is already a reality, as China's box office overtook that of North America in the first quarter of 2018. Patrick Prater, "China Box Office Overtakes North American in First Quarter of 2018," *Variety*, April 2, 2018, https://variety.com/2018/film/asia/china-box-office-global-biggest-first-quarter-2018-1202742159/.

19 Members of Congress Robert Pittenger, Mike Rogers, John Culberson, Chris Smith, Bradley Byrne, Walter B. Jones, Mo Brooks, Paul Cook, Duncan Hunter, Bill Posey, Dana Rohrabacher, Robert Aderholt, Rosa L. DeLauro, Ralph Abraham, Peter DeFazio, and Sam Johnson to Dodaro, U.S. Government Accountability Office, September 15, 2016, https://pittenger.house.gov/sites/pittenger.house.gov/files/letter%20to%20gao%20re%20cfius%20report%209.15.16.pdf.

20 Brent Lang and Gene Maddaus, "Lawmakers Raise Questions about Chinese Investments in Hollywood," *Variety*, September 22, 2016, https://variety.com/2016/film/news/wanda-lawmakers-raise-questions-about-chinese-investment-in-hollywood-1201868250/.

21 Peter Enav, "Hollywood Yielding to China's Growing Film Clout," Associated Press, April 25, 2013, https://www.apnews.com/6dbb6302fba9426ebad24ed9586bb09c.

22 Robert Sklar, *Movie-Made America: A Cultural History of American Movies*, rev. ed. (New York: Vintage, 1994), 174.

23 Zach Saltz, "The Newest Significant Medium: *Brown v. EMA* (2011) and the Twenty-First Century Status of Video Game Regulation," in *Rated M for Mature:*

Sex and Sexuality in Video Games, ed. Matthew Wysocki and Evan W. Lauteria (New York: Bloomsbury Academic, 2015), 72.

24 "Address Delivered by Will H. Hays, President of Motion Picture Producers & Distributors of America, Inc. before the Harvard School of Business at Harvard University," March 15, 1927, MPPDA Digital Archive, reel 3, record #330, 20, https://mppda.flinders.edu.au/records/330.

Index

About the Author

HYE SEUNG CHUNG is an associate professor of film and media studies in the Department of Communication Studies at Colorado State University. She is the author of *Hollywood Asian: Philip Ahn and the Politics of Cross-Ethnic Performance* (2006) and *Kim Ki-duk* (2012), as well as the coauthor of *Movie Migrations: Transnational Genre Flows and South Korean Cinema* (2015).